Praise for *You Don't Look Like a Lawyer*

"A powerful and much-needed book, with fine insights about black legal professionals that scholars, journalists, and the professionals themselves will find enlightening. This well-written and highly readable book makes innovative use of systemic racism theory to assess their racialized experiences and creative agency in difficult workplaces dominated by elite white men—legal worlds getting too little attention in current scholarship and mass media."

—Joe Feagin, Texas A&M University

"Capturing the poise and persistence of her subjects in a manner that quantitative studies cannot, Melaku's in-depth interviews with black women lawyers in law firms provide an essential critical examination of contemporary narratives of diversity in the profession of law. In this book Melaku explicates the challenges faced by black women professionals negotiating the white space of law firms, developing the unique concept of the *invisible labor clause*. The invisible labor clause is a tacit but essential contractual obligation required of black women lawyers, which results in unacknowledged and unrewarded work. This work includes tasks such as the management of physical appearance—for example, maintaining white aesthetic standards of hair care and styling—as well as the negotiation of racist and sexist networking practices. These forms of labor are not explicitly stated components of the work contract but are in fact mandatory for black women who are attempting to succeed in the elite and predominantly white male profession of law. This work exposes the intersecting mechanisms of systemic and institutionalized racism and sexism in the legal profession in a way that no other work has done to date. *You Don't Look Like a Lawyer* is poised to become required reading in the legal academy and intersectional sociology."

—Wendy Leo Moore, Texas A&M University

"Tsedale Melaku sheds light on the prevalence of systemic gendered racism in elite corporate work environments. Through the analysis of in-depth interviews of black female lawyers, she critically examines the nuanced experiences of these women as they try to navigate a career dominated by a white male elite who uphold a system that maintains and reinforces gendered and racial inequities. Melaku's firsthand account of these women lawyers provides a never-before-seen look into the inner workings of elite workspaces, particularly with regards to the emotional, physical, and psychological labor that black women have to exert in order to minimize the daily microaggressions they face. This much-needed book illustrates the incredible journey black women professionals often face in the workplace."

—Enobong (Anna) Branch, University of Massachusetts Amherst

PERSPECTIVES ON A MULTIRACIAL AMERICA SERIES

Joe R. Feagin, Texas A&M University, Series Editor

The racial composition of the United States is rapidly changing. Books in the series will explore various aspects of the coming multiracial society, one in which European-Americans are no longer the majority and where issues of white-on-black racism have been joined by many other challenges to white dominance.

Titles:

YOU DON'T LOOK LIKE A LAWYER

Black Women and Systemic Gendered Racism

Tsedale M. Melaku

ROWMAN & LITTLEFIELD

Lanham • Boulder • New York • London

Published by Rowman & Littlefield
An imprint of The Rowman & Littlefield Publishing Group, Inc.
4501 Forbes Boulevard, Suite 200, Lanham, Maryland 20706
www.rowman.com

6 Tinworth Street, London SE11 5AL, United Kingdom

British Library Cataloguing in Publication Information Available

Library of Congress Cataloging-in-Publication Data

Names: Melaku, Tsedale M., 1980-
Title: You don't look like a lawyer : black women and systemic gendered racism / Tsedale M. Melaku.
Description: Lanham, Md. : Rowman & Littlefield, 2019. | Series: Perspectives on a multiracial America series | Includes bibliographical references and index.
Identifiers: LCCN 2018045253 (print) | LCCN 2018045715 (ebook) | ISBN 9781538107935 (electronic) | ISBN 9781538107928 (cloth : alk. paper)
Subjects: LCSH: African American women lawyers—United States. | Women lawyers | African American lawyers
Classification: LCC KF299.A35 (ebook) | LCC KF299.A35 M45 2019 (print) | DDC 340.082/0973—dc23
LC record available at https://lccn.loc.gov/2018045253

♾️™ The paper used in this publication meets the minimum requirements of American National Standard for Information Sciences—Permanence of Paper for Printed Library Materials, ANSI/NISO Z39.48-1992.

Printed in the United States of America

In loving memory of Jerry G. Watts,
who reminds me every day that
we should strive to live the "life of the mind."
And for Christoph, Lukas, and Yonas: I'm better because of you.

This book is dedicated to my family.

CONTENTS

ACKNOWLEDGMENTS

This book is the result of brave black women taking a stand and speaking up about the everyday challenges they face working in elite white institutions. I am extremely grateful to each participant who took a chance on a graduate student hoping to shed light on their experiences. I am indebted to Joe R. Feagin for his support and insightful comments, which helped me formulate a more critical analysis of systemic gendered racism and white racial framing throughout the entire manuscript. I received invaluable feedback and critiques from senior colleagues and trusted friends: Erica Chito Childs, Rev. Traci C. West, Stuart Schulman, Carla Shedd, and Johnny E. Williams. A special thank-you to my reviewers, Joe R. Feagin, Adia Harvey Wingfield, Wendy Leo Moore, Robert L. Nelson, David B. Wilkins, and Enobong (Anna) Branch, all of whom have influenced my research through their scholarship. The support from Rolf Janke, Courtney Packard, Alden Perkins, and Niki Guinan, my Rowman & Littlefield team, was crucial to making this book happen.

On a personal note, I am grateful for the incredible village that supported me throughout this journey. I am thankful to all the amazing women in my life who supported me and this project, especially M. Elaine Johnston and Alison D. Bauer. Thank you to my friends and family for being the best cheering squad, and special thanks to Ian Jackson for his editing support. No words can express my gratitude toward my parents, Apufia S. Beko and Mekete M. Asfaw, who sacrificed everything to give my siblings and me a greater opportunity in life. Their love, encouragement, and support were instrumental in shaping my worldview and teaching me to stand tall, always reminding me that I am worth everything. I am grateful to my amazing siblings, Dawit, Stephanose, and Sarah, who never missed a beat in pushing me to the finish line. To my boys, Lukas and Yonas, thank you both for inspiring me to be better. And most importantly, I am indebted to my dear husband and intellectual sparring partner, Christoph Winkler. Your unconditional love, strength, insightful feedback and critiques, encouraging words, and constant championing are fuel for this work and our life together. We love, laugh, live, and learn together; working toward building a better world for our boys and others.

FOREWORD

In *You Don't Look Like a Lawyer: Black Women and Systemic Gendered Racism*, Tsedale Melaku brings us into the daily lives of black women lawyers in top corporate firms. These professionals offered Melaku rich details about their difficulties in this highly racist country. Social science and trade book authors alike have largely ignored the lives of the growing groups of professionals of color, but in your hands now is one of the few books to explore this important group.

Melaku's focus on black women lawyers helps restore them to a central place in US history. Black women professionals have long been central to the liberation movements of black Americans, and this book thus fits well with a recent historical book, *Outsiders Within*, about black female law professors and activists in the 1970s and 1980s, because it shows that the racist barriers these pioneers faced are still part of the major struggles black legal professionals confront today.[1]

In this powerful and much-needed book, we garner fine insights about black professionals that a variety of scholars, journalists, teachers, and black professionals themselves will find enlightening and helpful for their own analyses of, and responses to, persistent patterns of white racism. Well-written and consistently interesting, Melaku's text makes effective and innovative use of major elements of systemic racism theory, intersectionality theory, and other structural theories. It assesses the gendered-racist experiences and creative agency of these black women in difficult employment settings dominated by elite white men.

In particular, Melaku makes extensive use of the concepts of systemic racism and systemic gendered racism and coins her own useful concepts for certain dimensions of these black women's work lives. She introduces us to the "invisible labor clause," the labor that black women lawyers and other professionals *must* engage in as they try to navigate white-male-dominated organizational spaces. She also develops the related concept of the "inclusion tax"—the great and additional energy "resources black women are forced to 'spend,' such as time, money, and emotional and mental energy" just to be included in such important (and historically white) employment spaces.

Melaku's research and analysis contributes significantly to a deeper understanding of rarely assessed dimensions of the everyday worlds of African American professionals, not only in law, but also in other professional workplaces. She forthrightly calls out elite white male discriminators as those who most often, directly and indirectly, oppress these African American professionals. In many research and popular analyses, white male discriminators disappear into vague or abstract terms (e.g., "society discriminates") or passive tenses ("black women have been victims of racism"), but here they are foregrounded as mostly elite white male actors, with some (the partners) being more elite than others (the associates).

As Melaku summarizes, the "elite corporate law firms are typically white institutional spaces, traditionally only accessible to white men." Dramatic statistics provide a general context for setting much of the discussion. Presently, white associates and partners make up about 84 percent of those in US law firms, and about 91 percent of partners are white. Remarkably few black women are recruited as associates in elite firms anywhere, and recent studies show that, once hired, they have the highest attrition rate across all racial and gender categories.

Unsurprisingly, the respondents themselves are often cautious, as they have learned to be in professional lives as "othered" lawyers. Sometimes they, too, talk in the more abstract or passive terms noted previously, but one can see in their rich accounts that there are many elite white male discriminators whose racist and gendered-racist actions regularly restrict and harm their professional and personal lives. As Melaku emphasizes, "Fifteen out of my twenty participants admitted their firms either have a [white] club or have male partners who choose to work exclusively with male associates." Over recent decades, the usually modest diversifying attempts in these and other law firms have not generated "invitations to the boys' club being sent with any greater frequency to historically marginalized groups."

These commonplace, ol' boys' clubs, to be precise, involve powerful, white decision makers at the top of what I term the elite-white-male dominance system. That elite dominance system is not just an overarching institutionalized structure of this society but is also demonstrated and reinforced in the routine actions of actual white male discriminators. That overarching system constantly crashes into the everyday interactions in settings like those of top corporate law firms, including racist and gender-racist interactions that ensure the continuation of that larger dominance system. Melaku's interviews provide detailed evidence of the harsh reality: Most discriminators are powerful white men—and not just abstract or impersonal forces that many analyses keep vague. They are active enforcers of the systemic racism and gendered racism.

Account after account provides hard evidence that the path to promotions and partnership is seriously limited by this elite-white-male dominance system. One commentary from a fifth-year associate explains the common difficulty of not being able to fit into important male groups (termed "boys' club stuff"):

> [W]ithin corporate it was a group that worked together, they hung out together, and on occasion, I'd worked on deals with this group and I remember thinking. . . . I talk sports all the time, I hang out with men a lot and I'm fine in those situations. . . . But these guys, I felt very uncomfortable with this whole group. . . . I couldn't relate to them on any level. I don't play golf, nor do I care to. I don't have a country home. I don't have a wife at home who takes care of all my business. That was one thing that I think was very annoying to a lot of us women.

A third-year associate describes a related set of workplace issues this way:

> I know people say that about every firm, but I think [Firm Name] is really probably one of the last bastions of the old boys' club. . . . I came in prepared to kind of have to deal with issues in terms of my race, but I was not expecting to deal with issues because I was a woman. . . . There were also times where I would be around a partner during, let's say an outside work event and they would be talking about the good old days of the firm with the secretaries downstairs typing up notes and the men upstairs.

Reports of discrimination from these black professionals signal the importance not only of the elite-white-male dominance system (most of the powerful men they reference are elite whites) but also of the varying forms that quotidian discrimination can take—sometimes racist, sometimes sexist, and sometimes gendered-racist. Melaku's interviewees regularly note the complex realities accented by intersectionality theory, which often link systemic racism, systemic sexism, and systemic classism into an integrated whole.

Given the centrality and domination of these elite men, the respondents' accounts of numerous serious patterns of racial and gender discrimination in leading corporate law firms is unsurprising. These patterns include obstacles in law firm recruitment, mentoring and support, and advancement; obstacles in their performance reviews and assignments; and obstacles in everyday interracial interactions and in regard to inclusivity within the firms.

One fifth-year associate speaks of her unsuccessful efforts and difficulties in getting mentors in the firm, in contrast to what is typical for white male associates:

> I didn't feel like there was someone truly in my corner, not really. So, what I realized was that there were certain people that were kind of being taken under other people's wings, and for whatever reason, they were perceived as being better. Either better at their work or better because they fit a mold. . . . [The firm] laid off a ton of minorities. . . . And of course, they say it's random. But look, if you think about it, the people who got laid off were the people who had no one to vouch for them. . . . And my hours were good, despite that one year. I did all these things and it still wasn't enough.

Beyond the obvious institutionalized discrimination in mentoring, support, and layoffs, this respondent signals the reality of Melaku's "inclusion tax"—the extra time, money, and emotional and cognitive energy black women lawyers must expend to just attempt to be part of these historically all-white spaces. White male (especially younger) associates sometimes do additional labor to operate in these spaces, but much more substantial extra labor is always required of black women lawyers to gain a temporary or permanent place in these historically white corporate firms. Examples of these additional resources include the significant "number of hours and hundreds of dollars spent in the beauty salon to conform to white aesthetics" and, especially, the enormous emotional and cognitive labor required to deal with frequent "racist and misogynistic comments experienced in white spaces."

THE NORMALIZED WHITE RACIAL FRAME

Melaku's interview accounts demonstrate how the *imposed* expectations of white men commonly shape the occupational lives of black women lawyers.

Rarely in the respondents' commentaries do they note white male decision makers who demonstrate a significant understanding that they are operating out of the dominant white racial frame central to US racism. Such white framing is so normalized that it remains unnoticed by most white men. Consider this commentary from a third-year associate about a training session set up by one firm for associates of color:

> They were like, it is your job to make the majority comfortable with you. It is not their job. They are going to be uncomfortable, and if you're going to succeed in law, it is your job to put them at ease. . . It's exhausting you know . . . because I am the other. So I am the unknown. . . . I see it sometimes, and even diverse (people), . . . it's that person who makes the racist joke about themselves so that everybody else feels more comfortable.

In many cases like this, elite white men assume that people who are not white and male should adapt to *their* white framing of the societal world. In that racial framing, whites are central and generally virtuous as a group, while women of color are typically othered, disparaged, marginalized, and expected to conform to white male expectations. Not only is there clear evidence in this last account of how white discrimination operates, but we also again see the invisible labor required and thus the inclusion tax. Such accounts strongly signal the emotional and cognitive labor needed to navigate these predominantly white law firms. Of course, this workday reality is not unique to law firms and is widely reported by black workers in a variety of employment settings.[2]

Melaku's interviews make clear that white men in these firms routinely use numerous elements of an *extensive* white framing. Today, unfortunately, much social science and legal research on racial and gender issues heavily rely on such concepts as prejudice, stereotyping, bias, and bigoted discrimination. While useful, they are skewed in practice toward an individualistic, cognitive, or nonsystemic interpretation of racial and gender issues. Indeed, a majority of (especially white) social scientists and other professionals (e.g., lawyers and judges), especially since McCarthyism, have not wanted to go beyond a more or less individualistic interpretation of racial matters to a much broader framework accenting systemic racism. In this book, Melaku illustrates how far much of social science has gone from the everyday reality of actual white racial framing (including motivation) and frame-generated discrimination. Indeed, the recent psychological and other social science emphasis on "implicit bias," "hidden bias," and "microaggressions," while sometimes valuable, has taken the focus off the extensive, intentional, and

half-conscious white-racist framing and the macroaggressive actions docu-
mented herein and in other recent field-interview studies.[3]

For four centuries, this still-dominant white racial frame has provided a
broad white-generated worldview from which whites (and others) view US
society. It includes not only racial prejudices and stereotypes but also racial
narratives and interpretations, racial images and language accents, racialized emotions, and inclinations to discriminate. This collectively developed
framing has a positive orientation toward whites as virtuous and superior (a
central pro-white subframe) and a negative orientation toward black people
and other people of color as often unvirtuous and inferior (anti-others sub-
frames).

Melaku adds significant understanding through the accounts in this book
of how the white racial frame operates in professional employment settings.
Several associates make clear that most white men in these law firms have
traditionally racist frames of black women, including the classical stereotype of the "angry black woman." One associate put it thus: "[E]very now
and then, you'll get hit with a perception like black women are angry, black
women are strident, black women are intimidating. . . . You know, most
white [men] don't know any black women other than their housekeeper or
their secretary, like not a single one. . . . Most white men have no context
for interacting with a black woman."

CONCLUSION

Much white racial commentary on the United States still accents the er-
roneous notion that this is a "postracial" society in which black Americans,
especially those in the middle class, already have rough equality with
whites. From this perspective, government remediation, such as affirmative action in employment and education, is no longer necessary. However,
from plenty of hard experience, the African American professionals in this
book know this is an aging white fiction without visible, empirical support.

Joe Feagin
Distinguished Professor, Texas A&M University
Author of *The White Racial Frame*

INTRODUCTION

What We Talk about When We Talk about Diversity

Black women occupy a unique space at the epicenter of dueling tantrums and fearful outbreaks related to race and gender in what some identify as "America's culture wars."[1] The national political conversation teeters between the twin fantasies of postracial utopia and white nationalist revanchism. In the aftermath of the nation's serious contemplation of electing its first female president and apparently motivated by the misogyny on display during the campaign, a movement was born, exposing seemingly ubiquitous sexual abuse, bullying, and assault up to the highest echelons of American power.

It is crucial, therefore, to assess our most prized US cultural, business, and democratic institutions and their rate of progress at converting from archaic structures of white supremacy, patriarchy, and sexism. The advancement of black women, undoubtedly one of the most marginalized groups, offers up a unique vantage point from which to measure the entrenched obstructions to the social, political, and economic progress of women and people of color in all areas of American life. Being that business is of utmost importance in America, particularly for patriarchal institutions and those who profit from them, the US corporate world is a world of singular influence facilitated by the work of elite corporate law firms. And, to those interested in the present status of gendered racism, elite corporate law firms provide an illustrative, if alarming, snapshot of black female professional advancement in the post-Obama, neo-Nazi-normalizing, "grope and grab" Trumpian era.

As it stands today, women and men of color continue to experience systemic racial discrimination in every major societal institution. The current status of black female lawyers suggests that successes hailed by diversity scorecards have not materialized for this demographic. Upon closer examination of the actual numbers behind these self-congratulatory scores, one finds that many prestigious law firms are praised for having moved the pin further along than it actually has. Undoubtedly, there is progress being made: The number of black female associates has incrementally increased in the last forty years.[2] However, the statistics behind this increase reveal it to be highly limited at best. While progress exists for black female associates at the hiring level in elite firms, their rate of advancement to partnership has remained virtually stagnant for forty years.[3] This suggests hurdles in the advancement track of these organizations and raises questions about the level of egalitarianism that figures into their applauded efforts to create a "diverse workplace." Sheryl Sandberg, among others, encourages women to *lean in* to patriarchal institutional spaces.[4] Yet the evidence demonstrates that, even if we, black women, *lean in* with confidence, an embossed invitation, and accomplished work in our hands, it certainly does not mean that we will acquire a seat at the proverbial table. One of the important factors I therefore explore in my research is how the diversity efforts of prestigious law firms actually work to impede, rather than advance, diversity.

In addition to the issues of gender that must be examined, attorneys of color are grossly underrepresented in elite corporate law firms.[5] Not only are black men underrepresented in all positions, but also black female lawyers are virtually absent from the ranks of partner in these institutions, a phenomenon basically ignored when diversity rankings begin chiming the bells of celebration.[6] Take, for instance, the American Lawyer's (AML) 2017 Diversity Scorecard, which ranks firms based on the diversity of its associates and partners.[7] Given this distinction, it is troubling to find that the number-one ranked firm only had three black partners of either gender in their US offices.[8] In most fields, this would be considered a poor showing—and it is—with only 2 black male partners and 1 black female partner out of a total of 203 partners across five offices. Relative to other firms, however, this statistic is praiseworthy, despite the fact that this top-ranked "diverse" establishment can claim only 20 black associates (4.464 percent) out of 448 associates across the country.[9] Clearly there is something amiss, in terms of both outcome and expectations. If this statistic is supposed to reflect a reasonable standard of diversity in the profession, it invites us to take a closer look at the underlying racial rules of the game and how they curtail the professional lives of black female lawyers in elite firms.[10] In particular, understanding and acknowledging how elite white men create, control, and reproduce a racialized system run by white male actors is imperative to understanding the experiences of black female lawyers. The purpose of this book is to do just that.

Chapter 1 details the theoretical framework used to discuss the double burden black women face in elite corporate law firms, particularly how both race and gender create tangible barriers to their advancement prospects. I also summarize the relevant literature on black lawyers in corporate law, as well as studies on the experiences of women of color, to suggest that focusing on black women is crucial to understanding how being part of a subordinated race and gender group affects advancement. Specifically, I describe how systemic racism[11] and color-blind racist ideology[12] apply to the exploration of black women's experiences, extending the concept of the white racial frame[13] and systemic gendered racism to the dynamics of this elite context of corporate law firms.[14] I argue that systemic gendered racism and white racial framing affects the experiences of black women lawyers, bearing substantive consequences for their recruitment, professional development, and advancement. Additionally, in chapter 1 I introduce and advance the concept of the *invisible labor clause*, which references the added invisible labor black women, women as a whole, people of color, the poor, and LGBTQ members must expend to navigate white institutional spaces. I also introduce the *inclusion tax* concept, the additional resources black women are forced to "spend," such as time, money, and emotional and mental energy to be included in white spaces.

In chapter 2, I examine how systemic gendered racism and white racial framing are deeply embedded in accepted professional appearance and its influence on the perceived ability of black female lawyers. I also discuss the pressure to conform to the dominant Eurocentric aesthetic driven by white racial framing, thus affecting black women's prospects for advancement. The inclusion tax is examined through the in-depth discussion of black women's appearances in this chapter, particularly in the context of black hair. Managing, maintaining, and maneuvering black hair, which is often not experienced by other marginalized groups, such as white women or black men, is an example of the inclusion tax black women are forced to pay to be in white spaces.

Chapter 3 explores the "felt" experiences of black female lawyers, looking to transform their status as outsiders in these institutions. I focus on their lack of access to a network of family and friends who can help them navigate within the firm; how white narratives negatively label affirmative action, which contributes significantly to attrition rates; and how added invisible labor creates self-doubt. Systemic racism endemic to white spaces limits access to opportunity by actively isolating and creating self-doubt among black female lawyers.[15] This generates costly labor obligations, unspoken in their contracts, reinforcing the concept of the invisible labor clause.

Chapter 4 further investigates how systemic gendered racism affects the attrition rate through the perceived differences and similarities between black female lawyers and both black male lawyers and white female lawyers. I argue that, despite their shared gender or racial classification, systemic gendered racism provides a nuanced view of how combined dynamics of race and gender uniquely shape their experiences in elite corporate law firms. In isolating the experiences of black women, we illuminate how systemic gendered racism, white racial framing, and the invisible labor clause affect their ability to navigate white spaces and their particular career trajectories.

In chapter 5, I explore how the elite male dominance system (i.e., the boys' club) confers benefits on its members through its exclusionary practices, often excluding women (and sometimes men of color) from social and professional networking opportunities, directly affecting their ability to advance. I illustrate how the white racial frame's patriarchal structure negatively affects the interactions among women in the firm, specifically between black female associates and white female partners, to maintain white male privilege and power. Also, I discuss inequalities in the performance feedback and review process, which further strain black women's ability to obtain substantive assignments crucial to training and development. All of this speaks directly to the invisible labor clause and how black women are required to work harder for less access to advancement opportunities.

Chapter 6 examines how racialized social structures and the group ideology they reinforce systematically exclude black female lawyers from mentor and sponsor relationships. These relationships are crucial to professional development, training, and networking that would enhance the advancement prospects of black female lawyers.

Chapter 7 concludes the book by summarizing key points and discussing the implications of black female lawyers' lack of advancement to partnership. I provide a holistic view of how elite white male spaces, the white racial frame, and systemic gendered racism affect black women. Additionally, I discuss potential resolutions to address the subtle yet pervasive nature of gendered racist practices in law firms and provide suggestions for future research.

The invisible labor clause sheds light on the incredible amount of work required to maneuver elite white institutional spaces. Centering this research on the narratives of black female lawyers and highlighting the inclusion tax they must pay to be a part of a "diverse and inclusive" environment empowers their voices. The invisible labor required to navigate the firm is clearly substantiated in this book. I hope to give my participants a platform through which *they* can shift the discourse of diversity in professional settings toward the realities of subtle, everyday race and gender discrimination upheld and reinforced by elite white men. These racialized and gendered experiences reinforce the invisible labor clause, underscore the cost of the inclusion tax, and create concrete hurdles that prevent black women from reaching the top rungs of elite corporate law firms.

1

BLACK WOMEN'S BURDEN

"Black women face yet other serious forms of gendered racism —the double burden of suffering racial prejudices and stereotyping because they are *black and female.*"[1]

Legal scholars and social scientists, including David B. Wilkins, Mitu G. Gulati, Richard Sander, James E. Coleman Jr., Monique R. Payne-Pikus, John Hagan, and Robert L. Nelson, have engaged various theoretical frameworks to examine why so few black lawyers exist in elite corporate law firms, at the stages of hiring, retention, and advancement.[2] To take a controversial example, Richard Sander's human capital and merit theories, which alleges that associates of color experience high attrition rates as a result of their credentials gap within law firms, falsely leads readers to assume that lawyers of color in general and black lawyers specifically are simply not qualified to work in elite white legal organizations.[3] By not substantively examining how partners' and senior associates' racist thinking and practices place black associates at a disadvantage, Sander reinforces existing stereotypes of black inferiority.

From Wilkins and Gulati's discussion of the impact of pervasive stereotypes on black lawyers gaining access to the "royal jelly"[4] (essential training opportunities) to Coleman and Gulati's critique of available comparative data of white and black lawyers[5] to Payne-Pikus, Hagan, and Nelson's "institutional discrimination theory," the structural elements that determine the failure of elite corporate law firms to retain and advance their black attorneys are investigated from an array of viewpoints. *You Don't Look Like a Lawyer* lessens the gap within this discourse of racial inequity by illustrating the nuanced experiences of black female lawyers navigating elite corporate law settings. The in-depth interviews conducted and data analyses provided herein offer unique details about the work experiences of this demographic and how the intersection of race and gender define these professional women's lives.

Reviewing national data collected in the 2003 US Equal Employment Opportunity Commission (EEOC) study *Diversity in Law Firms* and the Foundation and ABF 2000 study *After the JD* provides us an aggregate sense of hiring, training, and advancement practices at elite firms.[6] It is important to note that this book examines large private law firms, excluding other legal practice settings, such as government, public interest, and nonprofit organizations.

The EEOC's 2003 *Diversity in Law Firms* examines the employment experiences of women and racially subordinated groups in medium and large law firms with one hundred or more employees, chronicling changes in employment for women and people of color at select law firms since 1975. It also assesses the correlation between firm "characteristics," their employment of people of color and women, and their prospects for attaining partnership.[7] What the EEOC study found is that the hiring increase of racially oppressed lawyers occurs primarily within private-sector law firms, ranked highly in prestige and earnings in top legal markets. The study further notes that the proportion of both people of color and women is higher in large, nationally recognized law firms than in other types of law firms, which corroborates Cynthia Fuchs Epstein and her colleagues' foundational research on the integration of women and people of color at the associate level in large elite law firms. They argue that, in the late 1960s and early 1970s, women's groups, black organizations, and government regulation pressured law firms to increase employment opportunities for these groups.[8] This progress is thus understood to have been catalyzed by this pressure forty to fifty years ago.

After the JD, a twelve-year longitudinal study, provides us with important statistical data on the career trajectories of lawyers across the United States, considering gender, racial and ethnic variations.[9] Evident limitations of the *After the JD* study center on the lack of substantial qualitative analysis of the experiences of racially subordinated lawyers in elite firms, which, I argue, would have provided significant insight on why firms with such extensive resources have failed to retain lawyers of color. Further diminishing its scope, *After the JD*'s "minority oversample" does not provide a representative subset that would allow us to make critical assessments of the experiences of black lawyers in corporate law firms in particular.[10] The lack of a larger pool of black respondents presents an obstacle to formulating coherent analyses of the qualitative experiences of black attorneys and how the dynamics of race and gender affect their advancement prospects. This book specifically highlights the narratives of black female lawyers and how they perceive their own career trajectories.

Although the number of studies that focus on the experiences of women of color are about as limited as their presence at the top of the hierarchy, there are some studies that reveal the interlocking nature of the oppression women of color confront in elite professional environments. Catalyst,[11] American Bar Association (ABA),[12] and Corporate Counsel of Women of Color (CCWC)[13] all share emerging themes that outline the unique nature of the black female experience within these environments, attributing high attrition rates among women of color to their fundamental lack of (1) access to mentors and sponsors, (2) substantive billable work, (3) networking opportunities within the firm and with clients, (4) advancement prospects, (5) effective diversity measures, (6) proper training, (7) work–life balance, and (8) the perception that their presence and work are valued institutionally. Combined, these factors perpetuate barriers to women of color, particularly black female attorneys, successfully achieving desired goals within elite corporate law firms.

Despite their merits, these studies do leave a number of questions only partly addressed, namely, why do black female lawyers continue to face significant obstacles, essentially setting their retention and advancement rates at distinctly lower levels than other marginalized groups? The research amassed in this book sheds light on some of these obscure and at times controversial corners by using an intersectional lens as its principal method of investigation.[14] In recent years, statistics from the National Association for Law Placement (NALP) confirm that in these settings, something causes black female professionals to lag behind all other groups when it comes to partnership attainment.[15]

Building on research concerning race and gender in the legal profession, this book assumes that the absence of black female corporate law partners, however normalized within elite corporate law culture, is a social problem worthy of sustained exploration.[16] Simply put, why are there still so few black female partners? To address this question, in 2019, post-Obama (Michelle and Barack), I postulate that systemic gendered racism and white racial framing heavily affect the recruitment, professional development opportunities, and advancement of black female lawyers in elite corporate firms.[17]

As sociologists and prominent critical race scholars Joe R. Feagin and Yanick St. Jean assert, black women experience a "double burden" of entrenched race and gender discrimination.[18] Therefore, the experiences of white female lawyers (which speak to race privilege) and black male lawyers (which speak to gender privilege) must be analyzed in isolation and as comparative resources highlighting the unique barriers confronted by black females. The interpretive frames of *race* (socially constructed beliefs and meanings used to distinguish between different types of human bodies) and *racism* (practices used to reproduce social structures and racial hierarchies that confer benefits, privileges, and power for some while simultaneously promoting oppressive actions and discriminatory behaviors for others) in elite corporate law firms aligns with the theory of systemic racism to reveal the historical and contemporary factors rooted within deep structures of American society that perpetuate racial inequality within most major institutions.[19] This racist reality rationalizes that exclusive economic, social, political, educational, and other privileges for whites maintain their power and dominance at the expense of other groups. The theory of systemic racism is reinforced by Feagin's concept of the white racial frame, an all-encompassing superstructure that includes racial stereotypes, assumptions, narratives, and interpretations embedded primarily within the minds of whites (though people of color can also buy into this frame).[20] This white racial frame establishes whites as superior and the racially oppressed as inferior, thereby justifying continued white dominance and oppression.

Eduardo Bonilla-Silva argues that a "new racism" permeates American social and institutional structures vis-à-vis a color-blind racist ideology that perpetuates racial inequality through a nuanced obfuscation of the racist framing behind institutional discrimination.[21] Such systemic and new racism theories are exhibited in Wendy Leo Moore's research, in which she examines the racialized practices, discourses, and outcomes embedded within the white institutional space of elite law schools.[22] Moore illustrates how students of color negotiate these spaces much as they do upon graduation—expending strenuous amounts of emotional and mental labor to resist the "white racial frame" and the hurdles it presents for the successful completion of their education.

In this book, I examine the beliefs and perceptions of black female lawyers vis-à-vis their elite firm environments and the cultures that rule them. I interviewed twenty attorneys from this population who do work or have worked in the top twenty-five elite corporate law firms in a major northeastern metropolitan city. My questions covered a range of subjects, including recruitment; professional development; inclusivity; and, of course, perceived obstacles to advancement.

COLOR-BLIND RACISM

The term *black female lawyer* describes three distinct socially constructed categories of race, gender, and class. Social scientists of various stripes have dedicated an enormous amount of resources to exploring the theoretical and empirical underpinnings of these elements in American society. Critical race theory, for instance, borne out of critical legal studies, offers an analysis of the relationship between race, racism, and power but from a legal perspective. Similar to systemic racism theory, it posits that racist bigotry is entrenched within US institutions and forms an integral part of the dominant culture. White supremacy, of course, drives the power structures that marginalize people of color in American society. Critical race theory centers the discourse on how the voices of racially subordinated people are silenced by the trappings of white power. In my research, I use critical race theory as a jumping-off point to grapple with the presence of so few black female partners in elite corporate firms despite their diversity rankings and efforts.[23]

A significant body of research addresses the contemporary character of racism and contends that its subtle institutional varieties are real and thriving in America today.[24] As sociologist and critical race scholar Eduardo Bonilla-Silva asserts, despite statistical strides made in the post–civil rights era, there is a new racial structure in place that perpetuates old structures of racial inequality in the United States. Bonilla-Silva describes this as the "new racism."[25] This sleek, sophisticated upgrade of traditional forms of oppression has superseded many of the more blatant, bulky, and thus more vulnerable categories of racism that existed during slavery up through Jim Crow. It has flourished in today's established, complex system of racial domination, which uses the white racial frame and the structures that nurture it to reinforce and maintain white privilege, power, and normativity.[26]

Race, as we know, is a particularly virulent strain of social construction that "produces real effects on the actors racialized as 'black' or 'white.'"[27] The social system built around this construction confers benefits on whites while disadvantaging nonwhites through practices and social relations that strengthen the systemic reach and durability of white privilege. Through racial ideology, the dominant group (whites) justify their positions and challenge subordinate group members (nonwhites) to maintain the racial status quo.[28] As Bonilla-Silva argues, there are several ways that color-blind-racist ideology manifests itself: specifically, through the machinations of abstract liberalism, naturalization, cultural racism, and "minimization of racism" frames.[29] Abstract liberalism, by far the most pervasive and insidious frame, permits whites simultaneously to adopt a liberal viewpoint, allowing them to appear sensible and unbiased, and to oppose practical methods of confronting and dismantling racial inequality.[30] An example that comes to mind is the "meritocratic" argument against policies designed to counterbalance the inequities perpetuated by systemic racism, arguments wielded against such policies as affirmative action.[31] The conceptual emphasis on "equal opportunity," catch-all "individualism," and the equally obscure notion of "choice" distracts us from directly addressing racial issues embedded within the educational, housing, economic, social, and political institutions that determine the mechanics of access for conventionally subordinated racial groups. Backtracking from intentional racist remarks and sentiments with humor is an example of abstract liberalism at its finest, working to create a sense of "unintentional" acts that suggest the existence of, as Bonilla-Silva aptly phrases it, *racism without racists*.[32] Daily microaggressions, such as those that fall under the umbrella of abstract liberalism, are effective at hiding overt racism because they are often so subtle that those who use them are able to passively assert their own dominance while upholding the illusion of neutrality.[33]

Naturalization, a method whites use to justify their limited contact with the racially oppressed, as well as their general racial preference for whites, defines *inequality* in terms of "natural occurrences." In effect, whites normalize racism by suggesting that it is universal among all racial groups to gravitate toward the familiar.[34] Racial matters are "naturalized" in a manner that reinforces racist beliefs without necessarily adopting overtly racist tactics. The idea that segregation and racial preferences are not discriminatory but are, instead, a natural socialization process inherent to all racial groups normalizes this type of color-blind racism.

Cultural racism is used to justify the social and economic status of people of color by relying on stereotypical assessments of the practices, family groupings, and values of their communities.[35] Whites view black communities failing as a result of the choices they make due to cultural deficiency rather than the racialized structure bearing down on their ability to mobilize politically, socially, and economically.[36] Minimizing racism, meanwhile, downplays the salience of race within institutions and daily practice. Whites can deny the significance of discrimination of racially subordinated groups and rely on alternative explanations to explain their failures, thus minimizing the impact of racism. This technique enables whites to argue that racism is no longer pervasive in the post–civil rights era and to suggest that people of color are hypersensitive to race issues.[37] The usage of color-blind-racist frames is not meant to label all white people as inherently racist. Although racial categorization is real, white people who do not acknowledge its existence, regardless of intent, endorse its policy of conferring benefits to whites over racially subordinated groups. This, in turn, sustains the racial status quo.[38] There is a deep-rooted racialized structure in American culture that works to benefit whites and to disadvantage nonwhites, while simultaneously upholding the pillars of patriarchal domination, exclusion, and misogyny.[39] The black women I interviewed are restricted by these frames, and their experiences can only be adequately understood through the prism of critical race analysis.

THE SIGNIFICANCE OF WHITE RACIAL FRAMING

Joe R. Feagin's *theory of systemic racism* provides a useful analytical tool for picking apart the mechanics of how elite law firms maintain their hegemony and control of the archaic superstructure that facilitates the elite-white-male dominance system.[40] For example, many associates of color argue that they are unable to develop organic mentor and sponsor relationships with white partners because partners tend to reach out to associates who "remind them" of themselves.[41] Systemic racism focuses on the reliability and depth of racialized ideas and structures historically embedded within institutionalized practices. In US history, recognizing the centrality of political and economic control whites acquired through the stolen land of Native Americans and the forced labor of enslaved Africans is key to understanding how racism persists over time, evolving within institutions and sharpening its tools against the wheel of progress, resistance, and social justice.[42] As a result, racist hierarchies continue to be systemic, normalized, and profoundly entrenched within white institutions. People of color experience very real and tangible effects of economic, social, and political inequalities that stem from centuries-old subtle, covert, and obvious discriminatory practices. In the context of law firms, for instance, associates of color are often viewed as "affirmative action hires," suggesting that they are unqualified for the job to begin with, leading to their exclusion from substantive assignments and networking opportunities.[43] More broadly, people of color from every walk of American life experience subtle racial discriminatory practices daily in housing, education, lending, and other major social institutions.

Feagin argues that this foundational racialized structure of oppression that manifests in antiblack racism has remained consistent throughout American history and is enforced and maintained by legal, political, economic, and other systems across society. He later builds on his theory of systemic racism by developing the concept of the white racial frame, consisting of the various racial stereotypes, prejudices, ideologies, images, emotions, narratives, and interpretations that justify and perpetuate daily racial oppression. The passage of time, of course, has a cumulative effect on the development of this frame, created by whites to defend and rationalize their social structures and ideology from a dominant white perspective that ignores, silences, or rejects outright the perspectives and views of people of color.[44] Furthermore, historical injustices passed down from generation to generation continue to prevent subordinated racial groups from accessing resources readily available to white Americans, including economic, social, educational, and political capital.[45] It is imperative to the resolution of racial inequality that the actors and agents of racial oppression, as well as its beneficiaries, be frankly named.

Systemic racism is the institutionalized form of racist attitudes against subordinated racial groups to obscure the levers that engender the dominant position of whites in American society. There is an overarching system of societal oppression at work here that includes systemic racism, systemic sexism, and systemic classism, which Feagin and Ducey describe as the "elite-white-male dominance system" mentioned previously.[46] Recognizing the benefits white men receive from subordinating black female lawyers in elite corporate law firms is integral to understanding their motives for ignoring or actively perpetuating these disadvantages. Elite-white-male dominance operates out of a racial frame that maintains its pro-white-virtue center and an antiblack subframe directly and indirectly imposed daily on women and men of color. The scope of its impact, which involves almost all law firms and major corporations and nearly all controlled by elite white men, is vast and devastating to those it targets, disadvantages, or discards.[47]

Drawing on Feagin's conceptualization of the white racial frame, sociologist Wendy Leo Moore develops a "white space" concept that extends the literature on institutional racism by examining the sociolegal construction of race as it has been historically linked to the preservation of white economic and political power in the United States.[48] Through a critical race theory framework focused on law schools, Moore effectively discusses the creation of a white institutionalized space that reproduces the racial hierarchy and maintains white privilege and power through the relentless reinforcement of white-dominant perspectives. Specifically, Moore theorizes that elite law schools, which are inherently white, use a white racial frame to structure the dissemination of legal knowledge through an "objective," "emotionless," and "neutral" strategy that ignores the historical relevance of race in the United States and further disadvantages students and faculty of color by indirectly attacking their experience. Moore suggests that law students of color must adopt a white racial frame and push their own experiences and views onto the back burner or out the window to be successful.[49] This overt racist teaching practice reinforces the structural organization of racial hierarchy prevalent in law schools and other US institutions, such as elite corporate law firms.

Moore also argues that the conflation of race and gender identity is problematic because of the various ways they operate in society.[50] This is key to understanding the experiences of black female lawyers in elite corporate law firms because the ways in which black female respondents express their raced and gendered experiences may not always reflect the expected intersection and overlapping of racial and gender categories. As Moore argues, the conflation of gender and race identity does not allow for a critical analysis of how these identities work in hierarchical contexts. Instead it illustrates the racialized landscape students and faculty of color must navigate, where white privilege and power shape their daily practices, rates of success, and racial discourse. This book builds on Moore's conceptualization of white institutional spaces, with their history of exploitation and exclusion, and applies it to elite corporate law firms.

SYSTEMIC GENDERED RACISM

Looking at the experiences of black women, we find, requires an intersectional approach. We cannot talk about race and gender without looking at how other socially constructed identities and categories, real or imagined, affect the experiences of black female attorneys. The interconnectedness of these various identities creates experiences that produce oppressive or disadvantageous outcomes for this demographic. Many scholars, from feminist theorists to critical race theorists, have employed intersectionality within their research to examine the interaction between race, gender, class, and other categories of difference in individual, social, cultural, and institutional modes—particularly with respect to power and oppression.[51]

What I hypothesize, therefore, is that both race and gender, at their point of intersection, create tangible barriers that affect the advancement prospects of black female attorneys in elite corporate law firms. I also argue that race is more salient than gender, or vice versa, depending on the specific set of structural obstacles respondents confront. What is clear is that systemic racism, the white racial frame, and color-blind-racist framing create circumstances that trigger the influence of race and gender, establishing a system of oppression that reflects the "intersection" of multiple forms of discrimination.

Gendered racism, first introduced by sociologist Philomena Essed, articulates the notion that the racist interactions shaped by gender produce unique forms of oppression. Essed argues that racism, being gendered, operates on black men and black women in different ways, depending on stereotypes and gendered assumptions.[52] Similar to Feagin's white racial frame, Essed's "everyday racism" theory encapsulates the favoring of the dominant group and active rejection or discrimination of racially subordinated groups due to white-centric ideology, shaping the personal and professional experiences of people of color accordingly.[53]

Sociologist Adia Harvey Wingfield's concept of *systemic gendered racism* brings us even closer to a holistic approach. Systemic gendered racism points directly to the inseparable linkage of race and gender, arguing essentially that the white racial frame that rationalizes systemic discrimination is also gendered.[54] Black female lawyers thus experience racial and gendered oppression in ways that are unique to their social identity.[55] Based on my respondents' accounts, I support this assertion that systemic gendered racism bears substantive consequences for the recruitment, professional development, and advancement opportunities of black female attorneys in elite corporate firms.

THE INVISIBLE LABOR CLAUSE AND THE INCLUSION TAX

In conducting the interviews, I quickly learned that black female lawyers engage frequently with the idea that they expend significant labor hours performing "invisible labor" that their white counterparts are not required to do in order to negotiate the ongoing meaning of their institutional role and presence, especially in relation to their advancement in the firms. The chapters to follow explore this added "invisible labor" and how its implications compare with the experiences of their white counterparts who are not subjected to the same type of added labor. The invisible labor clause is constituted by unwritten rules of social and professional contracts deeply rooted in the United States and global histories of white patriarchal domination. This traditional cultural narrative of success requires marginalized groups, including the racially oppressed, women, the poor, and LGBTQ members, to perform added invisible labor to navigate their daily existence within social and professional spaces.

The terms and mechanisms of the invisible labor clause are not explicitly outlined, but they manifest when marginalized groups are forced to negotiate their presence in institutional spaces created, controlled, and reproduced by elite white men. The invisible labor clause becomes evident through repeated exposure to required labor that is not recognized yet necessary to be in the space. For example, compliance or resistance to dominant narratives about marginalized groups, outward rejection of these narratives, or conformity to white narratives all require added invisible labor. Essentially, marginalized individuals are required to perform added invisible labor to navigate white institutional spaces regardless of which narrative is being perpetuated.

In the context of law firms and other professional institutions, the invisible labor clause is an unwritten contractual term that effectively conditions continued employment at will for professionals of color and women on a requirement that they perform added labor in their positions. Oftentimes, this added labor is required to navigate daily racial or gendered encounters or both, and more specifically microaggressions, in a manner to counterbalance or neutralize negative perceptions or presumptions of their majority colleagues and counterparties. The invisible labor clause speaks directly to this added emotional, mental, and physical labor black women are forced to expend in order to survive in the white institutional spaces discussed throughout the book. As concrete practices of systemic gendered racism and white racial framing create concrete hurdles to the advancement of black female lawyers in elite corporate law firms, the invisible labor clause becomes pivotal for how these women attempt to negotiate their very presence within the white cultural frame while navigating the firm.

The type of added invisible labor black women must perform to navigate white institutional spaces includes emotional, mental, and physical labor, such as expending energy worrying about performance, appearance, self-doubt, recognition, visibility or invisibility, organic mentor and sponsorship connections, and other issues. The added emotional and mental labor includes the considerable physical time that may be taken up by these concerns, creating stress in both professional and personal settings. White males may argue that they, too, have to expend additional labor in order to traverse institutions. However, it must be noted that the additional labor expended by black female lawyers can be seen as a tax they are required to pay to be included in white spaces. The inclusion tax is the additional resources "spent," such as time, money, and mental and emotional energy, just to be allowed in white spaces. For example, the number of hours and hundreds of dollars spent in the beauty salon to conform to white aesthetics, as well as the enduring racist and misogynistic comments experienced in white spaces, all count toward the inclusion tax. The tax is like a fee paid in added labor to be included in white institutions. Unlike their white counterparts, black female lawyers are, in essence, required to work harder to fulfill nebulous, shifting, identity-related job requirements to survive in elite white institutions by doing more work without the same guarantee of benefits.

The invisible labor clause and inclusion tax concepts provide a critical lens to highlight and analyze how systemic racism, white racial framing, and systemic gendered racism affect the experiences of black female lawyers in elite corporate law firms. It can also be used to analyze the experiences of other marginalized groups in US institutions. The invisible labor clause demonstrates how black women must perform added invisible labor just to be seen or recognized. It is important to distinguish that black women may not achieve the same, nearly the same, or perhaps only conceivably the same benefits, results, or consideration of their labor compared to white male actors who are not subjected to the same dynamic, which of course results from white patriarchal structures that operate to maintain white male privilege and power. That is how black women are disadvantaged, which focuses on how elite spaces have a pro-white center that effectively impedes on their potential to succeed. Therefore, understanding the difference between the kind of labor black female lawyers put into traversing the firm versus the labor white male lawyers put into traversing the firm is imperative for advancing the discussion of equity and advancement of this historically sidelined class of workers.

Through the inclusion—or tolerance—of people of color in white institutional spaces, the elite law firm is now artificially viewed as a space that promotes equality and opportunity.[56] But qualitative and statistical analysis of black female professional attrition and advancement rates suggest that there is, indeed, something seriously amiss in these elite corporate environments, where one is conceivably offered entry at the front door as a means for deliberately or inadvertently pushing another out the back door when every other passageway is structurally blocked.

The purpose of this book is to use the theoretical foundations described in this chapter to explain, through the voices of twenty black female attorneys, how precisely this discouraging phenomenon results in a disproportionately low number of black female partners in elite corporate settings. In the next chapter, we start with appearance and work our way in.

2

YOU DON'T LOOK LIKE A LAWYER

"So many people are walking around the law firm, totally insecure about their abilities to be there, disposition, where they are, if they're getting enough work, if they're meeting the mark. Associates in general have that, but the burden or the trouble I think that African American associates also have is, *Do the people think I'm smart enough? Are they looking at my hair funny? Am I dressed the part? Am I not as good? If I don't get this assignment and someone else got this assignment, are they saying that I'm incompetent? Is it because of the color?* That is very difficult, and so what tends to happen is people start to isolate themselves, and when you're a person of color and you isolate yourself, it's a death wish. You might as well throw in the towel because you as a person of color, right or wrong, on behalf of the firm's culture, have to be able to get past that to get work."

—Nikoleta, third-year associate

"I think that there's still enough of a thought that a lawyer looks a certain way. . . . They feel comfortable with you because you fit an image of what they actually think works."

—Hannah, fifth-year associate

Hannah is a single, thirty-nine-year-old lawyer who currently works as in-house counsel after leaving a top-ranked law firm in a northeastern metropolis. The interview I conducted with her took place in a beautiful conference room at the office of the firm representing the organization she now works for. The tables have turned, however, and now Hannah is the client.

A fascinating woman, really, Hannah has very sophisticated notions of race, gender, and the workplace. Donning beautiful, dark brown curls with perfectly placed blond streaks, she is often mistaken for Latina because of her light skin tone and fluency in Spanish—which she picked up during various experiences abroad. Make no mistake, however: Hannah clearly and proudly identifies as black—so much so that she questions how *non–African American blacks* are even able to grasp the complexities of the black experience in America.

Raised by her mother and father in a middle-class neighborhood in southern California, Hannah comes from the highest educational pedigree. She attended private primary schools, received an Ivy League undergraduate degree, and pursued her juris doctorate at one of the three top-tier law schools in the country. She is not only brilliant on paper, but she also simply lights up a room. Her anecdotes depicting her experience as an associate are clear and passionate. Although, by her own admission, Hannah struggles at times with the nature of those experiences, she is firmly convinced that it was absolutely necessary to leave the firm at which she worked in order to be successful in her field.

One of her biggest barriers we discussed was the perception that she did not "fit in" to the role of a lawyer based on her appearance. Like many black professionals across industry (from finance to technology, from law and medicine to the academy), Hannah experienced a debilitating apprehension: We, as people of color, do not look the part of the "typical" lawyer or doctor because we are socially conditioned to view individuals in highly prestigious occupations as white.

Regardless of how hard Hannah worked, how great the quality of her work, or how many compliments her work received from respected clients, it is her conviction that she failed to be viewed as a legitimate attorney. To receive *that* distinction, it was necessary to do more than conform to corporate aesthetics—which in the end did not seem feasible for her.

In Hannah's case, as in many, systemic gendered racism continuously worked to undermine her material successes and perceived capabilities in the eyes of white partners in the firm.[1] She could not be anything but herself, of course: a *black female* lawyer, which conflicted directly with the white racial framing of what a competent lawyer looked like, should, and could in fact be.[2]

In this chapter, I examine how systemic gendered racism is deeply embedded in professional appearance and how it influences the perception of black female lawyers' abilities, thus affecting their prospects for advancement. More than any other group, perhaps, the legal judgment of this demographic is inextricably tied to their appearance—the more "ethnic" they appear, the less capable they are perceived by their colleagues. Consequently, pressure to conform to dominant Eurocentric aesthetics is high and demanding, a loaded issue that female lawyers of African descent confront daily in elite law firms, as well as in many other corporate—and even noncorporate—settings. Yet this is not an accident or coincidence but instead is intricately tied to the racialized system created by elite white men that forces marginalized individuals to conform to the dominant white Eurocentric standard and that is constantly reinforced by elite white male agents using the white racial frame.

As alluded to in the epigraph of this chapter, there are potential ramifications of the disproportionate emphasis on difference, as evidenced by a recently publicized incident involving a black physician who attempted to assist a sick passenger on a Delta flight. Yet another example of how black women are not generally perceived as professional, the staff onboard ultimately rejected the physician's expertise with the simple explanation that she did not "look like a doctor" and that they were "looking for an actual physician," which of course she was.[3]

I discuss how the invisible labor clause is enacted through the ways in which black female lawyers are forced to expend more emotional, mental, and physical energy (not to mention time, which detracts from other enterprises) to cope with the pressures associated with maintaining a physical appearance that conforms to white corporate aesthetics. Fashioning one's hair and dress is an excellent example of how black women are forced to pay an inclusion tax to fit in to the existing cultural frame of elite white men in corporate law firms, yet many women of color remain unable to break through its prohibitive ceiling.[4]

This chapter extends the discourse on black women professionals' experiences in corporate environments by focusing on how they are affected by the perceptions of what legal professionals are "supposed to look like" and how black women scramble to conform to this desired image in white institutional spaces, essentially paying the inclusion tax. Moreover, I examine systemic gendered racist notions of beauty, the discourse surrounding black female lawyers' hair, and how they are confronted with (and often *forced* to engage in) the seemingly minor yet surprisingly corrosive racial dialogue attached to it.

WHITE CASTLE

Elite corporate law firms are typically white institutional spaces, only accessible to white men. Today this space continues to be predominantly white and male, with white associates and partners comprising approximately 84 percent of the total US lawyer demographic.[5] White partners constitute a whopping 90.79 percent of all partners.[6] As noted in the previous chapter, associates of color are drastically underrepresented in elite corporate law firms, which leads, quite logically, to their underrepresentation in partnership positions.[7]

Fewer black female associates are recruited, and attrition remains highest among black associates, which further reduces both the number of black female lawyers in law firms overall and the pool of potential partners of color.[8] Evidence clearly shows that the path to partnership is curtailed for this demographic by the manifold hurdles I explore in this book, preventing their professional development, limiting their advancement opportunities, and thus leading to such high rates of attrition. By including a nuanced account of black female lawyers' direct experiences, we are able to fully appreciate the unique intersection of race and gender in this dynamic, illustrating the barriers that prevent their entry to these institutional spaces.

Previous studies on black lawyers in corporate law firms have investigated the subconscious stereotypes and biases that proliferate in these environments and the culture within firms that dictates the schemata of mentoring opportunities, as well as various generalizations that lump racially subordinated associates together rather than assessing individual merit.[9] Such empirical research provides a crucial understanding of the conventional arguments used by firms to justify the small number of black lawyers and its impact on partnership acquisition. Further adding to the complexity of the experience for black *women* in these firms are gender barriers to advancement. Research asserts that women face much tougher obstacles to achieving overall visibility, developing sponsor relationships, becoming rainmakers, and accessing informal and formal networking opportunities, and they encounter even greater implicit and subtle prejudices.[10]

As indicated by prominent studies, high attrition rates among women of color in corporate environments can be attributed to such factors as the lack of substantive billable work, effective diversity measures, proper training, work–life balance, inclusion in firm culture, and the sentiment that the work they perform is actually valued.[11] These factors combined support and explain recent data results from Vault and Minority Corporate Counsel Association's *2017 Law Firm Diversity Survey*, indicating that US female lawyers of African descent have the highest attrition rate across all racial and gender categories.[12]

AMERICAN BEAUTY

In discussing corporate aesthetics, we must first acknowledge that white institutional spaces are created and maintained by elite white men to adhere to *Eurocentric* beauty standards that out of hand exclude many women of color—particularly black women. The European beauty standard affirms the belief that European features are universally more appealing and desirable.[13] Attributes linked to whiteness, such as light skin, thin nose, thin lips, straight hair, and light-colored eyes, are viewed as beautiful, as opposed to features that contrast with or complicate these standards. Black women's physical differences from white women, ranging from skin color to hair texture to facial features to body type, are pitted against the "normalized beauty standards" of American society.[14]

Derived directly from this predominant white racial frame of beauty, black women are viewed as *inferior* to white women, with particular markers, such as hair, triggering this toxic conception of racial inferiority and often lack of femininity.[15] Historically, in the United States and elsewhere, dark skin; natural hair (braids, locks, Afros); Afrocentric facial features; and voluptuous or curvaceous body types have been disfavored, where not outright stigmatized or banned. Such systemic gendered racist constructions of beauty and femininity have been tied together to obfuscate the humanity of black women *as women*, thereby justifying their physical, mental, and emotional abuse; forced exploitative labor; and sexual harassment—or worse—to which they historically have been subjected at the hands of whites.[16]

This Eurocentric standard of beauty is deeply embedded within the white racial frame, where a definition of beauty is foisted onto all racial groups that do not naturally conform to racial images of whiteness. Because the elite-white-male dominance system controls the social perception for society as a whole, those individuals who do not personify this white beauty standard are categorically deemed as both literally and figuratively unattractive.[17] Therefore, black women are often forced to conform to the Eurocentric standard of beauty, which is directly linked to "being professional," in order to be accepted outwardly in white institutional spaces. They must pay an inclusion tax through the labor and funds needed to conform to this "professional white standard."

This rejection of individual beauty is also an exploitative mechanism used to keep blacks and other people of color in subordinate positions and to reinforce white privilege and power, thus maintaining racial inequality in white institutional spaces.[18] Obviously, systemic gendered racism hence dictates that black women are negatively affected by these prevailing standards, while white women and their paternalistic counterparts are inordinately advantaged. The payment of the inclusion tax is required of black women, and women of color who are perceived as black share similar experiences conforming.

In historically white spaces, such as law firms, social relations and practices highlight these Eurocentric standards of beauty, which are enforced by white agents and the culture that then develops in such spaces.[19] We see this play out in popular media images of black women, which tend to reflect whitened representations of women of color—lighter skin, straighter hair, and slimmer figures—as beautiful *through* white markers, reinforcing the universality of the Eurocentric aesthetic.[20] Hair, a significant racial marker, thus symbolizes the inherent inferiority of black women and plays a role in how beauty is mandated in firms and other corporate settings.

As one might expect, these racial projections of beauty can have a deleterious impact on the day-to-day experience of black female lawyers and other black professionals. As Paulette Caldwell, professor of law, argues,

> [Black female lawyers] bear the brunt of racist intimidation resulting from western standards of physical beauty. This intimidation begins early in the lives of black female children, continues throughout adulthood, and causes immeasurable psychological injury and dignitary harm. Such intimidation also is a crucial instrument to limit the economic and social position of black women.[21]

Within the past two decades, research concerning black women's aesthetics in corporate environments has steadily increased, primarily focused on the surprisingly, if not absurdly, incendiary subject of hair.[22] Hair is clearly a distinct physical characteristic often used to determine or assign racial classification; historically, hair has established such explosive identifications as maternity; paternity; and the social, political, and economic factors that attend to them. Because of hair's physical malleability, blacks must decide whether to keep their hair natural, conform to prevailing white aesthetics, or change their hair in ways that do not reflect the dominant white standard; each choice is potentially problematic, depending on perspective.

For example, the decision to go *against* the existing social order through certain hair choices tends to create fear and loathing in both whites and conforming blacks. Studies have shown that black women who don Afro-centric hairstyles suffer negative effects to their economic status.[23] Experimental studies to determine whether particular hairstyles have a negative effect on the perception of a participant's professionalism reveal that black women who wear Afrocentric (versus Eurocentric) hairstyles are less likely to be hired or promoted than those who do not and are typically viewed as more dominant and less professional.[24] As suggested, some findings even indicate that black evaluators penalize black employees with Afrocentric hairstyles as harshly as or more so than whites. In other words, as critical race scholars Philomena Essed and Joe R. Feagin posit, no demographic is immune to the dominant racial ideology that maintains the status quo—including negative perceptions of black resistance to Eurocentric standards of beauty.[25] For women in particular, systemic gendered racism punishes those who choose to wear their hair in natural styles rather than conform to the white racial frame that inhibits, denigrates, conditions, and controls them.

As alluded to earlier, systemic gendered racism hinders professional development opportunities and obstructs the advancement of black female lawyers in elite corporate law firms through often daily microaggressions. In addition to expending more time and energy, both emotional and mental, in dealing with comments and anxiety about their physical appearance and how it fits in (or doesn't) to the white cultural frame, black female lawyers face pressures—and more labor and expense—that their white male or female, and even black male, counterparts simply do not face, which further burdens an already-cumbersome path to partnership advancement.[26] Taken in tandem with other factors, the cumulative effect of the stigmas attached to both blackness and femaleness are indispensable keys for understanding the factors that lead to high attrition and low partner rates for black female lawyers.[27]

Throughout the interviews, there were several emerging themes: first among them, as outlined previously, the notion that black female lawyers do not fit the standard image of what a lawyer looks like (reminiscent of the now-infamous "we're looking for an actual physician" shot heard around the world).[28] Among other things, this preconception results in the inevitable case of mistaken identity that black female lawyers endure, described in detail here. Finally, there is the trope of black female lawyers needing to engage in specious and often offensive hair dialogue with white associates and partners in their firm rather than in conversations that include substantive questions, such as those pertaining to mentorship, billable work, networking, and developing deeper roots in firm culture.

As detailed in the experiences of my participants, it is possible to confirm the belief that, in the case of black female lawyers, race and gender intersect, overlap, and combine in obstructive ways that create significant barriers to their prospects for advancement.

FITTING IN

Not only in day-to-day operations but also in the glittering world of elite corporate law overall, appearance is a core component to all phases of recruitment, professional development, and advancement. If the dictum state, "The clothes make the man," for females at work in this environment—not to mention racially subordinated groups—the notion takes on more complex dimensions. Paying an inclusion tax is necessary to fitting in.

In assessing what an ideal candidate needs in order to gain entry to an elite firm, all participants acknowledged that a standard checklist with "objective" criteria is used by the firm to gauge the fit of a potential candidate. The language for the criteria is significant: The concept of fitness ("fitting in" or being a "good fit," etc.) is, of course, a determination based on the subjective narrative of the interviewer. What we have, then, as articulated by prominent race theorists, is a form of the "neutrality" or "objectivity" within a color-blind-racist ideology that imposes a white racial frame inherently disadvantaging people of color in institutional spaces.[29]

The use of language to sanitize the dirty work of excluding subordinated racial groups is reflected in the terminology law firms use in their recruiting practices, as well. "Fitting in" (or being a "good fit") are frequently racially coded phrases to neutralize racist notions of who can occupy white spaces.[30] Prominent legal scholars David B. Wilkins and Mitu G. Gulati discuss the "fitting-in" concept in the recruitment and hiring processes that law firms employ and identify two stages: (1) the *visible stage*, where standard (meaning unbiased) signals are used to determine the eligibility of a candidate, and (2) the *invisible stage*, where subjective criteria are used to make the same assessment.[31]

Moreover, as expressed by one participant, there appear to be structural impediments to recruitment built into the hiring process itself. Lydia is a single, thirty-two-year-old third-year associate working at one of the top-ranked law firms in the Northeast. She grew up an only child with black professional parents—a dentist and a school guidance counselor—in a middle-class neighborhood in a Midwestern city. During the interview, she struck me as a very level-headed and calculated individual who thinks carefully about the impact of her decisions. Among them is the decision that landed her in law school after working in the business sector and deciding whether to attend business school or obtain a doctorate in economics.

When asked about the recruitment process and how law firms decide whom to hire, Lydia explained,

> I think the main thing that firms, what they look for is . . . people who fit in . . . who they think will assimilate well to the culture of the place. . . . The interview process is very bizarre. You're looking for a lot of things, but it's really hard to gauge those things, I think, a lot of times in the interview process because they say they want people who are creative, who are team-oriented, who can analyze complex issues well. And so, you try and figure that out in thirty-minute interviews with people.

Because this process is rigorous, high-stakes, and logistically limited in scope, the brevity of the interview leaves a gap often filled by an interviewer's preconceived notion of the potential candidate's merits and ability to assimilate into existing firm culture. This factor essentially gives a leg up to candidates who share a cultural frame of reference with the interviewer and sit within the privileged parameters of the white racial frame. Few black females, compared to white males, white females, and even males of color, fall into this category.

Again, I return to Hannah's illustration:

> I think that there's still enough of a thought that a lawyer looks a certain way. So when you say, "What are the ideal characteristics?" I mean, they've just got to look like a lawyer, act like a lawyer, sound like a lawyer. Law school is supposed to teach you to think like a lawyer. . . . What's interesting is we're still in a place where culturally people think lawyers—you know the Apple commercials where they got the guy who plays the Mac and the guy who plays the PC? We have concepts of what things look like to us, and we fill that concept. So that's why the human resources and diversity officer is a black woman. We have things, we think things, we conceptualize something. So there are a lot of smart people. There are a lot of good people. I think the thing that stands out is, when you speak, someone else is willing to listen because otherwise they don't really know what you're capable of. So how do you get somebody willing to listen? They feel comfortable with you because you fit an image of what they actually think works.

What Hannah described is how the image of a lawyer is shaped by the white racial frame, which is indicative of its pro-white center and antiblack subframe imposed on women and men of color by elite white men, operating to maintain the white status quo. As Hannah suggested, conforming to an image of what already exists takes added labor, enacted by the invisible labor clause and measured out in emotional, mental, and physical labor expended. This is another example of how the inclusion tax is levied against black women lawyers just to be in white spaces. The time, money, and emotional and mental energy spent trying to conform to accepted images of whiteness is costly to black women.

BUILT FOR COMFORT

The question of comfort lingers provocatively behind the issue of assimilation to existing firm culture and cultural practice. As I have discussed, the concept of fitting in, itself a lexical construct of the white racial frame, determines the mechanics of recruitment, professional development, and advancement. Here, I discuss in greater detail the nuances that dictate how this language of assimilation unfolds in material ways in these central arenas.

Again, with respect to the hiring process, the drama of recruitment is fairly simple: It feeds off the performer–audience dynamic.[32] Along with submitting one's academic or experiential qualifications, the interviewee *performs* the assumed role of "compatible candidate," which is intended to give an indication of how she will *perform* in a given position if hired and as an actor within the firm's existing culture. The goal of the interviewee is to present herself as someone who can easily fit this mold. Associates of color, particularly black females, may therefore find the interview process difficult because fitting in is often confused with sameness or likeness. Color-blind-racist ideology helps us to understand how this notion of sameness is used to accommodate subtle discriminatory practices within such law firms.[33]

The phenomenon is bolstered by what sociologist Eduardo Bonilla-Silva describes as a naturalization frame, which slyly reinforces the conviction that segregation and racial preferences are not discriminatory toward those who do not fit the preference group—hence, color-blind—but are instead the by-product of a natural socialization process characteristic of all racial groups, like "sticking to" and "most comfortable with." Although perhaps true to a certain extent, this frame discounts the fact that not all racial groups share the white racial frame's power, blind privilege, and conviction of its own cultural superiority. Being former targets rather than beneficiaries of the white racial frame's hegemonic sphere of influence, not all racial groups allow the same concepts to take precedence when filling the gaps in their knowledge of the other—particularly the same prejudices and preconceived notions of people of color's incompetence, laziness, and endemic inferiority.

Again, the white racial frame and its ability to normalize discriminatory practices by dressing them up in terminology that conflates the denial of racism and privilege with neutrality perpetuates racial inequality in corporate environments. Thus, we are able to identify how actors of oppression—in this case, elite white males—are able to claim an air of objectivity or neutrality while simultaneously carrying out persistent but subtle discriminatory slights against those who aspire to occupy privileged areas under their restrictive control.

The experiences of black female lawyers and how their accounts reflect the subtle dynamics of the recruitment process in elite firms facilitate how we understand the intersection of race and gender early in one's legal career. Stereotypes can and do significantly affect—both positively and negatively—how an individual is perceived without even necessitating a tangible or sustained interaction. The color-blind-racist ideology that has proliferated in the post–civil rights era craftily forgoes some of the more overt forms of racial discrimination prevalent throughout US history while producing many of the same effects.[34] The quieter style of color-blind racism allows for the maintenance of white power and discrimination in often subtle ways, one of the most influential of which is through language.[35] Here, the concept of fitting in at the firm might actually be interpreted as "Can this candidate *fit into the existing white cultural frame* without disrupting it?"

This white racial frame construct typically makes its appearance at the very initial stages of the recruitment process; at the first interview certainly, but even in the review of a résumé, it can be triggered by associations connected with something so innocuous as the racial or ethnic marker of one's name. Subsequent interviews further develop these perceptions; admittance into the firm and interaction with colleagues does not disperse but instead solidifies them. The burden of trying to fit in to the existing white racial frame is clearly on racially subordinated groups. With black professionals, particularly black female lawyers, the question is, How can you reach that goal?

Several participants in my study expressed the conviction that the recruitment process is geared toward hiring *specific* types of people, suggesting that the so-called objective criteria for hiring does not, however contrary to policy, replace the importance of subjective individual impression. Hannah, the fifth-year associate featured at the beginning of this chapter, had very strong opinions on the matter: The subjective biases that influence the recruitment process haunt an incoming cohort of associates even through its subsequent efforts at advancement. At her law firm, she asserted, the preferred candidate was clearly a "white male with contacts":

> I think that people get a feeling. It's about the trust thing. Somebody decides that they think that you're smart, and somebody decides that they think that they'd like to work with you, and somebody decides that they think that there's a niche that you fit that they need to fill. A white male with contacts. A white male with the deep Rolodex and a family connection or background. That's all it is.

As in any relationship, trust figures prominently in the development of connections at elite corporate law firms. Hannah went on to explain that this is reflected in the recruitment process; interviewers tend to have more trust and confidence in those who meet the "traditional" (i.e., hegemonic) cultural image of a lawyer (i.e., white males like them) and are thus able to maintain group privilege in these institutional spaces. In the case of hiring, in other words, it is safe to say that white male candidates have an *inherent* advantage over black females, as well as other subordinated racial, ethnic, and gender groups. White males are not subjected to paying an inclusion tax like black women. The elite-white-male dominance system operates seamlessly to empower white male candidates.

Furthermore, according to Hannah, this phenomenon can be easily traced to the table at which partnership decisions are made:

> Black people who made partner in the days of yore were people who either came with a Rolodex or they had a really specific skill set. I think it's the concept of people saying, *Can you rain make? Can you bring business?* It's the concept of, *Do we think you're somebody who can make a phone call and get deals or get business?* What I mean about trust and relationships is, there are white people who make partner who can't do that, but someone likes them enough to help them do that, who says, "I have enough business to share my business with somebody that I like, who I trust, that makes me look good and I feel good about."

What she described here is a barrier to success, in this case partnership, attributable to Hannah's insurmountable status as *other*—being *black* and *female* in a white-male-dominated space. Because elite white men mitigate access to advancement opportunities, she, as well as other racially subordinated candidates, are constantly in the futile position of struggling to fit the square peg of eligibility into the round hole of the white racial frame.

The aforementioned theme of trust falls under the rubric of emotions and narratives that hold concrete benefits for whites' privilege within that frame. Regardless of merit, this trust and comfort mechanism, developed through a history of domination, rationalizes social structures that subordinate people of color in ways that are so subtle we may not even consider them racially motivated. Hannah, among others, described their influence as "cultural programming."

Said programming, both conscious and subconscious in nature, not only operates by obscuring opportunities for black female candidates to attempt the uphill battle of assimilation but, as we will see, also has the propensity to lock them into an outrageous systemic gendered struggle for *acknowledgment* once they even reach the coveted path to advancement implied by a successfully navigated recruitment effort.

ACKNOWLEDGMENT: THE CHRONIC CASE OF MISTAKEN IDENTITY

Philomena, a single, twenty-six-year-old third-year associate, works at a reputable law firm in the Northeast. She is the eldest of three siblings raised in a middle-class home in the country's mid-Atlantic region. Like many respondents, both her parents worked in professional positions and routinely stressed that education as *the* key to success in life and career. A garrulous child who loved the sound of her own voice and a good argument, Philomena did not seriously consider law school, despite early encouragement to become a lawyer, until, as an early graduate from college, she decided to take the LSAT, at which she excelled—she'd found her calling. When discussing how the interview process reflects the given priorities of elite firms, Philomena was clear that, although assimilation (fitting in) seemed to be the criterion she observed most strongly, it was acknowledgment that proved the most consistent barrier to visibility once employed there:

> I was in the elevator with X partner, and he thought I was a secretary. That happens all the time. I think it's little things like that. The head of the firm, whenever he comes here, he sits on this floor, every time he mistakes me for a secretary, every single time, and I'm just kind of like, "Whatever, I'm over it." . . . It's little things. Again, I don't think there's any maliciousness behind it. I'm sure if I made a point of being like "Hi, I'm an associate in this department" and giving him my whole bio, he'd remember. But I'm not going to do that . . . because, you know, when you see my white male colleague, you do not assume that he is support staff. You just don't do it.

Theodora, a fourth-year associate of Caribbean descent, was proudly raised in a working-class family with seven siblings, all of whom were instilled with a solid sense of self-worth and equality to others, despite the humble nature of their early circumstances. Also employed by a prestigious northeastern law firm, she describes how the taxing racial slights experienced daily are never overt but subtle enough in nature and couched in just enough ambiguity to avoid the outright charge of racist motivation.[36] In one of many examples, she recounts how just recently a white male counsel identified her via e-mail as "the paralegal" working on a major corporate transaction.[37] An event such as this, she unequivocally interprets the mistake to be based on gender and on race.

Like the perhaps apocryphal but conceivably authentic story of former Time Warner CEO Richard Parson's case of mistaken identity as support staff at his own board meeting, the white racial frame and its precepts "accidentally" relegate black professionals to subordinate positions within elite organizations and serve as another quietly racist means for asserting the dominance of the white male superstructure.[38] How female lawyers are culturally and socially depicted in the environs of elite corporate law firms directly connotes the ways in which people of color are excluded from professional development by being forced to relentlessly assert the achievements they have already made, let alone their eligibility for opportunities and contacts leading to advancement. The way one looks, one's ability to adapt to existing firm culture, and the ability to *obtain a visible status there* are constantly challenged, almost like psychological warfare.[39] Pervasive cultural perceptions about what a lawyer looks like—not *you*—aligns with the cultural emphasis on difference that reinforces the inviolability of the biases propping up the elite-white-male dominance system.

These incidents pressure the participants to maintain an überprofessional presentation at all times, not only to avoid these awkward interactions, but also to preserve their own sense of dignity and perceived value to the firm on a daily basis. As has been demonstrated, black female lawyers already have to work harder to be seen as professional, which again burdens them in ways that neither their white counterparts nor their superiors experience.[40] The inclusion tax black women are forced to pay to be in white spaces is constant, while they are simultaneously expending emotional, mental, and physical labor maintaining "white professional" standards. Data reflecting this trend's impact on attrition rates is speculative at best, yet we can reasonably assume that the phenomenon adds significant stress to black female lawyers' already-cumbersome efforts to clear a space for themselves within the exclusive confines of privileged white institutional spaces. The invisible labor clause is continuously in effect for black female lawyers attempting to navigate the firm.

As reflected in Philomena's testimony, the "little things" that point to systemic gendered racism burdens her with the responsibility of dispelling the blatant stereotype that blacks cannot occupy high-status positions within the firm ("I'm sure if I made a point of being like 'Hi I'm an associate in this department' and giving him my whole bio, he'd remember").[41] While the partner who issued the injury is relieved of accountability and allowed to fall back on the cushion of color-blind-racist ideology, this system, through intentional or unintentional ambiguity, categorizes such slights as "honest mistakes" ("Again I don't think there's any maliciousness behind it") and slyly blames the victim. It burdens her to achieve visibility and to acknowledge a never-quite-adequate representation of self. She must take on the formidable challenge of confronting the white racial frame's deeply entrenched hegemonic influence on all actors. Philomena continues, "You get tired of feeling like . . . you have to dress like an attorney so you don't get mistaken for a secretary."

Rhebekka, a thirty-five-year-old lawyer, who defied the odds and became the first black female *partner* in the history of her firm, wove a similar narrative:

> It's just this perception that I'm here to tap for your amusement. Or people asking me, "Barack Obama was elected. You must be super happy today." Just little crazy things that they don't necessarily view as problematic but that are. Or people asking me about other black women's hair or somebody on the other end of a negotiation continuing to use the phrase "tar baby."

Exhaustion, depletion, attrition: a cycle that obstructs invisible black female pioneers in elite professional settings and in advanced insidious ways—before the mirror, by the water cooler, at the conference table—even on planes.

In this chapter, I detail how black women's professional appearance is linked to their perceived ability and centers on conforming to Eurocentric ideals of beauty, created and upheld by elite white men, that negatively affect these women. I give examples of how black women are forced to pay an inclusion tax to be in elite white spaces and how the invisible labor clause is continuously in effect. Next, I turn to how exclusion works to make black women hypervisible and invisible in white spaces. I posit that black female lawyers' lack of access to a network of family and friends, sentiments of internal exclusion, and negative assumptions about the circumstances surrounding their presence play a significant role in their inability to advance in the firm. These emerging themes reflect the realities of white racial framing and systemic gendered racism at work within the firm. It further reflects the pervasiveness of the inclusion tax levied against black women in white professional spaces.

3

THE OUTSIDER WITHIN

"People don't know what to say to you. They literally just don't know what to say to you because they are afraid of saying the wrong thing. They don't want you to get offended. They have no concept of what your life looks like, and that puts the onus on you. And I even went to an associates of color training session where they said that. They were like, 'It is your job to make the majority comfortable with you. It is not their job.' They are going to be, and if you're going to succeed in law, it is your job to put them at ease. . . . It's exhausting, you know . . . because I am the other. So I am the unknown. . . . I see it sometimes and even diverse [people] . . . it's that person who makes the racist joke about themselves so that everybody else feels more comfortable. It's that feeling."

—Philomena, third-year associate

During her interview, Philomena was very expressive about her experience in elite white spaces, confessing that it took some adjustment to comply with the expectation of making others comfortable with her "difference." What she seized on here is a common theme among my respondents: that one of the prominent but little-discussed difficulties of being a black female seeking access to predominantly white male spaces is relatability—being an "outsider" whose attributes and life experience are poorly understood or valued by the white racial frame, if not outright dismissed, diminished, or denigrated. The inevitable dynamic of fitting in, however, harkens back to the invisible labor clause, the added emotional, mental, and physical labor that must be exerted to carve a maneuverable space for oneself within the confines of firm culture. This not only forces subordinated racial groups to sometimes participate in their own subjugation to make the dominant group comfortable with their presence, but it also forces them to contend with a set of hurdles suggestive of the fact that diversity is often more tolerated than embraced in these environments. We are reminded about the inclusion tax that black female lawyers pay, exacted in the time, money, and emotional and mental energy in order to be included in white spaces structured and operated by elite white men.

The previous chapter introduces the aesthetics of white racial framing in elite corporate firms and some of the challenges of the effort to fit in to its conception of what a lawyer "looks like." This chapter explores the "felt" experience of black female lawyers operating inside these institutions, looking to transform their status as outsiders into a viable platform for sustainable careers and advancement. I examine some of the barriers that keep them entrenched in this outsider status and argue that factors, such as relatability and negative labeling attached to white affirmative action narratives, contribute substantially to the attrition rates at the heart of this study. I also explore, through my respondents, the ramifications of some of these outsider feelings themselves, as well as some of the more logistical barriers to getting inside the partnership track from a disadvantaged outside position (i.e., the restraining influence of entering these institutions without the same network or networks of family and friends that often facilitate the professional development of their white counterparts).

I argue that these particular issues black lawyers face are part of the systemic racism created, controlled, and reproduced by elite white men and embedded within law firms, continuously limiting black female lawyers' access to opportunity.[1] This regulated system of oppression inevitably invokes a crippling matrix of obstacles that generate extreme added labor, self-doubt, and high attrition. The first matter I attend to in this chapter is the question of networks.

THE SOCIAL (AND PROFESSIONAL) NETWORK

Having access to a team of family and friends in a position to enhance one's advancement prospects is a marked asset in any industry, particularly in those elite fields dominated by an exclusive number of players performing high-stakes transactions with a propensity to lean on crony networks—where the price tag of one's Rolex often corresponds directly with the breadth and depth of one's Rolodex. Black female lawyers, like other subordinated racial and ethnic groups, tend to have limited access to such networks due to historical, political, and socioeconomic factors that have limited the professional and educational mobility of racially oppressed groups across generations.[2] Throughout the interviews I conducted, I found a prevalent social capital deficit among black female lawyers reflecting this trend and spotlighting how systemic racism perpetuates the inequalities that sustain the white racial frame, white privilege, and white power. What results is a stark imbalance of resources preventing black female lawyers, among others, from accessing the means to develop their human and social capital, thereby shaping the nature and trajectory of their professional "connections," networking capabilities, and overall grasp of how to navigate the social and political end of success in the legal field. In such a context, an "insider" or "outsider" status can, if not make or break careers, certainly lubricate the development of some more than others.[3]

As third-year associate Chloe, who attended both an Ivy League college and a tier 1 law school and thus no stranger to the prevalence and ubiquity of such networks, explained:

> I just also don't have anyone in my direct family who is a lawyer who I could have asked for advice. . . . I assume that most white females come from more privileged backgrounds than I do or have family members who are in law and could have advised them throughout the process, whether these are female mentors or male mentors. My former officemate, her dad is a partner in a law firm. I think she knew stuff that I didn't know or she knew how to do her work. And her dad is a partner. I didn't know these things, and I had to learn all this stuff from scratch. I don't know if that made me a worse associate, but it does help that you have some other kind of guidance.

The privileged backgrounds Chloe referred to here, often shared between partners, sponsors, mentors, and associates, facilitate the development of crucial relationships for career-track mobility, stemming not only from the common cultural reference points alluded to in chapter 2 but also from common contacts that arise from moving through similar social and economic circles. Not only do these networks assist in navigating the terrain of firm culture, but they also act as mills for generating the opportunities that lead to the work that leads to the establishment of reputation and advancement. This shared sense of background among privileged actors in elite corporate law firms, and the social and political networks cultivated by it, provide an indispensable tool that white associates are more likely to possess, especially given the historical legacy of excluding racially subordinated groups from primary labor markets, schools, neighborhoods and social clubs.[4]

Delia, a fifth-year associate, depicted in detail how her particular social capital "deficits" impeded her experience piloting the same landscape:

> I think one area where I could do better is the networking piece. I mean, part of the issue is . . . it's not that I'm not outgoing, but when you come from what I come from, you really have to go harder at it because a lot of people can just call their friend's dad, you know what I mean. And I don't really have that sort of network where the people I grew up with are going to be helpful in my current career. They're just not. And so then the question becomes, "What do you do with that?" And you have to be more—I think a little bit more deliberate about that. It's not to say that I don't have any networks because you can have networks with people from high school and college and law school and you do have that. But, there's a definite bifurcation, where some people, they have their schoolmates and then they have family and friends, which is also a source of positive network.

The benefits of such networks fall into categories as diverse as finding the guidance to resolve specific work problems to the contacts that effectively bring the work. Knowledge is power, in this context as in others—not just *what* one knows, of course, but also *who* one knows. For Delia and Chloe alike, this "definite bifurcation" hones in on what advantages associates of privileged, often white, backgrounds enjoy versus those of more modest backgrounds without the same "network resources"—a category in which the average black female lawyer finds herself. The gap thereby is powerful and, where not a liability fatal to advancement, almost certainly involves the commitment of substantial added labor, often invisible, to arrive at the same destination career-wise. This is another example of when the invisible labor clause certainly takes effect, with black women lawyers attempting to fill this gap in their networks. Finally, networks tend to create larger networks, though not necessarily involving a more diverse set of participants. This lack of access points not only to the limited number of blacks in elite white spaces but also to the perpetuation of narratives and cultural biases that make these institutions both impervious to "outsiders" and disconnected from the cultural and sociopolitical landscape of an evolving nation. Because very few lawyers of color are able to challenge the prevailing narrative favoring the dominant group, many of these institutions become locked into damaging—though not necessarily unremunerative—discriminatory cultural biases and practices in a seemingly never-ending loop of the white racial frame.[5]

This pervasive superstructure is fundamental enough to the legal field that, as Wendy Leo Moore notes, even in law school, students of color are trained to "think like a lawyer" or even "think white," which, for reasons touched on in chapter 2, relate to the architecture of the white racial frame's monolithic image of what a lawyer is—an image created and perpetuated by elite white men.[6] Without these networks that could potentially ease their transition into white corporate spaces—networks that are regulated and maintained by white male actors—black female lawyers are not only at a logistical disadvantage, but they also often experience intense feelings of isolation stemming from the status of being altogether cultural, historical, typically socioeconomic, racial, and gendered outsiders in an insider's game.

THAT OLD OUTSIDER FEELING

As alluded to earlier, one of the obvious questions raised by the fundamental lack of diversity in elite corporate law firms is the extent to which such organizations actually place a value on said diversity. Certainly, these limp statistical trends in hiring, advancement, and retention, whether related to black women or racially subordinated groups as a whole, are due to factors other than a lack of resources, which these powerhouses clearly possess in significant quantities. This fact is not lost on the black female lawyers who navigate these spaces daily and are thus regularly forced to contend with the operation of the elite-white-male dominance system, which cultivates and exploits the white racial frame to maintain the status quo and justify the propagation of its interests and attributes.[7] Philomena's experience, as quoted at the beginning of this chapter, captures the comforts—or lack thereof—of being the "other" in this environment, at the busy intersection of systemic race, gender, and class oppression. Being the only black associate in a room, for example, describes a position that clearly defines one's outsider participation in such a space. It also contributes to the alienating sense that their role, reception, and individuality are merely caricatures of insider biases, habits, and narratives aggregated by an alternately hostile or dismissive but inevitably controlling and subordinating superstructure. Two of my respondents, Elissa and Kallisto, illustrated this point succinctly.

Elissa is a thirty-three-year-old fifth-year associate in an elite law firm who was raised in an inner-city community, along with four siblings, and educated in public schools. She attended a high-ranked undergraduate institution, where she majored in finance and political science, and then took two years off between college and law school to work as a research assistant for a government official. During this period, she also bore a son. In spite of this diverse life, work, and educational experience (not to mention a long-held enthusiasm for the work), which in certain contexts would certainly be an asset to a career, Elissa, after five years, nevertheless is still acclimating as a perennial outsider to what should be a familiar, if not comfortable, environment:

> I carry with me . . . this comfortability being in this corporate law environment because that prevents you from really engaging—that engaging aspect with the people here and with your clients. So there's several challenges that have to be overcome but I'm working on.

What she and others described is the hindrance of being constantly made to focus on difference instead of one's ability to perform. She is placed in the undesirable—and perhaps even impossible, if not ultimately tragic or traumatic—position of trying to establish one's own comfort. To do so, black female lawyers, to a great extent, must promote the comfort of one's white colleagues, clients, and superiors and in turn sometimes participate in their own subjugation because their white colleagues, clients, and superiors are not comfortable with narratives and practices that defy the white racial frame that has maintained, however questionably, the entire superstructure. The invisible labor clause is evidenced by Elissa's feelings of being an outsider. She struggles with having different experiences that are not valued, which forces her to negotiate her own comfortability along with making others comfortable with her differences. Elissa expends emotional and mental labor managing her comfortability while trying to fit in to the existing white space.

Several factors put white male and female lawyers at an advantage in elite law firms: (1) the history of the institution, (2) the reproduction of whiteness in this elite space, (3) the way the white racial frame operates to advantage the dominant group, and (4) how white privilege and power are maintained as a result.[8] As the dominant group and by virtue of their racial affiliation, white lawyers are assumed to belong in the institutional spaces they have created and are (when unchallenged) commonly comfortable there—even if those creations are at the expense of other groups or were historically enabled by the direct subordination of other groups. This is a very complex dynamic that burdens black female lawyers and others (as outsiders, no less): the task of making the dominant group more comfortable—to this class's continued privilege and benefit. And that is precisely what takes place and is even normalized in these spaces. White lawyers are not burdened with the task of making others comfortable with their existence; they are the norm in institutional spaces, while *others* are included. They do not pay a tax but instead enjoy the tax paid by *others*, which maintains the status quo.

Again, one central disadvantage of women of color in elite corporate institutions is the immense mental and emotional labor exerted just to obtain and maintain a seat at the table. Meanwhile, white actors can advance their own careers without the challenge of maintaining the confidence and motivation to progress in their work. The benefit of using one's finite store of energy on a daily basis to advance one's career prospects rather than surmount structural racial and gendered obstacles (let alone recover from the damages they propagate) cannot be overemphasized. The invisible labor clause systematically works against the efforts of black female lawyers while advantaging whites, particularly white men. White men are not burdened by the added invisible labor that professionals of color must manage on top of the *actual* work they are all required to perform.

In her research on elite law schools, Wendy Leo Moore explores the discourses that affect whether aspiring associates of color are afforded the same sense of "comfort" or "acceptability" as the dominant group. Moore notes that "white students are not burdened with having to work to create an institutional space in which they can feel like insiders; the white institutional space provides these students with social and cultural capital to succeed as soon as they enter the institution."[9] As former white law students, white associates basically undergo a process of graduating from one set of institutional privileges to another, which inherently places those from outside such circles (i.e., the vast majority of lawyers of color) at an embedded disadvantage.[10] The significance of this circularity becomes palpable when we revisit the previous section's discussion of networks and the ways in which social and cultural capital convert to material career advances.

Kallisto, who was a sixth-year associate at the time of our interview, confirmed the chilling sense of isolation in both spaces—top-tier white undergraduate and graduate institutions and the elite firms they allegedly prepare individuals of color to succeed in. She further depicted the impact of a lack of connection between insiders and outsiders deriving from differing social and cultural capital resources that are valued quite differently by an elite work environment:

> I think that people feeling comfortable with me as an attorney versus other attorneys was different. I think backgrounds come into play a lot, and people

want to work with you because you're smart but also because they know you and they felt comfortable with you. I don't think people always felt comfortable working with me because I could not talk to them about skiing or, even though I have skied, I wasn't a skier. I couldn't talk to them about things that they did in their regular [lives]. I'm talking about partners; these are people who were giving out work. So, the people who were giving our assignments, I did not relate to them in certain ways that my white female associates related to them. So, if an ideal candidate is someone who gets a lot of work, right, and I'm not getting that work because I can't talk to you about certain topics in the same way, we haven't built a relationship because I don't have the same life. My life was just so different. My experience was a different one because I couldn't relate to people as, like, the urban black girl who didn't have the experience of the country home, skiing. I went to good schools, but those schools were my outlet.

Although Kallisto discussed her experience in particular reference to social class designations, it is clear that these designations are closely linked to race. Like in any other space, associates who share similar experiences with partners or potential sponsors are able to build comfortable, mutually beneficial relationships based on commonality. Kallisto finds herself locked out of that dynamic because she is precluded by her "urban black girl" background and, implicitly, does not see the value of her background in the experiences of her white counterparts, nor does she receive access to the benefits that their experiences provide them. The inclusion tax Kallisto is forced to pay to be in the firm does not reap the same benefits that her white counterparts enjoy, precisely because she is the "other" with differing experiences that are not equally valued or even valued at all.

What Kallisto's report also points to is the need for outsiders to execute the added labor required to bridge the gap (i.e., deficit) implied by their status to the "people who [give out] work." Again, the invisible labor clause comes into effect. This harkens back to the idea of both "fitting in" and "thinking like a lawyer." While we may assume, with some risk, that elite firm stakeholders are savvy enough to realize that distinctions of temperament, ability, motivation, and so forth cut across racial, class, gendered, and other lines, the essentially racist, classist, and misogynistic underpinnings of the white racial frame often prevent those in power from giving those with diverse or unfamiliar backgrounds an estimation of value and capability unencumbered by its influence. If I am a partner allocating a high-stakes assignment and I have a choice between a white male whose father is a judge, who went to the same prep school as my child, and who grew up in the same suburb as my sister Sarah, I may reasonably feel more comfortable giving a potentially career-enhancing assignment to him rather than Tanya, a black woman from Detroit, raised by a single father in the inner city, whose hair I cannot entirely grasp the nature of and whose way of thinking is not apparent to me.

For this reason, akin to Moore's findings with students of color, lawyers of color are pressured to work harder than their white female and male colleagues to prove that they can "think like a lawyer," which according to Moore "requires a manner of thinking that acquiesces to a white normative framework and simultaneously facilitates the invisibility of whiteness by precluding forms of argumentation that seek to identify the power and privilege that mark it."[11] Systemic gendered racism works in this scenario to exclude Tanya from connecting with both the white partner and the work he controls based on a perceived dearth of shared personal experience fomented by the divisive constructs of the white racial frame, continuously pitting black women against predominately elite white male privilege and experience.

Because this superstructure operates directly and indirectly, deliberately and inadvertently suppressing blacks and other nonwhites, black female lawyers are not afforded the luxury of being comfortable in elite white law firms, which would foster relationships with partners and senior associates, bringing them in from their "outsider" status and facilitating their professional development and success. It does nothing to diminish the exhaustive mental and emotional labor required to deal with their "difference" and the impact of this difference on whites at the office, specifically white males. It does not reduce the rates of attrition that result from this dynamic. Moreover, the insider–outsider opposition invoked here creates a formidably vicious cycle, whereby the scarcity of black lawyers in elite corporate law firms makes their difference and outsider status hypervisible and threatening and even more detrimental to their success, while creating even more discomfort for white actors in control of eliminating the structures and practices in law firm culture that directly limit access for and often ostracize the few lawyers of color who gain entry.

WHEN IN DOUBT

> "I almost didn't apply to [my firm] because I didn't think my grades were good enough. I've kind of always been very self-conscious about that and whether or not I'm intelligent enough, and so I'm not sure where my grades stack up in terms of other candidates or candidates that I even interview."
>
> —Nikoleta, third-year associate

Throughout the interviews I conducted, the toll of outsider feelings exacted on the confidence of my respondents, even after several years of solid practice in elite firms, was almost staggering. As is well known, the pervasive shadow of American bigotry follows people of color from childhood through adolescence and into the various spheres of adult life. But what is less well known, or at least less broadly discussed, is how this shadow affects the prospects of those who are even able to break through the barriers that discourage or dismantle the mobility of a majority of black and brown aspirants. In the legal field, a crucial element that appears to be at work in this regard is self-doubt inculcated by one's perception of how other lawyers, as well as staff and management personnel, perceive one's qualifications. It is anyone's guess the extent the anxieties attached to this phenomenon are a consequence of earlier stages of one's educational and career development, but following Wendy Leo Moore's examination of law school students, we can extrapolate that, from the time black female lawyers are in training, they are made to feel as though they do not fit into the law school environment, whether they are questioned about their qualifications for enrollment, it is insinuated that they are affirmative action beneficiaries, or they are silenced in the classroom through the "neutral" and "objective" teaching practices that ignore persistent US systemic racism in history and society. Law students of color transition to elite white law firms that carry the same practices and beliefs, with substantial seeds planted for the self-doubt that steers how they maneuver once employed and affects their prospects for advancement, thus increasing the likelihood of attrition.[12] The invisible labor clause manifests in law schools for students of color and continues in practice at law firms.

As we know, white racist framing and ideology has historically characterized blacks as intellectually inferior, a tenet that has been challenged with an odd lack of robustness even in some of the politest white progressive circles.[13] At any rate, the suspicion, if not outright endorsement, of its accuracy permeates law firms and other white institutional spaces, causing black female lawyers, like Nikoleta, to, at best, feel (at times crippling) pressure to prove its fundamental wrongness or, at worst, to feel as though they may, in fact, be as inadequate, incapable, and underqualified as they are charged with being. Black women lawyers find themselves in such spaces due to the bounty of the white racial frame's narrative of affirmative action, which basically likens it to a "reverse racist" entitlement program rather than a deliberate federal or institutional effort to repair the gross, devastating inequities and legacy of a thoroughly racist system based on equally deliberate economic exploitation, enslavement, and sociopolitical oppression.[14] As Moore argues for the case of racially subordinated law students, the "white narrative of affirmative action . . . places continual scrutiny upon the presence of people of color in the law school and causes students of color to question their own abilities."[15] In elite law firms and among lawyers of color, the same measure of self-doubt is encouraged by firm culture and creeps into black female lawyers' professional development at any stage. Out of twenty lawyers interviewed, three acknowledged outright that they were not confident in their law school grades but believed themselves to be equal to the majority of their peers in terms of performance and ability. Some, like Kallisto, even fall prey to the white racial frame's narrative that, in spite of their educational and professional achievements, diversity outreach more than talent is responsible for their employment:

> I don't think I was the top ten of [my law school], but I do think that diversity had a weight in me getting my job. They were looking to hire . . . more diverse attorneys. I think I came from a school where you got a little bit more credit. And also my school did not release your grades until after your interview, so I probably was not in the same—received the same treatment because other law schools you'll see their grades before you pick the candidates. I was picked and interviewed, and then they got to see my grades, so they got to see my personality before I was judged for my GPA. But my GPA was pretty good coming from a school at the time that was like number 7 I think in the country. I got a fair shake, and everyone thought I was smart because I came from [my law school]. I got that benefit of the doubt.

A case such as Kallisto's reflects the subtle influence of this narrative, in that, while admitting her grades were "pretty good" for the top-ranked law school from which she acquired her degree, she still believes that diversity played a more prominent role in her position than her qualifications did.

Again, Nikoleta exhibited the manifestation of self-doubt that can easily hinder an associate's ability to develop her craft and build the meaningful relationships with partners, mentors, and sponsors crucial for advancement. Although she attended a law school that is not ranked in the top ten, she was able to secure a job at one of the top law firms in the country. We note from Nikoleta's quote at the start of this section how her insecurity about her grades compared to other job candidates—even candidates she is qualified enough to interview—takes a heavy toll on her intellectual confidence. Having less confidence in one's abilities compromises how and even *if* one is able to foster the kinds of productive work relationships that make or break a lawyer's ability to receive quality work assignments and billable hours, establish a reputation, make essential contacts, and continue to develop professionally (as set forth in chapter 2's introductory quote).

Nikoleta's story confirms that associates of color are tremendously burdened by the threat of negative perceptions that can and do affect this development. These negative perceptions perpetuated by the white racial frame affect attrition rates and are generally ignored by whatever diversity measures exist within corporate law firms and firm culture leading up to and beyond the hiring stage. Whether these perceptions are about their ability to perform, as described earlier, or their physical appearance, as described in chapter 2, many of my respondents indicated that these unspoken tensions often force them to retreat from interacting with others or assault them with pressure to overcome, through extreme added labor of various types, the affirmative action and tokenism discourses that challenge their ability to "fit in," undermine their comfort, dog their advancement, and diminish their accomplishments.[16] Olympia, a third-year associate who, in contrast, comes from a middle-class suburban background, echoes the same conviction about the notorious legacy of self-doubt stemming from her law school educational experience and haunting her navigation of firm culture, even years later. Even with Olympia's educational pedigree as an Ivy League college and top-ranked law school graduate, she asserted in our interview:

> I do think that the partner I work the closest with, he is Cuban, and we haven't had that many conversations about race, but we have had discussions about both of our backgrounds in terms of going to elite undergraduate institutions and feeling like we didn't totally measure up in comparison to other students because we did go to public high school and hadn't had all the same experiences. And speaking about, kind of building inner confidence in a way that's really important to thriving as a lawyer. And so, I think having conversations like that, I think that he looks out for me. I don't know if that's the only reason why, but I do think when you recognize a little of yourself in somebody, it makes people just think a little extra about developing you.

In contrast to most associates of color, Olympia was fortunate enough to build a relationship with a partner who shared similar, relatable life experiences. This gave her an opportunity to discuss difficulties she was facing at the firm, as well as air some of her own insecurities. Olympia was able to receive constructive feedback, which, by her own admission, had a salutary effect on her confidence rather than the reverse and far more common experience of moving in isolation, as one's outsider feelings insidiously dictate the course of one's career track. This particular partner was, if not a Cuban of color, at least someone of a national or ethnic background or temperament who was able to facilitate a safe space within the firm, in which she was able to counter the white racist framings forcing her to question her own abilities.[17]

Central to what we gather from these accounts is the fact that white associates, male or female, do not experience this form of self-doubt. Because of the pervasive pro-white center reflected in the elite corporate superstructure, whites are generally presumed to be qualified based on their privileged position in the racial hierarchy and the common cultural signifiers established by the white racial frame and its constant markers of value. This notably antiblack (and anti-other) framing juxtaposed with pro-white normalcy perpetuated by elite white male actors is a core component of the insider–outsider dynamic in white institutional spaces across the nation. For black female lawyers, it takes shape as systemic gendered racism, obstructing their access, compromising their confidence, and leading to alarmingly low rates of hiring and retention, while rendering the prospect of advancement to a labyrinthine quest of psychological, social, and political labor worthy of a late Kafka fable.[18]

This chapter discusses the reasons black female lawyers have an extremely difficult time breaking into law firm culture and assimilating into the existing structure that advantages white lawyers. The lack of diversity in elite corporate law firms perpetuated by white male actors has a significant impact on how lawyers from subordinated racial groups are able to maneuver professionally and socially within white institutional spaces created, controlled, and reproduced by elite white men. Targeting three important aspects of black female lawyers' experiences, I discuss why and how black female lawyers are at a disadvantage in elite white law firms because of the ways in which systemic racism, white racial framing, and systemic gendered racism operate. First, lack of access to networks of family and friends resulting from the systemic nature of US racial oppression has created a gap of perceived and actual social capital resources for black female lawyers. Second, outsider feelings are prevalent in institutional spaces that privilege and value the experiences of whites over subordinated racial groups. Last, self-doubt among black female lawyers is a destructive and often self-perpetuating by-product of white narratives of affirmative action. Each of these elements contributes handily to the rates of attrition for this demographic.

By exploring how social capital deficits, outsider feelings, and white narratives of affirmative action factor into the experiences of black female lawyers, we can illuminate the operational effects of systemic gendered racism and white racist frames. If law firms promoted the value of difference in a way that was inclusive of individuals who do not come from the privileged group (primarily white men but also increasingly white women), then subordinated groups would not feel ostracized based on race, gender, class, sexuality, or other salient identity categories that are not privileged. Furthermore, the ways in which subordinated groups are linked to low performance and affirmative action policies often lead some partners and senior associates to view them as unqualified, reinforcing the white racial frame and perpetuating racial inequality.

The issue of diversity is never addressed in a way that can actually influence positive substantive change. This is another way in which the white narrative of affirmative action works to further disadvantage black female lawyers within elite white law firms. Therefore, the struggle to prove oneself in the firm can be a self-defeating struggle that leads to self-doubt among associates of color. As law professors David B. Wilkins and Mitu G. Gulati suggest, it would be expected that the self-doubt exhibited by some participants is a direct result of the pervasive and negative prejudices toward blacks when interacting with partners.[19] Diversity is complex, and not having real diversity when it comes to race has deleterious consequences for black female lawyers and other subordinated racial groups. Systemic racism continues to be prevalent, thus privileging whites, maintaining the status quo, and reinforcing white racist frames that support and justify white male (and female) claims to privilege and power. Black female lawyers' lack of access to networks, outsider feelings, and self-doubt reflect the pervasive impact of systemic gendered racism on their experiences in elite law firms. Additionally, the invisible labor clause and the inclusion tax play a significant role in the experiences of black female lawyers. This allows us to see the various ways that black women are working harder to be *seen* or *recognized*, while being forced to spend additional resources just to be *in* white spaces. Without the potential, and certainly not the guarantee, of similar, equal, or any benefits, black women are confronted with tremendous obstacles to compete with their peers. The following chapter goes a step further to discuss the similarities and differences between the experiences of white female and black male lawyers compared to black female lawyers.

4

ALL THE WOMEN ARE WHITE, ALL THE BLACKS ARE MEN

"Yes, both white women and black men can be ideal candidates. However, there are different barriers for both. Black females experience two hurdles, race and gender as barriers, while black men experience only race, and white women experience only gender. It's automatic."

—Sophie, third-year associate

"As a fellow woman, I can identify with the tensions around gender and sexuality, and I think all women, whether white or blue, can all speak to that in a general way. But once you do look past the gender and the other things that impact on how someone interacts with that particular woman, there are nuances, nuanced differences between the way folks in a law firm deal with a white woman, an Asian woman—I work with no Latin women—an African American woman, an immigrant woman, an Indian woman, so on and so forth."

—Xena, partner

"I think it's like that, where the black male, black female kind of breakdown happens in some ways, and then obviously there's like social stuff. . . . I think that's really basically what it comes down to. I think at least in my experience and even at [my firm], though we only had one black male associate. I think that's where their experience was easier because it's like, apart from the skin color, I can look the part, I can talk the part.

And I think generally men don't have necessarily as much of a family responsibility that's on them because they are out being men. As opposed
to when you're a woman, and then you're a black woman, and then it
just becomes . . . exhausting, and it's hard when you don't have someone
to talk to. Or even when you talk to people about it, . . . the conversation will be very negative; there's competition. Just between the black
women, we kind of all knew. It was like we are not competing against
the rest of them; we're competing against each other because they don't
need all of us; they just need enough of us."

—Philomena, third-year associate

In this chapter, I further explore some of the ways in which systemic gendered racism's unique impact on the attrition rates of black female lawyers
may be better understood by comparing and contrasting their experiences
with those of two other "minority" demographics: white women and black
men.[1] While both groups demonstrate attrition rates exceeding those of
white men in the legal field, it is important to note that they are also advancing at higher rates than black women, suggesting that gender and race in
isolation do not provide sufficient explanation for the phenomenon of black
female attrition or their lack of advancement at elite firms.[2] In fact, it is the
intersectionality of black females' experience in these settings that dictates
the nature of their relationship to white women and black men.

I begin by illustrating some of the general, though by no means insignificant, hurdles faced by women in elite corporate firms overall—which goes
to explain why women's attrition rates exceed those of white male lawyers,
irrespective of color.[3] According to my respondents' accounts, I am able to
break these gender barriers down loosely into several categories. Expand-
ing on chapter 3's discussion of self-doubt, I spotlight the influence of
confidence here with a more detailed analysis of the "gap" that arises from
corollary patriarchal narratives built into the white racial frame affecting all
women.[4] From there is an excellent vantage point from which to explore
the decisive gendered differences in the work–life balance expectation that
disadvantages women of all colors on the career track, including demanding more time from them, more pressure to sacrifice personal goals for
professional opportunities, and the added labor of shouldering responsibility for familial support and maintenance—the so-called double shift many
professional women uphold.[5] All of these differences add up to a substantial
gender burden that the patriarchal structure of most firms neither acknowledges nor works to dismantle to create a more equitable atmosphere for the
professional development of all associates.

While applicable to women of all racial and ethnic backgrounds, the intensity of the gender burden described here is exaggerated for black females. To illustrate this point, I examine some of the ways in which racial privilege advantages white female colleagues over black female colleagues pursuing the same career goals. These differences are crucial in explaining why white women, despite considerable gender oppression, nevertheless enjoy higher rates of partnership acquisition and associate retention; for example, such differences as cultural relatability sustained by white racist framing.[6] Although the similarities between white and black female professionals discussed here are important, it is rather the distinctions I uncover that reveal the most about why it is black women who still reside at the bottom of all pyramids: income, training, access to networking and mentorship, and overall advancement.

From there I circle back to delineate how race, while certainly a powerful determinant of any lawyer's career trajectory—as reflected by the many similarities between black female and black male lawyer experiences in elite firms—does not go far enough in isolation to adequately pinpoint the gap between black male lawyers' advancement in these settings and that of their female counterparts.[7] Thus, I complete this chapter by using our respondents' accounts to argue that variances within the black racial group related to gender privilege further enable us to measure the weight of intersectionality; its impact on black female lawyers' development; and how the notion that "all women are white" and "all blacks are men"[8] renders black females hyperinvisible and hyperobstructed, critically accelerating the attrition rates of this demographic in the field of corporate law. In doing so, we engage with the reality that systemic racism and sexism, created and controlled by elite white men, reproduces white male patriarchal power. The invisible labor clause and the inclusion tax are key in providing examples of the differences between the experiences of black women as compared to white women and black men.

THE CONFIDENCE GAP

One of the foremost ways in which our respondents identify their experiences with those of their white female colleagues pertains to confidence, or the lack thereof, available to those excluded from the elite-male-dominance system.[9] It is important to note here that, when I speak of confidence, not only am I speaking of the conviction that one's work is adequate or their abilities are sound enough to make the grade, but also, essentially, that said quality work can and will be received in such a way as to promote one's career development. Hence, when third-year associate Chloe mentioned the confidence issues she believes all females in these environments struggle with "in terms of speaking up; being confident in what they're doing," she speaks not only to how they assess their own merits but also to the various ways in which confidence plays a crucial role in how women at these firms prosper and advance.

Being confident in ones' abilities—and their efficacy—aids success in any area, while self-doubt, of course, is useful in certain contexts but extremely inhibiting in others. Evidence shows that, as one would expect from a rigid patriarchal society such as ours, women are less self-assured than men and that, to succeed in one, confidence often matters as much as competence.[10] Confidence issues stemming from continual challenges to women's intellectual aptitude or questioning their "natural" propensity to succeed at activities outside the home often hinder women's abilities to be as outspoken and self-asserting as men in work contexts. Perfectionism, fear of failure and taking risks or of being disliked and "overthinking" are other nonstructural factors that may prevent women from gaining a stronger foothold in historically male-dominated institutions. The emotional and mental labor exerted here takes a toll on the confidence of women and is reflected in their experiences, an example of the invisible labor clause.

Based on my own experience in graduate school, I can certainly affirm the stifling anxieties that attend the prospect of vocalizing questions or comments in such settings: for fear of being wrong—*or worse*—of being judged as incompetent. In an elite alien environment that sometimes seems to tolerate diversity rather than embrace it (whether gendered or racial), that pervasive "imposter feeling" can easily eclipse one's own sense of personal authority. This is another example of how the inclusion tax is paid out.

For this reason, the professional world is rife with examples of the phenomenon so described: men inclined to speak up and exude confidence, even in areas in which they may not be as knowledgeable. In this vein, men are more likely to apply for promotions and demand pay raises regardless of whether they meet all attendant requirements. Conversely, women tend to be more reserved for fear of appearing underqualified; they are more self-critical and less likely to apply for advancement opportunities or ask for raises until utterly certain that they meet all relevant qualifications.[11] These trends taken together produce a net result of less women in positions of power and less overall parity, particularly in law firms and other corporate institutions.

Whereas the elite-white-male dominance system imbues men with a logical overconfidence in their abilities—encouraging them to take the risks that lead to better opportunities—as an oppressed group, women tend to shortchange their prospects, thus inadvertently conspiring with structural obstacles to prevent them from pursuing important opportunities that could lead to advancement. What I describe are, in part, the psychological barriers that derive from the color-blind chauvinism of the white racial frame. In the field of corporate law, the *After the JD* study found that women tend to underestimate their ability to become partners, thus confirming a significant "confidence gap."[12]

Self-perception is obviously a crucial instrument in building confidence. However, one must also acknowledge that women who exude this quality, overriding their male counterparts (tending toward outspokenness, for example), often face negative consequences in hierarchical patriarchal settings. As mentioned, because of prejudicial racial and gender framing, white males on the whole typically enjoy the comforts and confidence of authority regardless of the ultimate accuracy of their statements or position.[13] For women, this confidence may be viewed as arrogance, aggressivity, or worse. Errors committed by a male in a given work situation are interpreted as a reflection of a natural "learning curve"; for women—and particularly women of color, which I return to—such errors are frequently interpreted as confirming stereotypes of incompetence or lack of intelligence.[14] The stakes are high: One false move for a female professional, particularly one of color, can relegate the achievements of an entire professional or educational career or both to the no man's land of a disparaging designation like "affirmative action hire"—whereby one is conceived to have been recruited for a position based more on gender, color, or quota than capability or experience. The threat of such a designation, fairly unremitting in elite corporate settings, goes a long way to undermine success: by shaking a female professional's confidence, inhibiting her ambition, and exaggerating the risk of error for those pioneers seeking recognition for potential and actual contributions to firm work and firm culture.

Chloe's observations here reflect how female professionals' efforts, regardless of color, are restricted by the male-dominant narrative component of the white racial frame. Perception here, as always, wields a uniquely strong influence over how we behave; the decisions we make; the enterprises we undertake; and, as I show, often determine the character of important social interactions in these settings. Before I discuss how the confidence gap plays out differently for black and white female lawyers, with crucial ramifications for the former, I explore in depth a significant obstacle common to both groups, as articulated unanimously by our respondents: gendered differences in demands on time and personal obligations, the work–life balance.

GREAT EXPECTATIONS

Based on my respondents' accounts, it is safe to say that the majority of elite corporate law firms fail to adequately acknowledge the double standard foisted on female lawyers in terms of work–life balance expectations. Part of this failure has to do with the invisible labor performed by women overall and the extent to which the demands made on wife, girlfriend, and mother by patriarchal structures in a heterosexual framework are historical. This refers to a time, however misty, class-specific, or ultimately mythological in nature, in which the office and factory labor of the dominant male "provider" was perceived to be counterbalanced by the "natural" labors of the female partner at home. (Part may have to do with the fact that it is not necessarily in the interest of the elite-white-male dominance system to acknowledge this double standard.) The pervasiveness of the invisible labor clause is that those affected may not necessarily acknowledge their added labor, as it has become so ingrained within their daily lives, while those in power (employers) appear blind to its existence. Nonetheless, the added labor is required to survive within institutions.

In any case, in 2019, contrary to many other countries in the world, the American sociopolitical landscape has yet to adjust either the will or consciousness to the reality that women now occupy a significant portion of the full-time workforce—in a wide variety of industries. Simultaneously, women maintain responsibilities allocated by such factors as patriarchal social programming, misogyny, personal choice, and traditional gender framing, without substantial formal or institutional structures to support them. Thus, in examining any field in which attrition rates for women outpace men, such as corporate law, it is useful to assess the degree to which this double standard affects the female professional. The invisible labor clause is enacted in the employment contracts of women, forcing them to manage the contradictory views of being in both the public and private spheres without adequate support from corporations. Corporations must address the differences between the genders as it relates to the added invisible labor women expend in order to navigate law firms, manage work–life balance expectations, and maneuver the advancement trail.

Speaking to this point, several interviewees stressed that, unlike their male counterparts, many female lawyers do not have the convenience of someone else (a partner, for example) to ensure that home and hearth are maintained while they maintain equally indispensable, equally demanding work responsibilities. Most male lawyers, they argue, have wives or girlfriends who can take on essential daily responsibilities, such as cooking, cleaning, picking up or dropping off dry cleaning, doing laundry, grocery shopping, managing health- and child-care obligations, paying bills, and more.[15] Jocaste, a single associate, described this disparity, again poignantly phrased as the "double shift":

> I don't have a wife at home who takes care of all my business. That was one thing that I think was very annoying to a lot of us women. Because most of the men worked late, and male partners assigned work. And it was great that they [men] got stuff done at home because they had a wife at home who could take care of all their stuff. Not us; we don't have wives. We're the wives, or we're single or what have you, so laundry doesn't get done, cooking doesn't get done, bills don't get paid. All of those things that they rely on their women, I hate saying that, but their wives to do. We just didn't have the liberty, and it was very frustrating because there was no recognition of the fact that women, for better or for worse, have this sort of double shift. We need to work, but we also, to the extent we have someone at home, we're still in that role of wife, girlfriend, mother, whatever it is where we have things to do at home. There was no acknowledgment of that and not at the other firms I was at, either.

Once these professionals leave the office, in other words, their second shift begins, inevitably affecting some of the networking and development work that takes place off hours, basic tasking, and the availability of discretionary time central to one's general life balance.[16] The argument that Jocaste made here is that female lawyers are thus dually disadvantaged, set with an unenviable, perhaps impossible, dilemma. They must either allow their personal lives to be negatively affected by the exigencies imposed by elite firms' work demands in a manner distinct from males there—meaning they must effectively neglect this "home" work for the purposes of career advancement—or they must prioritize their personal responsibilities to the detriment of professional development, causing them to lose out on opportunities to advance and maintain a competitive stance at the firm and on the partnership track. This dilemma, the lack of space for it in firms, and the general difficulties of addressing it for women who seek to balance a rich professional life with a stable home life and relationships—in a culture that both normalizes and undervalues their invisible labor, expecting and profiting from it daily—plays a central role in heightened attrition rates for women lawyers, as in other corporate and noncorporate professions.[17]

Jocaste illustrated how the predominant patriarchal categorization of gender roles (i.e., the double *standard* that establishes the foundation of or justification for female professionals' double *shifts*) does not permit men and women to operate on an equal footing when managing personal and occupational expectations. That this fact remains unacknowledged and unaddressed by elite corporate firms—which certainly possess the resources to do so—following the lack of such recognition in cultural discourse overall forms one of our respondents' principal vexations:

> I mean, now, the thing that I think we talked about as women constantly was the sort of lack of recognition. Not that we were women but the fact that all of these men were working these crazy hours and had someone to take care of their stuff for them, and we were expected to work the same hours, and [we] didn't have the support that they had, and they had no concept of that. I think that just frustrated us because it was kind of like, "I can't get my dry cleaning." "Well, why can't you get your dry cleaning?" "Because I'm here. Because I've been here every single day, and you don't understand that that's a problem." Just there's no acknowledgment of that, and I think we all have expressed frustration with the fact that, this is just societal, that it's perfectly fine for a man not to be available because he's working. So if your boyfriend can't come to dinner with your parents because he's working, everyone understands, but if you can't go to dinner with your boyfriend's parents because you're at work, people don't understand; it is too much. "Oh, is she just going to work all the time?" . . . In society women, I think, have to, we just have more roles to play in a job working at one of these firms. I think it just doesn't allow us to really take on more than one role a lot of times.

In line with this argument, most of my interviewees concurred: The majority of male associates appear immune to worries about how late they work or if choosing work over home will negatively affect their personal relationships because traditional gender framing, designed to abet male advancement, supplies a synergy between the acceptable image of male work habits and their historical expectations as lone, and even heroic, breadwinners. Third-year associate Athena, for instance, reported:

> No, never. I have never once in my life, during an elevator conversation or in the cafeteria or one on one, ever heard a male associate talk about their concern about getting home on time [to take care of familial responsibilities].

Sixth-year associate Kallisto, whom I introduced in chapter 3, vehemently acknowledged the gender privilege that advantages men, supported by a system they have at home, traditionally accepted but institutionally invisible outside the bounds of marriage. As an only child raised by a single mother, Kallisto witnessed firsthand the demands of working a full-time job, maintaining a household, and caring for a child—for those who have not closely witnessed such a delicate and wearying exhibition of human fortitude, inconceivably hard work. Part of the issue seems to arise from a lack of recognition at the top of the food chain, that a different reality exists at competing stations of the socioeconomic jungle. At the top,

> [men] can rely on their wives to take care of the family life. The men, their wives are having the babies, and they are the breadwinners, and they're making all the money, and wives can stay home and stay home for a year or more. They took care of that, and they can still go to their meetings and do all the work, and they can become partner. It's easier.

When stay-at-home wives and mothers facilitate opportunities for men to gain access, and the men who benefit in this way rise through the ranks until they are themselves in a position to dictate the factors by which others are able to climb the so-called ladder of success, a gendered echo chamber is typically created, as with race, that reinforces the status quo; excludes entry to outsiders (i.e., women); and bars associates with different attributes or different trajectories from obtaining the necessary income bracket to profit from the same set of circumstances. The name on the doors may change, but the characteristics of those who put them there remain the same.

Without the everyday burden of running a household, male lawyers have access to longer work hours, free from the threat of jeopardizing their personal relationships; more discretionary time; and more time for career-enhancing networking activities that often lead to partnership-track opportunities. Most women do not have the luxury of doing both, or doing both well, because of significant constraints on their time imposed by traditional gender framing of what that time should rightly consist of and the invisible disadvantages this obstructive bias propagates.[18]

TIME WAITS FOR MEN

> "I think men's families expect that they're making more money or that they're working long hours. I don't know. I don't know how partners do [inaudible]. I don't know how their wives do it actually because they're

[men] never home, and the partners' wives are always with the kids alone. But men just seem to, it's just more of a given that men are going to be working hard and work long hours, while women, the reverse is not necessarily true. You may not find someone or be married to someone who's comfortable with that, and I've had a friend here who left because her husband told her, 'You need to leave this job. I never see you.' She would come home, and he's getting ready to go to work in the morning, . . . so it's not seen as something that's expected of women."

—Chloe, third-year associate

Tacitly, Chloe is one of the respondents to suggest that firms may in fact discourage the hiring or promotion of female lawyers due to the extreme pressure the double shift places on their time and personal lives. (We might consider this a form of negative consideration.) Certainly, work demands place a drastic strain on one's ability to manage relationships, particularly for women, and even for single women on the dating scene, a recurring theme among a good majority of those interviewed. Finding and maintaining meaningful personal relationships while engaged with long and often strained hours is no mean feat for anyone, regardless of gender. Chloe further expressed just how much the lack of work–life balance significantly steers women lawyers' decision about whether to date and, if successful, often start families and feel compelled to resign:

I don't know if I'd say it's supportive for women attorneys because of the work–life balance. We work crazy hours. People here are very friendly, very nice, but the work is intense. The firm has been very busy since I've started in 2010, and so we've just always been working very, very long hours. And in that way, I don't think it's conducive to females' working lifestyle. For example, the two black female counsel I know, I think they're both single, and they're much older than me. And I don't think it's conducive to me finding someone if I'm always in the office or just long-term growth in that way. Most of the females, like I said, a lot of my friends have left already. And some of them were married; some of them weren't married, but it's just not a sustainable lifestyle.

Not that it is guaranteed that someone else picking up your dry cleaning, children, or groceries will launch a successful career in elite corporate law, any more than the ability to work long, relatively care-free (at least in terms of neglected domestic duties) hours at the office will land you that coveted client. However, the flexibility to maneuver in the best possible direction toward the realization of work goals is obviously a key ingredient to the confidence and capitalization of opportunity associates need to advance. Having such a support system in place, at least on par with those you are competing with for a conceivably finite number of professional development pathways, goes a long way to alleviate the significant labor required of a high-profile occupation in general. The reduction of added labors provides the opportunity to focus on professional development and gain further access to channels, leading to reputation building, networking, mentoring, sponsorship, and partnership. As I show, this dynamic is only intensified when race is added to the equation.

SACRIFICES

A sad but telling consensus among my respondents was that, to achieve the level of success enjoyed by the average male lawyer, it is basically necessary to sacrifice one's personal life completely until making partner. Several participants, in fact, expressed the belief that female attorneys tend to have children after making partner in order to avoid delays that could potentially interfere with their professional development. Clearly this trend is a matter of personal choice for many; however, it is not a dilemma faced by male associates, with an accompanying litany of social, cultural, and biological ramifications.

Delia, for example, acknowledged that female associates who decide to have children are disadvantaged on the partnership track because of time "lost" during maternity leave. These absences sometimes lead to unforeseen results, she suggested, such as hindered skill development or even colleague resentment:

> If you were on partnership track, you'll be delayed in the time that you were out [on maternity leave]. It also hampers your client relationships of course, . . . you leaving the client for six months. A lot of our clients are males, as well, and I don't know how they perceive you leaving again and again for maternity leave. It also stalls your development, your learning curve as an associate. I guess maybe the associates, the male associates or female associates left behind, kind of say, "We were here the whole time, slugging it out, and you left, and you had six months off." They kind of maybe feel resentment in that respect because some females do hold off. It's a personal choice. And then you kind of lose deal continuity because you leave off a deal. [There is] just a whole process in transitioning, and you're not available for six months, no one knows what's going on on this thing, and you kind of lose that client tie like I said. And it just causes disruption. It's not convenient.

Not only colleagues but also the less kindly disposed among one's client base may react negatively to associates who take leave after working closely on a particular transaction, breaking the continuity of deal work and flow. Because elite corporate firms generally go to great lengths to cultivate the impression that clients and client workload is the firm's top priority and concern, women who go on leave to bear children often face issues pertaining to the firms' perception of their commitment to the institution. And the pressure does not end there. As Delia reflected,

> Most of the female partners I see here I think had their first kid after they were already partner, just by their age and how old their kids are. And it also is not perceived as well when you're a single person or your marriage, your marital status, is uncertain, and you're a female, and you have a kid [i.e., are a single parent]. And, that I think is whispered about here at the firm.

Beyond the category of "white male" from a "particular background," the parameters leading to opportunity thus seem to grow narrower and narrower. Delia suggested that the firms' perceived moral policing, in relation to what is viewed as a proper "fit" within firm culture, can cast a wide shadow on the perceptions of potential sponsors and mentors, partners, and other associates. As she suggested, women whose marital status is uncertain can become the subject of rumors and negative labeling, which can have conceivably fatal consequences for their professional success.[19] This is not true for male attorneys, who, if they have a child through a former marriage, outside of wedlock, or by some other human configuration, are unlikely to be the primary caretaker.

Forcing women to jump through certain hoops, including major life sacrifices not required of their male colleagues, forms a core component of preserving the elite-white-male dominance system, just as it does with race. Fotoula, a first-year associate, gave a brief but poignant description of the sacrifice required of women to break through the glass ceiling to partnership in her firm:

> In terms of the people making partner while I was there, they were literally workhorses. There's just no other word. No children, usually no boyfriend, no husband, no nothing. I rarely saw the light of day. I say that, and I think, I feel like that's in contrast to maybe some men's experiences. I feel like some men didn't have to be that extreme.

Jocaste elaborated,

> I think women, as far as I can tell, can't have any outside interests. . . . I feel women have to demonstrate above and beyond that their number 1 priority is the work. Men can get married, they can have families, and that's not an issue. And I think I definitely saw this in a number of women who made partner or who were brought in as partner. I mean, it just seemed like there were a lot of women who were single when they made partner and who worked all the time. And then there were women who were single and worked all the time who didn't make partner, but it definitely seemed like a harder road.

Again, according to my respondents, it is imperative to note that, while such sacrifices are unquestionably required to advance, there is no guarantee of reward for one's enactment of them.

Discussing the matter with Philomena, a third-year associate, produced the confession that, at this stage in her career, she is not even contemplating dating or building a family due to the demands of working in elite corporate law as a black female. Yet her response speaks to a category broader than race:

> I'm single. I'm not even worried about pregnancy and kids and the familial issues that most people talk about when they have that conversation about women and the law and why we're leaving in droves. Sometimes it's literally just I don't have the energy. It takes so much more energy for me to just compete with you on a very basic level. And I know it's not just black women because a book just came out recently where she [Debora L. Spar] talks about how women spend on average five years of our career on just appearance versus men.[20] That's the president of Barnard [College, Columbia University] in her book. She talks about that. . . . She talks about it in the last month's issue of *Glamour*.

While other advancement challenges certainly exist for women attorneys in elite corporate firms, these respondents outlined pervasive work–life balance issues that advantage males in these settings and tip the scales of attrition, often at the expense of their female colleagues, regardless of color. Confidence wears thin in the face of a historical set of gendered obstacles, as one's opportunities diminish, or as one encounters some of the structural and nonstructural barriers erected by traditional gender framing at the institutional level. Women in this context, burdened by cultural norms and the extraordinary level of personal sacrifice required, with less time and support, seek to balance invisible labor with hypervisible scrutiny.[21] For women of color who choose to participate in this taxing marathon, there exists no guarantee that such intensive efforts will lead them anywhere near the coveted medal of partnership. The invisible labor clause is continuously in effect and exhibited in these various ways for women traversing white-male-dominated institutions.

What is guaranteed is that women will have an additional burden when trying to maintain professional and personal relationships, that, in spite of the stark imbalance in work and home obligations chronically disadvantaging their development, law firms will impose the same work expectations on female attorneys as they do on males, with the same "neutral" provisions, and that the net result of these disparities is higher attrition; less females in positions of authority; and, ultimately, the reinforcement of male power and privilege at the highest levels of the institution.[22]

In the next section, by contrasting some of the crucial distinctions between white and black female lawyers' experiences of this already-bleak and strikingly inhospitable gendered landscape, I further explore how the racialized social structure—and ideologies that buttress it—effectively lead to even higher attrition rates and an intensified set of hurdles for black women.

GENDER IN BLACK AND WHITE

Clearly the most decisive factors distinguishing black and white female attorneys' experiences navigating the rocky patriarchal terrain at elite firms are the following: the obstructive influence of the white racial frame on the former and race privilege as it operates on the latter. Exploring this divide provides important insight into the mechanics of intersectionality—where gendered racism directed at black females in such spaces departs from the elite-white-male dominance system's treatment of women from a similar or identical racial and socioeconomic background.[23] Although certainly not intended to be an exhaustive analysis of the toxic impact of white males on white female sexism (there is a significant body of solid scholarship devoted to that particular subject, relative to the number of studies of the intersectional angle), my discussion touches on several core aspects of the dynamic as perceived by respondents of color.[24]

Dorothy E. Roberts, prominent race, gender, and law scholar, succinctly captures the uniqueness of black women's experiences, arguing that women as a whole experience gender in different ways. However, Roberts argues, "Black women experience various forms of oppression simultaneously, as a complex interaction of race, gender, and class that is more than the sum of its parts."[25] Therefore, focusing primarily on gender and simply adding race to the equation forces "women of color to fragment their experience in a way that does not reflect the reality of their lives."[26] Racism and patriarchy interact in manifold ways within the lives of black women that are unique to their social positioning.[27]

Some of the questions posed here take the following form: What are the major factors, for example, that lend systemic gendered racism (versus traditional sexism) its fatal impact on firm retention and advancement rates for black female attorneys? How does white women's racial privilege facilitate their ability to fit in to firm culture versus those women denied access to those same coveted corridors leading to sponsorship and networking opportunities? How does the white racial frame exacerbate black female attorneys' experiences of sexism, deepening the already-formidable obstacles that disadvantage women of color in elite institutions that serve the interests of the elite-white-male dominance system? Ultimately, what are some of the important distinctions between the two groups that burden black females such that their attrition rates far outmatch any other demographic within the white racial frame's sphere of influence?[28] And what does this teach us about the intersection of race and gender?

Sociologist Enobong Hannah Branch argues that

> race and gender must be considered along a continuum that recognizes how individuals are gendered or raced according to the degree of privilege they have and the degree of their disadvantage; for example, whether they are members of a dominant or subordinate racial or gender group. This interlocking nature of oppression creates a complex hierarchy of privilege and disadvantage, in which, generally, White men are privileged, Black men and White women possess conditional privileges, and Black women experience near-absolute disadvantage.[29]

White women are able to cash in on their white privilege, just as men are able to cash in on male privilege.[30] Recognizing that particular privilege means acknowledging that you receive benefits that others do not, often disadvantaging them as a result. As such, finding similarities and differences of their experiences with white women's really does not paint the full picture of black women's experiences. What we are able to see are some of the ways in which female associates find parallels in their experiences dealing with white male dominance in law firms, but black women face a much more difficult road in white male spaces. The invisible labor clause and the inclusion tax are heavily experienced by black women in these spaces and are demonstrated by the examples provided by the participants.

Similarities were noted with the confidence gap, sexual tensions, gendered differences in work–life balance expectations, demands on time, and sacrificing the personal for the professional.

THE WOMEN

Given the nature of elite white institutional spaces, it should come as no surprise that white women still outpace black women in partnership and associate rates.[31] As expressed earlier, black women are still at the bottom of all pyramids: income, training, networking, access to mentorship, and advancement rates. The reasons for this trend, as it contrasts with white female attorneys, are diverse, from the foreseeable to the controversial. Xena, for one, suggested that, due to the privileges of in-group status, white women are coddled by male partners or senior attorneys.[32] They cash in on white privilege:

> [White female associates] are able to elicit sympathy and comfort and protection in a way that that same senior white male attorney wouldn't give to any other woman or any other white or black male. And so that's a big difference, . . . and what that means in terms of how that impacts the environment for a black woman is, I think, that we don't get that same sympathy. We don't get the same "Get Out of Jail Free" card.

One interesting element of Xena's report is the suggestion that white female associates may garner, in limited doses, I suspect, a form of privilege that is even withheld from males. Regardless if this is true, the general effect of the "coddling" they receive under such circumstances certainly provides grounds for a level of confidence, however compromised by gender, that is not meted out to other females. This could have very significant implications in situations where errors are committed, training opportunities are allocated, or the distribution of substantive assignments leading to high-quality billable hours and contacts.[33]

Elite corporate law firms, like many white institutional spaces, operate as racialized social systems, where those perceived as insiders are conferred the benefits of that status (increased opportunity or income, insulation from censure, etc.), which essentially reinforces white privilege and power by disadvantaging those who do not receive the same perks.[34] The basis for this preferential treatment is, of course, rooted in fundamental similarities. Black women, unlike white women or black men, are required to pay an inclusion tax in order to be in white spaces, which is not facilitated by either gender or racial class membership that would provide an easier terrain for navigating a dominant white male environment.

MORE OF THE SAME

"In terms of white female associates, the biggest advantage, or the biggest thing, the difference that I think that there is socially, people are calm, more comfortable dealing with people that look like them. And there are often perceptions. I still think the rule that my mom gave me a long time ago still applies which is, 'When you walk into a classroom, you have to prove you deserve an A. A white female or your white counterpart or your white peer will walk into the same classroom with you, and they have to prove that they don't deserve an A.' And that is, to me, the fundamental difference. . . . I understand that, I've accepted that. Do I think it's fair? Of course not! But, I've accepted that, in my life, there are things that I'm going to have to prove that other people are not. And I think that, that is one of the key differences between myself and just perceptions about who I am and someone else. . . . So that is part of the difference, I think, between a white associate and an associate of color or black associate in particular."

—Nikoleta, third-year associate

The theme of comfort and how it manifests within and between social groups, as well as in the decisions such groups make en masse or individually, unquestionably bears on the development of relationships. People are more comfortable interacting with those with whom they are familiar, who look like them, who act like them, who speak a similar language, and who derive from a similar cultural milieu or a perceived value system, and so on. Thus, the argument goes, it is a natural characteristic of human behavior to give preferential treatment to one's own gender, class, sexual orientation, religious, racial, or ethnic group.[35] As an Ethiopian, therefore, I may prefer my child to marry an Ethiopian over an American; I can defend this preference by asserting that it is not a reflection of bigotry but a simple reflection of sociobiology, an evolutionary mandate. Maybe other primates even echo it.

While clearly true in some contexts, one of the many holes in this theory is revealed by asking ourselves the extent to which all human groups at all times analyze the merits, cultural validity, or even humanity of other groupings equally. For example, the US chattel-slavery-originating white racial frame generally denigrates the intelligence, aptitude, work ethic, and capabilities of nonwhites and women—particularly blacks, without irony—for a variety of social, political, economic, psychological, historical, and other reasons because it simultaneously attaches to nonwhites a complex of often-contradictory narratives and stereotypes that may include anything: being hypervirile, hypersexualized, animalistic, unreliable, docile, unstable, violent, cunning, and thieving. It is no wonder that white Americans, themselves often from insulated communities in which protracted interactions with people of color are limited, might feel more comfortable collaborating with those of their own kind.

Thus, when third-year associate Nikoleta observed that white partners are "calm," exhibiting an affinity for engaging with individuals they are comfortable with as a result of particular commonalities, she speaks to the ongoing racist legacy and institutionalization of the white racial frame.[36] This confers notable benefits on white female associates, who have more flexibility when it comes to developing organic relationships with partners, unlike their black female counterparts, who typically struggle to cultivate such interactions and the connections fomented thereby. White women are invariably excluded from paying an inclusion tax similar to that of black women in white spaces because of their whiteness.

Nikoleta concluded that being black is a disadvantage due to the stigmatization requiring black female attorneys to perform added labor to compensate for the deficits propagated by an elite-white-male dominance system in concert with the edifice of the white racial frame—multiple systems of oppression operating at once.[37] Black women work harder, again, for a more remote shot at the same benefits.[38] As my parents often emphasized, it was necessary to "excel in my excellence" because a black immigrant woman has three strikes against her walking right through the door. Or as Rowan Pope (of the popular television program *Scandal*) might phrase it, "You have to be twice as good as them to get half of what they have," as powerful a commentary as any on the plight of the black laborer at all levels and in all fields.[39]

A BOOST AT THE START OF THE RACE

Whereas Nikoleta focused on the comforts of sameness, Chloe returns us to chapter 3's discussion of networks, where, by her observation, white female associates are more likely to come from a privileged background that extends to them an advantage at the outset:

I think, or I guess I assume, that most white females come from more privileged backgrounds than I do or have family members who are in law and could
have advised them throughout the process. Whether these are female mentors
or male mentors or, my former office mate, her dad was a partner, is a partner
at a law firm. And she's a female, and I think she knew stuff that I didn't know,
or she knew how to interact with partners, and she knew how to do her work.
And, her dad is a partner. I didn't know these things, and I had to learn all this
stuff from scratch. I don't know if that made me a worse associate, but it does
help that you have some other kind of guidance.

There is luxury in avoiding the initial bend of the learning curve and the
access to guidance on how to maneuver law firm and corporate culture.
For Chloe, as for many of my interviewees, one of the primary distinctions
between the resources available to black female attorneys and their white
female colleagues lies precisely in the concept of what must be built "from
scratch" and what is already available to someone due to family or other
personal connections. This specifically is something most black women in
corporate law do not possess: the background of legal, financial, or other
corporate dynasties. Access afforded to white female associates in these areas through various professional networks is typically the direct or indirect
result of white supremacy or the systemic racism embedded within white
social, educational, and occupational institutional spaces.[40] By normalizing
the trajectory and experience of a particular class and race in elite corporate law firms, moreover through a male-dominant perspective, space fails
to be carved for "outsiders," such as black women, whose trajectories and
resources differ and whose experiences are effectively rendered invisible
by this exclusion. One of the greatest resources white women have is access
to white men—who have access to power. Therefore, white women are not
forced to engage with the invisible labor clause to the same degree as black
women because of the access they enjoy due to race privilege.

GENDER IN BLACK AND BLACK: PART I

The parallels between all black students' experiences at elite schools and
the firms that absorb them after graduation and how this path from education to occupation factors into attrition rates in the professional world probably merits its own dedicated study. I touch on several points of contact
here, none more applicable than Louwanda Evans and Wendy Leo Moore's
conclusion from their landmark research into elite law schools that blacks
in such institutions "experience an unequal distribution of emotional labor

as a result of negotiating both everyday racial micro-aggressions and dismissive ideologies that deny the relevance of race and racism."[41] Regardless of gender, black attorneys confront this dynamic as an inevitable feature of their daily work life.[42] In this section, I explore how our respondents—females—identify with their black male colleagues' negotiations of the same taut racial superstructure in elite corporate law firms.

Some interview participants, in fact, felt that there was no notable distinction between genders in this area. As fifth-year associate Hannah offered:

> I never felt anything but camaraderie and support from the black male associates at [my firm]. They may have been treated differently in some respects, but for the most part, I think we were all suffering the same slights, just in different ways.

One of the interesting trends observed, which is contradictory in light of what is known about gender privilege, black male lawyers' presence in elite firms is often fairly scarce, yet their advancement rates still outpace black females.[43] The experiences of both genders come together when we again discuss the thorny subject of fitting in to firm culture; of the psychological as well as practical need to "manage" their behavior and language in front of white lawyers through code switching; and, lastly, of confronting the manifold, often all-consuming pressures of a similar socioeconomic background amid a sea of insiders perceived to be unencumbered by the same responsibilities.[44]

"If It Don't Fit . . ."

Due to the insider–outsider mechanism that typically develops in elite firms once they open the box of inclusion, black males typically encounter a similar quandary, despite their gender privilege, when it comes to fitting in to the white racial frame's projected image of what a lawyer is, looks like, and sounds like and how this image operates in firm culture, promoting a similar sense of alienation and "outsider" feelings. Iris, a forty-year-old counsel at an elite firm, described this shared phenomenon, suggesting that black lawyers in general are never made to feel quite at home in elite corporate firms:

> It's that feeling of—the black males that I've gotten close to, it's the feeling of never feeling like you're belonging. People give you work, will do that, but then—never goes further than just sort of giving—someone giving assignments to them. I think the culture of this place is you sort of just have to fit in

within the grooves of it. And I think people figure out, like some women figure out early on which small departments are good for them so they know which groups to go into to feel like they can make those bonds.

Underlined by Iris's observation is a central weakness at the heart of elite institutions' diversity efforts, which are generally focused on hiring and much less effectively geared toward retention and the factors that complicate it, regardless of gender. Both black male and black female lawyers, like any professionals, want to feel that their presence is valued, not tolerated—neither the mere result of political maneuvering nor a human statistic simply providing evidence of an institution succumbing to social pressure. They prefer to feel that their contributions are or can be, with mutual leaning in from the institutional side *as well as* the individual side, integral to the broader success of the organization. For this reason, workshops that instruct black attorneys of both genders on how to best fit in to firm culture may actually perform an alienating function, at least in isolation, when not coupled with an equally robust effort to teach white colleagues and higher-ups the finer points of dismantling institutional racism for the benefit of firm culture, practices, and even the bottom line.

Code Switchin'

Code switching, as applied here, refers to a complex sociolinguistic phenomenon whereby a speaker elects to alter her dialect, mannerisms, idioms, language, and more according to audience. In US history, code switching among black Americans has served a number of important functions, manifested in various compelling ways, particularly in white-dominated spaces. This term often refers to the use of African American vernacular English (AAVE)—a variation of standard English (SE) that includes different inflections, tones, vocabulary, slang, and style of speech—over the use of SE or vice versa.[45]

Jocaste, a fifth-year associate, described to me how she and other black associates found it a "relief" in this high-pressure environment to communicate in a more comfortable manner using code switching. Undoubtedly, this is comfort black attorneys of either gender seek in each other, allowing them to maintain the desired image that supports "professional" (i.e., white-normalized) speech while offering the opportunity to create a safe space for black cultural expression inside a setting dominated by the white racial frame. In accord with Elijah Anderson's study of code switching in inner-city neighborhoods, black attorneys' ability to alternate as needed is

an indispensable survival skill essential to the black professionals' "reper-
toire of behaviors that do provide . . . security," allowing them to maintain
control over identity presentation with and away from whites and the white
racial frame's racist categories.[46] Jocaste elaborates:

> I don't think it differed a lot [black male versus black female experiences].
> . . . But I think there was a lot of code switching. One of my friends, who's
> a black male associate, he used to come in my office, and we'd eat a lot and
> talk, and the way we would talk with each other was very comfortable, and the
> minute a third party would come in, we'd switch; there was just a lot of that
> going on I felt, a lot of code switching, which seemed very normal for me. You
> know, you're just moving from place to place, community to community, this
> person gets this response. And actually, I think that was helpful, truth be told,
> because, if I had to perform as an associate at a top law firm all the time, I
> would've lost my mind. So, it was good to have an outlet for that expression,
> those discussions that people need to have sometimes.

Generally speaking, use of AAVE in a corporate environment is frowned
upon and can lead to troubling stereotypes and labeling (not to mention uncomfortable interactions with white partners, clients, and colleagues) that
can challenge one's potential to succeed.[47] For this reason, code switching
provides a handy tool for the navigation of these spaces for black female and
black male lawyers alike.

Blue in Green

Across all lines, finance, in one respect or another, plays a defining role
in most American lives. Almost all of my interviewees concurred that their
particular anxieties and preoccupations regarding finance were shared by
their black male colleagues. Nikoleta, married and pregnant with her first
child at the time of our interview, spoke candidly about the financial pressures that tend to fall on the shoulders of all black associates:

> We are first-generation lawyers, meaning . . . there's very few of us who, I
> think, don't have debt, meaning that your parents are wealthy enough or
> fortunate enough to pay for your law school and/or your college experience;
> so there is that burden. There is also, most of the people that I know either
> still live at home and/or supporting their home. It is not just that you could be
> living in the city; . . . you are also slightly, on some level, the person in your
> family that supports home. That is very common. There are very few people
> that I meet that don't have that family construct.[48]

Given the history of inequality in the United States and the fact that black people were intentionally excluded from building generational wealth by a host of systemic racist practices and policies discussed intensely in Feagin's research, we can understand how whites are at a significant advantage over black Americans when it comes to wealth—even discounting the history of slavery.[49] Whites, unlike the black population (ironically), have benefited from government programs that provide crucial resources and the redistribution of material rewards and acquisitions from one generation to the next. Not only do black professionals as a whole have less access to family funds that can be steered toward education, but also they are often in a position in which it is necessary to care for their families' financial well-being, regardless if they are able to obtain professional degrees. These pressures do not, one can easily imagine, make a large purse available for building finances generationally.

Therefore, despite the promise of financial mobility broadcast by corporate firms, many black and Latinx lawyers find it extremely difficult, if not impossible, to build economic security as quickly as their white counterparts. This phenomenon cannot be understated and afflicts both black female and black male associates equally.

Same but Different

"Well, I think, first of all, if you're a black man, you're golden. . . . Not necessarily. I shouldn't say *golden*. You're golden in a particular way. People, in my opinion, once people decide that a black male is not dangerous, they adore him. It's always this sort of like, black men are commodified to be the cool guy. They're supposed to be fun, . . . and then they're supposed to be great athletes. And so, I see people drawn to black men in particular, in a race-based way, in a positive race-based way, positive to excluding the notion of stereotyping, in a way that people aren't drawn to black women in a positive race-based way. . . . I guess the social excitement around black men doesn't exist around black women. So that would be the first piece as to how my experience would differ. And then this isn't really based on race at all, but the fact that the majority of partners and counsel are men . . . still majority men in the higher ranks."

—Delia, fifth-year associate

Nearly all perceived differences between black female and black male lawyers expressed by our respondents seemed to suggest that gender privilege affords black males an advantage because of the patriarchal orientation of the elite-white-male dominance system. While the focus of this study did not include investigating the degree to which *being* a black partner at an elite firm compares to the difficulty blacks face in getting there, studies show that black males advance to partner at far greater rates than black females.[50]

While some positive stereotyping does exist for black males—particularly stereotypes that involve entertainment, profits, or both historically enjoyed by whites (i.e., athletics, music and dance, manual labor, sexual prowess)— the vast majority of scarce positive stereotyping related to black females has evolved very little since the days of chattel slavery (i.e., strong caretaking ability, will, capacity for manual labor, sexual objectification).[51] This has consequences that play out socially and professionally for black associates in occupational settings and situations. Because the white racial frame places value on athletic ability—versus, say, its views on caretaking ability, which are, I would argue, either nonexistent or inconsequential—there is a certain respect such stereotyping may afford black males as opposed to females.

The problem here lies in the fact that, as with most racist stereotyping, any positive designation heaped on blacks is routinely double edged. For instance, black males' athletic ability correlates directly with the intellectual inferiority also assigned to them.[52] As partner Rhebekka noted,

> There is a mystique surrounding the black man's sexuality which plays itself out in so many ways socially that you find coming into these professional settings. And so, there's this thing where on one hand, black men are seen as cool but then on the other hand there is a reticence to really accept their intellectual ability, and that's where I'd say there is a huge difference between the way black men are treated and black women. Black women, you know, we can be smart, that's OK. A black man, it's kind of like, he's really smart? Damn, how did that happen? But can he run, too?[53]

While women's athletics are a less mainstream form of entertainment and thus figure less prominently in the value system of the white racial frame, it can be argued, however tentatively, that black females benefit somewhat from not having their sports overshadow or negate the stereotypical prospect of their intellectual aptitude. But as I show, the advantages accrued by black females over males in elite corporate firms more or less stop there. And the white racial frame's acceptance of their intelligence certainly does not do much for placing black women's names at the main entrance with greater frequency.

GENDER IN BLACK AND BLACK: PART II

A number of respondents reasonably perceived black male associates as having an easier time navigating firm culture due to the benefits of gender privilege discussed in the previous sections. Chloe, for instance, explained,

> I think . . . black males and all males, are just more confident, more outspoken. I think better at networking. The black males that I see here at the firm, they seem to be able to relate to different groups of people more easily.

Here we see the gender-based confidence gap operate on the experiences of black male and black female lawyers, potentially influencing their respective career paths—as the former possesses the biology that enables them to engage and identify with other males at the firm: white males. What Chloe herself identified here is not only the confidence of gender privilege but also the social lubrication provided by this shared gender trait. While it might not make a black associate and a white partner best friends, according to the white racial frame, it does, however, assume a space in which "male interests" can connect. Several respondents, furthermore, ventured that male partners and senior lawyers seem more "comfortable" interacting with black male attorneys than with themselves.

Lydia, a third-year associate, is one of them:

> There is a difference. For a black male, I think, sometimes it is still easier for them to identify with the male partners just because there's a different level of comfort. I think a lot of times just on a strictly gender basis, the male partners are afraid of the female associates thinking that, if they're harsh with them, we're going to cry or something. Or if they're working late, it's going to be awkward or something like that, where they won't have that issue with a black male associate.

The stereotype invoked by this assumption, referring to women's perceived emotionalism, sounds trivial until one realizes that discomfort in providing feedback to an employee with less seniority could very easily influence a superior's decision whether to advance someone he is not comfortable managing. Going further, Lydia imparted that some male partners seem to feel awkward working on assignments late in the evening with women attorneys, a gender-related awkwardness that is only exacerbated when relatability is perceived to be even lower because of the white racial frame's categorization of blackness. This can, of course, be a tremendous disadvantage because it can mean being passed over for specific assignments, opportunities, and even the invitation to social occasions. Again, black men can move beyond racial barriers, relying on gender privilege to connect with such figures; white women can move beyond gender barriers to fall back on their race privilege. What might a black woman fall back on? Certainly not hair care. As Rhebekka elaborated,

> [Y]ou have to deal with all of the black things; then you have to deal with all the woman things. And then, every now and then, you'll get hit with a perception, like black women are angry, black women are strident, black women are intimidating. I also think the difference is white men are very used to interacting with black men in sports teams, so it still feels very natural to them. You know, most white [men] don't know any black women other than their housekeeper or their secretary, like not a single one. It's just coming from a completely different, they don't socialize with them, they don't see them at the sports bar, they don't play pickup basketball with them in the gym. Most white men have no context for interacting with a black woman.[54]

Nor is the advancement of black female professionals well served by the white racial frame's hackneyed but remarkably relentless stereotype of the "angry black woman," alluded to by Rhebekka. A surprisingly effective weapon in the war to silence alternative, countervailing voices, the depiction works by using a caricature to invalidate the substance of an individual's articulation a priori, thereby shielding white patriarchal hegemony, privilege, and power and perpetuating the structural inequalities that derive from them.[55]

Several of my interviewees acknowledged feeling the necessity to be very careful in expressing their emotions because they might be labeled as "angry." When wronged in certain work scenarios, they felt they could not react in a manner that would fuel this reliable, centuries-old stereotype, like its cousins in the area of sexuality, which dampens black women's perceived power. Some of my respondents' anxieties about the label, as Wendy Leo Moore describes, may be held over from law school (and also true of most other white-dominated spaces in American life), where black law students were often characterized as "angry" when resisting or challenging racism.[56] According to Moore, emotion itself in these settings is frequently viewed as a sign of nonbelonging, of not fitting in—especially in a self-described "neutral" and "objective" institution. Therefore, black law students (like black lawyers) who displayed anger or frustration due to racial inequality only amplified their outsider status in such elite white spaces, where, as inconceivable as this may seem, emotion is evaluated as a sign of "otherness."[57] The inability to address one's grievances in a natural manner is yet another, if negative, example of the added labor of black female professionals in what is already a precarious environment for them. The invisible labor clause applies to the experiences of black women, white women, and black men alike. However, like white women's advantage of race privilege, the degree to which black men expend added invisible labor is mitigated by advantages of their gender privilege.

BLACK WOMEN ARE UNIQUE

Our comparative analysis of black female, white female, and black male attorney experiences provides important insights into how the elite-white-male dominance system and white racial framing coalesce to create unique intersectional barriers for black women. Acknowledging that this system of racial and gender oppression created by elite white men and perpetuated by white male actors disproportionately affects black women is crucial to understanding their unique experiences. Although there are strong similarities with both white women and black men, we find the experiences of black female lawyers to be incomparably shaped by both their racial and gender identities' conflict with white patriarchy. This intersection, overlap, and combination of subordinated racial and gender identities creates nuanced experiences that *only* black women encounter. On the one hand, black women, like white women, struggle with confidence, outlandish work–life balance expectations, the confines of stigma, and more. However, the perceived differences between black and white women create definite obstacles that significantly hinder black women's ability to rise through the ranks at elite firms.

The differences in treatment described by my respondents reflect how whiteness is normalized in white institutional spaces, while the contrast with black male lawyers demonstrates that, in spite of racial identity, black males are still perceived to receive better treatment and access because of their shared gender with the white men in power.[58] Many respondents argued that their experiences as black women actually create different circumstances as a professional of color in which they are forced to negotiate their access to opportunity differently.[59]

Black men and white women do not face the same inclusion tax levied on black women precisely because black women negotiate both a subordinated racial and subordinated gender identity. The identity of black women in elite corporate law firms is already viewed as a marginalized identity. Comparing this identity to black men and white women underlines the dynamic processes of multiple forms of oppression. This angle from which to examine the intersectional experience makes visible unmarked categories that highlight power relations within elite firms and their effect on black female associates' advancement and attrition experiences.[60] These antiquated power structures are bolstered by the white racial frame of white male actors in positions of power to create a matrix of domination in which racism and sexism act on each other to normalize and propagate discriminatory practices and policies.[61]

The next chapter focuses on the various ways women are excluded from social and professional networking opportunities and how this element affects their career trajectories within the matrix of domination.

5

WHERE THE BOYS ARE

"[Firm Name], and this is not something that I realized before I came, is very much an old boys' club. And I know people say that about every firm, but I think [Firm Name] is really probably one of the last bastions of the old boys' club, and I think that they stick to it really, really well. I think they did a good job kind of covering it up over the summer [while I was a summer associate], but once you get there, you see. I mean, it's kind of crazy because I came in prepared to kind of have to deal with issues in terms of my race, but I was not expecting to deal with issues because I was a woman. I thought we were past that. So that was really interesting. There were also times where I would be around a partner during, let's say, an outside work event, and they would be talking about the good old days of the firm, with the secretaries downstairs typing up notes and the men upstairs. The partners getting to write and think about things and smoke because you were allowed to smoke in the building at that time. . . . The partners seemed like they lost something in the good old days. And they would say these comments out loud, regardless of who was around."

—Sophie, third-year associate

"Yes, sometimes would they go on recruiting lunches, take only guys to steak restaurants, like Peter Luger's—yes . . . sometimes will they take them to sports stuff. There was some old boys' club kind of thing happening in the corporate finance group, and there was some weird power thing happening in M&A."

—Fotoula, fifth-year associate

"There is a bit of a boys' club, but like any good fraternity, they'll let women in for a party."

—Rhebekka, partner

The exclusion of women from full participation in the activities of elite corporate law firms stems, as we know, from the foundational influence of traditional white patriarchy. The boys' club referred to by these respondents is a beloved relic of the "good ol' days"—prior to black and women's liberation, sexual harassment and assault lawsuits, indoor smoking laws, affirmative action, and the scourge of political correctness, an era when the US corporate world, still vastly white and vastly male, was blessed with a golden age unencumbered by scrutiny and consequence for its drastically prohibitive set of actors, operations, immunities, and beneficiaries.

Although the lingering power of the white racial frame ensures that most of these dynamics are still so firmly in place as to appear inevitable, or at least unassailable, to the majority of Americans, some progress has been made to dismantle its superstructure and the gross inequalities, even violations, it perpetuates.[1] While white women, however, unsurprisingly, constitute the largest payees of affirmative action programs and practices and a small share of black men have been able to capitalize on their skills and gender privilege to achieve their own small presence at the executive and partnership levels, as I show in chapter 4, black women lag behind both demographics in gaining access to the boys' club for reasons that extend beyond the elusive mysteries of their hair. What remains fact is that this system of racial, gender, and class privilege created and controlled by elite white men is in place to benefit white men, which is further evidenced through the existence of the boys' club.

To illustrate the unique position black female lawyers occupy in this matrix, this chapter expands on the previous discussion by exploring how the elite-white-male dominance system (i.e., boys' club) confers benefits on its members while disadvantaging nonmembers directly and indirectly. I also examine how the boys' club forecloses access to outsiders and exhibits racism and historical gender framing, which inhibit its own ability to adequately manage the black and female elements of the organizations under its confining umbrella.[2] Last, I illustrate some ways in which the pervasive chauvinism of the boys' club and bigotry of the white racial frame that undergirds it (both perpetuated and performed by white male actors) negatively affects relations, even between women in elite corporate firms, namely, the complex relationship between white female partners and black female associates.

I also discuss discrepancies in the feedback and review process women of all colors face and, crucially, the role this and other factors play in determining the all-important assignment allocation. I wrap up this chapter with a brief discussion of the income gap faced by women in these institutions.

MEMBERS ONLY

One of the more common iterations of exclusion described by our respondents pertains to "traditionally" male-centered social activities, such as attending sports events with clients, partners, and senior associates. As I have discussed, these are activities during which substantial business is conducted and important networks are anchored. Therefore, not only does the exclusion reflect patriarchal gender biases at work (yes, women like steak and basketball, too), but they also form a de facto means of barring intraorganizational competition from capable female colleagues for contacts, opportunities, and other resources that increase one's partnership and advancement potential. The "tournament," as discussed in David B. Wilkins and Mitu G. Gulati's 1996 seminal research, is skewed toward men.[3]

As you can anticipate based on the earlier analysis of intersectionality and the intensification of basic gender barriers imposed on black women attorneys by systemic gendered racism, it is clear to see how an environment already predicated on male dominance and female exclusion catalyzes higher rates of attrition rather than advancement for this demographic, thereby preserving the corrosive structure of white male privilege and power.[4] Fifteen out of my twenty participants admitted that their firms either have a boys' club or have male partners who choose to work exclusively with male associates.[5] The small uptick in diversity precipitated by affirmative action does not, as I have stated, result in invitations to the boys' club sent with any greater frequency to historically marginalized groups. The boys' club has been defined elsewhere as a "powerful circle of men, usually white, whose connections and alliances help advance them within an organization or silo."[6] Yet unlike affinity groups that develop to help address the types of barriers created by the boys' club (as well as other issues pertinent to such women, blacks, Latinxs, etc.), the boys' club itself is like a fortress, an unofficial affinity group for white men, the primary concern of which is the management, consolidation, and development of power within institutions it has created. Gia, a fifth-year associate, acknowledged that such an entity may exist in some organizational spaces but not in others:

It varies by practice group. . . . If you look at M&A [mergers and acquisitions], and there's a deal team, which are more traditionally like the investment banking type sort of environment, you'll overhear a conversation: "Oh, yes, we went golfing, this partner and I went," and women aren't a part of that conversation. So yes, there is that socializing outside of work that women aren't necessarily a part of.

From her response, we can infer that, although boys' clubs may not exist in every practice group, the spaces in which they exert the strongest presence are often the most influential—such as M&A, which involves sustained interaction with investment bankers, finance groups, and other money-controlling boys' clubs. Kallisto, a sixth-year associate, elaborated,

I felt certain departments were very much boys' clubs, and I avoided those departments. The M&A group was very much known as a boys' club, and people felt very uncomfortable in that group.

EXCLUSION. ALIENATION. DISCOMFORT. DISADVANTAGE.

Jocaste, a fifth-year associate, recounted how she usually fits in quite well with traditional male enclaves because of her own personal interest in sports and history of social engagement in male-dominated environments. However, Jocaste described how she was unable to find common ground with a particular group of males, in contrast to finding common ground with a group of males who were *not on the partnership track*:

Within corporate, it was a group that worked together, they hung out together, and on occasion, I'd worked on deals with this group, and I remember thinking, I happened to be very much a guys' girl. I talk sports all the time, I hang out with men a lot, and I'm fine in those situations; I like them a lot. But these guys, I felt very uncomfortable with this whole group. They just had such a different experience. I couldn't relate to them on any level. I don't play golf, nor do I care to. I don't have a country home. I don't have a wife at home who takes care of all my business. That was one thing that I think was very annoying to a lot of us women. . . . But I meant that's kind of just the reality. But the boys' club stuff, it's interesting because I did fit in with another group of males, but they were not guys who were going to make partner. Not that they were outcasts. They were just different people, and they were just much more down to earth. . . . And I think there's some men who've felt, "OK, I have to get in with this group, I have to adopt this, I have to act like I like these things," and I would watch that a little bit.

One of the more salient points illustrated here is the causal relationship between career advancement and affiliation with the boys' club. And it is no coincidence that the less approachable of the two subgroups—the less "comfortable" for a black female, Jocaste—is the one comprised of (white male) associates on the partnership track. This exclusivity is a reflection of historical, socially sanctioned forms of exclusion within white institutional spaces by white males.[7] Racial and gender framing justifies their existence and acts as a buffer against forces of change. From elite schools, firms, political groups, and influential places of leisure to services, resources, and other insider information, such spaces that are predominantly only accessible to affluent white men, and to a certain extent their families, outline the workings of the modern-day boys' club and its very pervasive and archaic standard of exclusion. Given the discussion in chapter 4, the invisible labor that is necessary for any nonwhite male or any female attempting to penetrate the boys' club is significant. However, when analyzing the experiences of black women, we find that the invisible labor clause that requires black women to perform added labor just to be seen or recognized, aside from the inclusion tax paid to be included in the general white space to begin with, is nearly unfathomable.

Its historical roots wend so deeply into the American industrial and socioeconomic landscape that, at times, the boys' club may seem a deterministic institution unto itself, divorced from the control of its beneficiaries and, even to our participants, a self-operated power-reinforcing machine. The challenge of its ubiquity, at least for those seeking access to some of its privileged spaces (i.e., advancement at elite firms), is that normalization, as we know, becomes confused with inevitability, and trends that disadvantage marginalized groups continue to do so with impunity, further reifying the tenets of the white racial frame's social Darwinist undertones.[8]

The benefits bestowed on men who are a part of the boys' club automatically disadvantage women from developing and nurturing organic relationships with clients, partners, and networks, while simultaneously adding to the soft skill and practical work skill deficits for already disadvantaged groups, who consequently miss out on substantive assignments. But tokenist tendencies within the club can be just as inhibiting. Similar to Wendy Leo Moore's findings that law students of color are forced to attend social events at all-white spaces, we find that black female lawyers, like other female attorneys, often find it uncomfortable, reasonably, to be in particular male-centered, utterly white-dominated spaces.[9] Moreover, while firms cannot be expected to invite all female associates to, say, an off-hours strip club foray with a high-profile client, they can create opportunities for female associates to connect with the same clientele in other mutually advantageous ways, as well as encourage dialogues and policies to address some of the contradictory aspects of doing business in such manner in a field putatively seeking to be more inclusive of women and other groups at all levels. (Of course, the easiest way to dismantle such relics of the "good ol' days" is to hire and advance more women anyway.)

Lydia, a third-year associate, described the boys' club as influential partners working with a select group of male associates, but she succumbed to a certain fatalism about the plausibility of reconfiguring the dynamic:

> Particularly in my group, it's a big group, so there are different factions, and there is definitely a boy's club within the group. And I'm sure that's the same in other groups, too. . . . There is a group where it's some of the top men in the group, top revenue generators, and then they have their group of favorite associate males, and they're all men who they work with all the time. And figuring out how to break into that isn't really an easy task, as you know. Those people are able to operate without going through the normal channels of going through the staffing partners and doing the normal thing. And I don't think they're actively saying, I don't think it's them intentionally excluding women, but they aren't trying to include them, either, in the process. I think it's things like that that are missing. There are definitely people at the firm who want to make the effort, but there's only so much you can do without people changing their normal, everyday habits.

The sense of futility inculcated by this element within firm culture can be a deterrent to the retention of black female attorneys, and not necessarily grasping the cultural and economic value of diversity in no way discourages the operation of the boys' club, which benefits from high attrition rates and the lack of competition, scrutiny, and competing perspectives on its operations that result from it. From its vantage point, the fewer supplicants seeking entrance to the citadel, the better.

A few associates, such as Athena, though, did question how deliberate and countervailing the boys' club's influence is:

> I think there's a boys' club. I don't think it is intentional. I don't think it is as bad as anywhere. I mean, I don't think it's as bad as that term suggests, but I do think that the men socialize amongst themselves a lot of times, not always,

in a much freer way than they socialize with the women. And also a lot of the activities, for example, golf, I think are sometimes limiting for women.

It is important to note that the selection process for its membership is not arbitrary. Men are more likely to be eased into the club and receive this distinction once they develop the skills to maneuver within firm politics, further distancing them from those who do not have those skills or contacts. The inclination to accept this dynamic, or perceive it as inevitable, as Philomena did here, again only reflects how deeply ensconced white male privilege is in our broader culture, how common such behaviors are in work culture in general, and how normalized restrictions on racially subordinated groups are in elite corporate firm settings:

> I mean, it's big law. Big law is a boys' club. If clients want to go out for drinks, the first thing, they'll reach out to the partner or associate, he's going to round up his boys, and then maybe if you're on a deal or if there's a specific reason to invite you, he'll invite you. But you know, I don't even think it's intentional. I just think that it is a boys' club, and that's how big law is, especially in finance because the investment bankers, it's a boys' club over there. . . . I mean, men are men, so I think in a way it's easier for them to break into the boys' club once they learn the language.

None of my respondents espoused the fatalistic "Boys will be boys," but the "Big law is big law" mentality went as far as "Whites will be white." So one wonders why it is easier to accept normalized gender barriers than it is to accept biased US racial norms—especially if the allowance of one, as many would argue, typically engenders the propagation of the other. While intent may make a difference on an interpersonal basis, as such prominent sociologists as Eduardo Bonilla-Silva and Wendy Leo Moore emphasize, taken more broadly, intent is irrelevant to the social outcomes of action.[10] Regardless if associates of color and white women are consciously or subconsciously excluded from joining the boys' club, the effects of this exclusion create substantial obstacles to their advancement. And then, of course, there is also the impact of overhearing conversations reminiscing about the "good ol' days," back when women were secretaries, and men did the "thinking work." We miss poodle skirts, too.

MANAGING WOMEN AND BLACKS 101

The boys' club may be difficult to assail because of the patriarchal tradition that power and wealth is a zero-sum game pitting white males and white male institutions against the less capable but nonetheless cunning other (comprising most of the known world). But one argument for introducing workshops, policies, and practices to dismantle racism and sexism, thereby promoting greater inclusivity in elite corporate firms, is that educating white males about exactly who the other is and establishing firmer lines of communication and understanding between them can have a salutary impact on important relations with clients, foreign entities, stake-holding communities, colleagues, markets, and associates who would traditionally fall under diverse categories that are not white and not male. Many of my respondents painted a picture of common exchanges with senior associates and partners that clearly reflect discomfort interacting with, let alone effectively managing, females, blacks, and especially black females.

A workshop devoted to teaching white males how to interact with black women might, one imagines, do more harm than good, but dispelling the toxic narratives, subconscious framing, and biases that often dictate the tenor of interactions between potential and actual members of the boys' club and other groups could actually benefit areas of firm culture and productivity weakened by these factors. For example, the discrepancies often cited by my respondents pertaining to developmental feedback and performance reviews for black females not only do a disservice to their advancement prospects but also prevent firms from developing the skills of these employees and strengthening specific facets of their operations.[11] Due to its importance and the frequency with which the matter was raised in my research, I take a moment here to further characterize this problem.

Not surprisingly, systemic gendered racism plays a significant role in the ways in which black female lawyers' performance is weighed and evaluated. The annual review is a time when constructive developmental feedback is given to improve attorney performance, as well as an opportunity for attorneys to engage with senior management about their own progress and training concerns. The expectation is that, if an employee performs the responsibilities of her job satisfactorily, the review process should be straightforward, with logical corollary discussions that lay the groundwork for assignment allocation, mentorship and sponsorship issues, substantive billable hours, and advancement—no small thing. Unfortunately, several lawyers I interviewed expressed critiques of how they measure up, as women who are black, because of the framing that manipulates *their re-*

viewers' performance during this straightforward, albeit impactful, corporate ritual. As Hannah forthrightly put it:

> Because being a lawyer is an apprentice business, you're looking at various stages of your career for feedback of what you do well, what you need to get more of, and how you need to grow. And we get such piss-poor feedback that it's very difficult for you to actually really even evaluate your own skill set.

The belief that males are assessed differently than females was cited numerous times by my respondents, who argued that women receive developmental feedback in a manner that puts them at a significant disadvantage for improvement and engagement, basically giving them another handicap. Lydia explained,

> Actually, one of the black male partners, who, he's very candid about things, and he'll have conversations with us, he talked about how, particularly for the black female associates, he said the firm, particularly a lot of the partners are just afraid of us. Those were his words. He said that they're just afraid, that if they do the wrong thing or say the wrong thing, we're going to cry or get upset, so they're afraid to be too critical, to give the same criticism that they might give one of their . . . positive or constructive feedback they would give to one of their white male associates. They are reluctant to give that kind of feedback to us because they're afraid of the repercussions. He was speaking specifically of black women because either we'll, I don't know, get emotional or we'll say that they're racist or who knows what we could possibly say. So, it's little things like that, that are beneficial to your development that we might not be getting because they're afraid of our reaction to it.

Who knows what the mysterious other will say? Who knows what the mysterious other will do? By not providing women with candid evaluations of their performances, they are less able to learn and develop their craft than male (and white) associates, who are given more accurate, constructive reviews and information and are able to have an authentic back and forth for a better understanding of how particular strengths or improvements may relate to opportunities. The facile concession to female emotionalism, not to mention general fear of black women, no doubt associated with the white racial frame's bizarre treatment of its own "angry" caricature, leads to this costly barrier.[12] Other than frustrating for black female attorneys, it can also be a bewildering handicap because it renders them unable to assess their own progress. Not only do they face differential treatment producing inequitable results for their professional development, but also, at the same time, the racial frame, vis-à-vis the caricature that attempts to obfuscate or preclude charges of racist actions or intent, blames them for the way they are treated by saddling them with a label that undermines their voices.[13] What antiracism and antisexism programs would offer is the opportunity to unpack much of this subconscious and structural distortion, paving the way for black women to receive the honest, constructive reviews they require and for firm managers to strengthen their staff, operations, and the relationships between associates and higher-ups. The boys' club may not benefit directly from such improvement, but the firm will, increasing its relevance to the global market and modern social realities.

BOYS DON'T CRY

As mentioned earlier, affiliation with the boys' club bears a direct correlation to the allocation of substantive work assignments, secluding particular contacts and channeling access to those cloistered within the club's network. Insiders get first dibs on the more desirable opportunities; outsiders, which often include the majority of female attorneys and attorneys of color, pick up the remainders. An alarming number of my respondents, in fact, argued that women are frequently reduced to playing a "service role" in firm activities. As partner Xena described,

> I think to a lesser extent, at least in my group, although I guess it happens sometimes, is the way responsibilities are divvied out, who's responsible for sending out calendar invites, making sure that things are in place for the big meeting, stuff like that. I think female associates probably feel like they get the bulk of that type of work.

By requesting female associates to take on traditionally gendered tasks, a division between male and female associates is established that disadvantages the latter, perpetuates stereotypes about their "inherent" abilities, and of course reinforces male privilege to the ease and benefit of the patriarchal structure. When one is an attorney out "getting refreshments" or "organizing a client dinner," effectively support staff functions, one is clearly not doing the "thinking work" of an actual lawyer or is competing with those male associates who are.

Apart from the outright damage of relegating accomplished female professionals to such an archaic articulation of sexist framing, the tendency to divide unskilled support staff tasks in this manner begs the question, What work are female associates finally allocated once the boys' club has received

its first glance, all the refreshments have been acquired, the meetings have
been organized, and the copies have been made? It reflects the counterpro-
ductive myopia of traditional gender framing, which saddles firms with an
inability to recognize, use, or even adequately manage the skills of a team
of diverse men and women.

Kallisto, a sixth-year associate at the time she was compelled to leave her
firm for this and similarly confining reasons, described an encounter with
a male superior that elucidates the subtle ways in which stereotypes about
the roles of women, and black women in particular, seep into everyday
interactions:

> I was on a deal one time with a partner who I absolutely loved. This partner,
> he was great, and we're on the phone, we're trying to reach counsel on the
> other side, and he's like, "Oh, she's probably out just getting her nails done.
> Why is she not answering her phone?" And I thought to myself, "If this was a
> male, he would never assume that the reason why this male is not answering
> this call is because of anything other than something being work-related." But
> for a woman, and this happened often, and this is just a small example because
> this used to always happen with women on the other side of deals in positions
> of power, the partners would always assume that they were not responsive for
> superficial reasons. But the males, it was because they were busy with other
> clients, and they were just busy. They must be busy. And that bothered me so
> much. And it happened often, but when it happened with this partner, it made
> me particularly upset because . . . even a good/bad situation, it's still bad. It
> still stinks, and even the best of the partners here think of women subtly in
> a way, that women in positions of power are dillydallying and off taking care
> of their kids, when I know clients have called you [the partner], and you've
> asked me to redirect the call because you're on a roller coaster right now. So
> why are you assuming?

Kallisto's experience clearly illustrates how gender stereotypes, which
effectively lead to negative labeling, influence how females are not only
perceived but also valued in these organizations amid the profusion of
regressive patriarchal narratives and biases.[14] Such barriers, which I argue
block the managerial view of the organization, as well as its members, proliferate unchecked and unchallenged because of the deliberate invisibility
implemented by the boys' club, the toxic and obsolete legacy of the "good
ol' days," and their controlling mechanisms.

Because most elite corporate firms are fully supplied with support staff,
the failure to identify, develop, and capitalize on the skills of female associates represents a structural underutilization of resources fomented by

conscious and subconscious gender discrimination. Add to this stew the litany of racial tropes, stereotypes, and preoccupations built into the white racial frame there, and again, one wonders how women, especially black women, are able to maneuver through this labyrinth of systemic archaic framing encountered daily in such settings, simply seeking to do a decent day's work in an equitable environment. The extra labor required of them, craftily inserted in the employment contract under the invisible labor clause, is meant to be exhausting; it is meant to be discouraging; it is meant to be practically impossible to sustain—and it is.

CAN I HANG OUT *WITH* YOU GUYS?

The calculus of steering this terrain deftly enough to maintain one's position and equilibrium is, as I have established, extremely delicate; to lay the groundwork for advancement in this context while negotiating so many bizarre artifacts and hurdles, while lacking the networks and equal access to sponsorship and mentorship opportunities that their white male colleagues and competitors enjoy (which I discuss further in the next chapter), only complicates the onerous but commonplace calculations black female attorneys must continually master. One anecdote that drove the point home for me embodies the extent to which even the most banal setting, a company barbecue, devolves, thanks to the "traditional" boys' club orientation of work politics, into an almost absurdly thorny dilemma for third-year associate Philomena:

> Another situation I personally encountered that actually made me so uncomfortable, . . . the chair of our department has a summer series, and he'd invite a mix of partners and associates in the group with their significant others . . . to his house. . . . It was a small group dinner so that we could all mingle, get to know each other. . . . And I just happen to end up in a group where I was the only female associate from here. So, it was all male partners and male associates, and it was a barbecue. So what ended up happening was we get to the partner's house, I brought my boyfriend, and everybody else brought their wives and their kids. And we get to the partner's house, and the guys go out to the grill, and they go grill and smoke cigars, and the women all stayed inside. And they're with the kids, and we're watching the Olympics at the time, the Olympic trials. And at one point, I started getting real uncomfortable because I was like, "Well, my boyfriend is out there with all of my coworkers, I'm in here with all of the wives, and is this going to subconsciously make them kind of associate me with [the wives]?" And all the wives happen to of course have

been former big lawyers who married partners and are bankers or along that line. But then I didn't feel necessarily comfortable going outside and joining them. And so, it was that kind of moment where you're like, "What am I supposed to do because I also don't want to be the person who snubs my nose to the women and is like, 'I'm here to network, so I'm going to go out and network'?" But that is kind of the point, . . . and I felt like, well, that's sort of a missed opportunity, and had I been a male associate, I would've been out there, and my wife or girlfriend would have been inside. It's little things like that, and part of that was me, too, because I didn't have another female associate with me to kind of follow her lead or to be like, "It's two of us."

Coming to the fore here is the associate's need, as a breadwinner, to break out of a disadvantaging social category framed by patriarchal gender stereotypes that is inhibiting a chance to create an opportunity for herself in this situation. Here, the dominant white racial frame and its patriarchal presumptions posit her gender above her profession and subject her to its archaic narrative about a woman's "place" in relation to the place of breadwinners, universally understood to be males despite countless generations of evidence to the contrary. In this particular account, Philomena's exclusion from the boys' club basically annihilates her agency, unlike for a male associate who, perhaps mildly pressured by social norms, would very easily be able to make a decision based on his own preference and perceived interest.

The traditional landscape of the law firm is revealed here as dramatically skewed in favor of men, forcing Philomena to risk her rapport, not only with the partners, but with their wives and girlfriends, as well. The more she might try to break away from traditional gender divisions, the more precarious her position would inevitably become. Needless to say, at a potentially harmless and fruitful company gathering, she was extremely uncomfortable with the circumstances and set of options before her. Philomena was unable to make the choice she so desperately wanted to make to ensure that she, too, received the same opportunity and access as male associates attending the same event.

MENTOR, FRIEND, OR FOE

Thus far, I've analyzed some of the ways in which female associates, irrespective of color and particularly black, are curtailed by the categories erected by the racist and sexist system that propagates the boys' club at the expense of those groups it excludes. Even firm managers, presumably members of the club, may find they, along with their institutions, are restricted by its biases from fully using its labor force's human capital and productive potential. One of the interesting aspects of this mechanism highlighted by Philomena's anecdote is the effect of these biases and framing on relations between females, a subject broached by a number of my interviewees regarding colleagues, partners, and mentors.

Before I enter into chapter 6's expanded discussion of sponsorship and mentorship dynamics and how black female attorneys perceive their access to the "royal jelly" restricted by systemic gendered racism, I introduce the theme of mentorship here because the same corrosive forces of the boys' club dichotomy has a manifest influence on two marginalized groups.[15] These groups seem to be natural, if not comfortable, candidates who are both excluded from the boys' club, though to varying degrees, and unable to use their affinity as excluded groups to join forces: again, white and black women.

Mentors can be anyone who has a little more experience or knowledge than the mentee, such as an associate or partner.[16] They take an interest in the professional development and training that go into building an associate's legal career, while sponsors, which I also discuss in greater depth shortly, focus on the advancement opportunities of their protégés. Most of the lawyers in this study indicated that developing mentorship and sponsorship relationships has been particularly challenging for them. While the difficulties of building relationships with white male partners are largely explained by the prohibitive character of the white racial frame and the boys' club, a surprising number relayed that they also confronted very restrictive challenges receiving support from white *female* senior associates and partners, a demographic one would expect to be a reliable source of mentorship and sponsorship opportunities.

Ironically, though not surprisingly, it is the exclusive nature of the boys' club itself that appears to lie at the root of what divides these two marginalized groups linked by gender. One interviewee postulated a feeling of resentment that exists for many female partners, who had to fight against these gender barriers, "shatter the glass ceiling," and so on to arrive at the positions they are in today and exhibit a certain reticence to offer to other females assistance they themselves did not receive.[17]

The highly competitive arena of elite firm culture overall, and the limited space for excluded groups within them to achieve power and access, essentially reproduces the same Darwinist dynamic among outsiders that allows the boys' club to separate itself and prosper within an insider's paradise.[18] Meanwhile, black female associates contend that, because white female partners and senior associates were forced to endure gender prejudice and discrimination, they should be more sympathetic to the issues that female lawyers face today.[19] Here is Hannah, a fifth-year associate:

> Now, the gender piece, which was interesting to me was, I've found that there was an antagonism between women who were a generation ahead who felt as if they'd done everything they did by themselves, and so they were less likely to help us. But this is the conundrum. . . . In order for the generation of women, white, who are now partners at law firms and managing partners, to get to where they were, a white man championed them, OK. As much as they want to think it was super, super hard and really, really difficult and nobody likes them, they would actually not be partners unless someone put their name up.

In truth, respondents like Hannah argued that the fact that white female senior associates and partners do not provide further support to women seeking their footing along the partnership track actually makes the path *more difficult* for the younger generation of female lawyers. The reason for this is the fact that, as she explained, male partners who have promoted white females tend to back away from promoting women associates thereafter, the assumption being (no doubt in part fueled by the discomfort they feel managing females and black women in particular) that female partners will, or should, promote and mentor female associates. Because female partners from an earlier generation could not have advanced without white males to advocate for them, black female associates, and female attorneys from the younger class in general, are thereby left with even fewer options than their predecessors.

If systemic gendered racism is giving black female lawyers an extremely difficult time forming organic mentor and sponsor relationships with male partners and they remain unassisted by white females at the same level, who is to advocate for them and help steer their advancement? As is true of these settings in general, there aren't enough black males to go around.

The competition at elite corporate law firms is tremendously intense among all associates, regardless of gender or race. Given the fact that women are dramatically outnumbered in partnership positions, an amplified sense of competition commonly develops among female associates vying for limited partnership positions and other opportunities.[20] The winner-take-all attitude operative in boys'-club-dominated institutions mainly leaves crumbs for those who cannot count themselves lucky enough to possess the benefits and security of being members. It would appear that the difficulty of surmounting their outsider status and the barriers they faced have left them, even at the highest level, with a palpable sense of still remaining under threat and needing to compete with mobility-seeking female associates. Again, Hannah, our most vocal respondent on the subject:

> Until there are enough white women who give a damn about creating opportunities for women and recognizing that the legal profession has a whole lot of people, women of color, that are not their enemies and not their competition and that they can create a safe space for us, we won't have a safe space. And white men no longer do it because the expectation is that white women should or will, and they should, and they won't, and they don't.

The bottom line here is that the intergenerational shift in expectations leaves many female associates, and particularly women of color, in a position where they are ultimately left to fend for themselves; as Hannah proceeded to note,

> The strides in the legal community advance white women, and there's really very little else or anyone else out there [for the rest of us].

Thus, because of the divisive atmosphere perpetrated by the boys' club and the lion's share of opportunities it absorbs, black female lawyers are doubly excluded from developing organic relationships with white partners of either gender, which sensibly burdens their advancement and retention. Because the white racial frame also renders the achievements, abilities, and hard work of nonwhites virtually invisible, a belief to which white females are equally as susceptible as white males, the suggestion that black female associates simply work hard until their efforts are acknowledged discounts the harsh reality of the manifold obstacles they face.[21]

In this chapter, I focus on how the boys' club and its various impacts determines the career trajectory of female associates, with an emphasis on black female lawyers. In the following chapter, I explore in greater detail how the white racial frame factors into black female lawyers' uphill battle for institutional support and how the "royal jelly," that crucial lubricant of advancement, is systematically withheld, summarily forcing these women into the frustrated position that leads all too often to their attrition.

6

"CAN YOU PLEASE PASS THE ROYAL JELLY?"

"I don't know if I'm getting the same opportunities as, like I said, my white counterparts are in terms of being in front of clients, leading deals, learning opportunities, running conference calls, or running deals."

—Chloe, third-year associate

"When I think about, 'well, why didn't I ever want to make partner?' . . . I think if it hadn't been for this one partner, when I think of the opportunities that men junior than me who have made partner and how quickly they made it, and I think, 'Have they been shown sort of a different path than me?' As opposed to just saying, 'Yes, you can make partner.' And me being worried about, once I make it, what am I going to do with it? Had I been given the same opportunities really that this person almost was hand-held about? This is what you need to do to sort of be a successful partner once you make it. . . . Some people are shown the path. . . . I still haven't put my finger on what it is, but I think part of it is from them [the partners], but then also, someone who's coming up as a midlevel, you realize, 'Well how open is this to me?'"

—Iris, counsel

"No, [I don't have a mentor]. Because we are in a very relationship-driven [place], a law firm is relationship-driven, a hierarchy, I guess. You need to find or you, as an associate, you work with partners who choose whether they see something that you are not. And, well first of all, you, as an associate, you work, and as long as you do the work, presumably, depending on the place you work and that of a certain caliber, you will advance. But in order to ultimately continue advancing, you need to have a partner and/or senior associates that take a liking to you. And in terms of taking a liking, that's a very personal choice. You can't tell a person, 'Oh, you should take an interest in that person, or you should take an interest in that person.' You just know that people tend to gravitate to people who are similar to them, and I know I'm different than a lot of the people at the firm."

—Elissa, fifth-year associate

In this chapter, I examine how racialized social structures and the group ideology they reinforce systematically exclude black female lawyers from mentor and sponsor relationships crucial to their professional development and advancement. All of my respondents, including Xena and Rhebbeka, the two pioneers who successfully braved the torrent of hurdles described in this research to become partner, stated unequivocally that *the most important factor* in achieving partnership is having a sponsor. Not having a mentor or sponsor, meanwhile, makes an associate vulnerable to bad assignments; negative reviews; and further exclusion from networking, internally and with clients outside the firm. It signals to others that the associate may not be "worth" the time and effort required to develop these types of relationships, all of which may inevitably lead to dismissal. The pressures associated with finding, developing, and maintaining mentor and sponsor relationships creates added labor for all associates, but black women tend to have the hardest time gaining ground. This inevitably forces them to work even harder, continuously enacting the invisible labor clause.

In the tournament structure of elite corporate law, mentorship and sponsorship, or the lack thereof, can make or break you.[1] Furthermore, the "royal jelly" ("jelly")—described by law scholars David B. Wilkins and Muti G. Gulati as the training that allows lawyers to shine and develop into potential stars for partnership track—is produced, manufactured, and distributed by such relationships.[2] This is the main ingredient that gets an associate to the door, knocks on it for her, and lets her in. It guides and teaches an associate how to navigate the professional complexities, as well as providing networking and business-generating techniques in a high-stakes law firm. In this chapter, I explore how systemic gendered racism, created, reinforced, and perpetuated by white male actors, functions to withhold the jelly from this demographic that, due to the proliferation of structural barriers, needs it the most. I investigate how billable hours fit into the equation and what the larger picture ultimately reveals to us about attrition rates for black female attorneys, who, craving the jelly, receive little more than peanuts instead.

CHEAP FRAME

The discussion of mentors and sponsors cannot be understood without understanding how Joe R. Feagin's theory of systemic racism is fundamental to the preservation of racial inequality, as well as how the white racial frame operates to maintain white privilege and power in this context.[3] It influences perceptions of who is worthy of being mentored or sponsored through its insidious web of "stereotypes"; "narratives and interpretations"; "images and language accents"; "emotions"; and, most consistent of all, "inclinations to discriminate," finally depriving black female lawyers of an equal shot at obtaining the royal jelly and merit-based advancement.[4]

Before I delve into the thick of this discussion, I clarify a few terms herein. Support in the form of mentoring and sponsorship is indispensable to the lawyers in any law firm of any size and in one form or another, formal or informal, for most corporate professionals of any kind. Although the terms *mentor* and *sponsor* are often used interchangeably within corporate and legal fields, they do embody some important distinctions. For instance, a mentor relationship is generally not as driven and focused as that of a sponsor relationship. Mentors can have several mentees, while sponsors tend to focus on individuals they consider to be rising "stars," usually taking on only a few protégés for the grooming process.[5] Sylvia Ann Hewlett, an economist, provides a clear distinction between the two terms and describes their significance: "[M]entors act as a sounding board or a shoulder to cry on, offering advice as needed and support and guidance as requested; they expect very little in return."[6]

Some of the common functions of mentors is to introduce and acquaint mentees to the organization, its institutional practices, and its culture, as well as act as an advisor on ways to navigate these practices. Various research provides an in-depth analysis that distinguishes the particular roles and related functions associated with being a mentor.[7] These roles include being a host, teacher, advisor, facilitator, protector, coach, role model, sounding board, confidante, publicist, champion, and so-called catalyst. Mentors primarily focus on career *development*, while sponsors focus on career *advancement*. It is important to understand that sponsors, particularly, tend to wield significant power and are able to influence other actors in positions of power. A sponsor's primary goal is to advance the career of their protégée because "sponsorship [more than mentorship] is predicated on power."[8]

While of course, a mentor would like to have his or her mentee be successful, they do not necessarily proactively seek ways to ensure their success.[9] In that variation, the onus is generally on the mentee to seek out advice and interactions with the mentor. Sponsors, on the other hand, are more invested in the development of the individuals they choose to foster: "Sponsors advocate on their protégés' behalf, connecting them to important players and assignments. In doing so, they make themselves look good. And precisely because sponsors go out on a limb, they expect stellar performance and loyalty. A sponsor can lean in on a woman's behalf, apprising others of her exceptional performance and keeping her on the fast track."[10] A sponsor relationship is reciprocal, in that the individual being sponsored must do her part to maintain a level of excellence that reflects positively on the sponsor, especially because sponsors will be viewed and judged based on this relationship. Reputations must be kept high.

Finally, a sponsor plays a very influential role in the career of a lawyer working to become partner, acting as an advocate or conduit on behalf of the lawyer to the partnership apparatus. Sponsors can do all the things a mentor can do. However, they also ensure that the attorney under her steerage obtains quality assignments that help to train her, that she engages with other senior associates and partners, and that she becomes visible to clients and helps them develop the necessary skills to be successful in the firm. A sponsor puts their reputation on the line to help the lawyer advance, which is, at the end of the day, the key difference between a mentor and a sponsor. This type of relationship cannot be assigned like that of a mentor relationship, making it particularly vulnerable to biases inculcated by the white racial frame; it must develop organically in order to flourish. It is based on mutual trust, whereby the sponsor trusts that the protégée will meet their expectations, and the protégée trusts that the sponsor will commit to helping her reach her desired goal of advancing.[11]

HOW TO MAKE FRIENDS AND INFLUENCE PARTNERS

Ida O. Abbott, a leading expert on mentorship, focuses her research on how sponsorship works to advance women lawyers.[12] Whether male or female, mentors can be anyone inside or outside the firm with more experience and knowledge than the mentee, such as a former partner or a third-year associate taking on the role of a mentor for a first- or second-year associate. In most cases, the third-year associate, based on his or her position, will not have adequate experience, knowledge, or power to influence firm partnership and advance a mentee. Therefore, to be a sponsor, one "must have sufficient organizational clout to make good things happen for the protégée"—often a partner or individual in high management located internally.[13] Abbott summarizes the importance of a sponsor in developing, tracking, and advancing the career of his or her protégée:

> An ambitious woman needs a special kind of mentor who serves as a champion or sponsor. A sponsor is a strong advocate who has power and influence to make that advocacy produce positive career results for you. A sponsor endorses your qualifications and takes risks on your behalf, arguing that you should move up to a higher compensation tier or urging that you are ready for equity partnership or a significant leadership position. A sponsor alerts you to the opportunities and appoints you to key posts. Sometimes they put their reputation on the line by calling in favors or putting pressure on colleagues for your benefit. Sponsors may not guarantee success, but they make it easier and improve your odds of receiving a coveted leadership appointment, a fatter paycheck or a new client.[14]

Some elite corporate law firms, to their credit, recognize the importance of mentorship, if not sponsorship, and thus implement formal diversity mentoring programs. While the efficacy of such programs varies widely and clearly requires significant improvement once one examines the attrition and retention rate data that inspires this book, a firm at least acknowledging an alternative trajectory can go far toward helping associates feel that their success is desired, that they are recognized in this environment, and that they are somewhat more comfortable in a typically hostile white institutional space.[15] The problem with such programs (a full account of which goes beyond the scope of this book but deserves mention here) stems from two factors: (1) Very few firms appear to have measures in place to assess the efficiency of such programs, so when they are dysfunctional for any reason, they usually remain dysfunctional. (2) Perhaps foreseeably, issues arise because the pool of partner and senior associates of color is extremely small.

Sophie's experience with her firm's formal mentoring program speaks to the disproportionate responsibility that some racially subordinated partners may face because of the shortage of partners of color. She explained that, because only diverse partners were tasked with mentoring diverse associates, the commitment ultimately may have become too burdensome for many mentors. Such a situation can be disadvantaging, not only for the diverse associates affected by the lack of partners of color, but for diverse partners, as well. Because their load of mentees is so extensive, they are obliged to dedicate a significant amount of time away from their practice in order to mentor. As she described:

> You had a regular mentor; then you had the diverse mentor. But I think it became too much of a strain on . . . three, four diverse partners. . . . They can't mentor all of us.

Viewing this tableau, one might wonder why white partners and senior associates do not opt to supplement the pool of available mentors and thereby relieve this taxing burden from their colleagues of color. There is no non-racist reason, other than simple convenience, to explain why white partners cannot mentor or sponsor associates of color, seeing that it is, in fact, in the interests of the organization to do so. The problem is that the divisive boys' club mentality, itself nurtured by the divisive social constructs of the white racial frame, prevents them from seeing it as within the scope of their own interests, or even responsibility, to do so.

The abdication, in this case, operates precisely in conjunction with Eduardo Bonilla-Silva's color-blind racist ideology because it provides whites, through an abstract liberalism frame, an escape from materially dealing with the lack of diversity in positions of power.[16] The burden of mentoring the associates of color is left on the shoulders of racially subordinated partners, which further disadvantages them because they are doing work that takes away from the work required of a partner; it also disadvantages the associates of color because they do not get the quality time needed to develop their craft and skills as lawyers.

In chapter 2, I discussed how fitting in was manipulated through coded language to obfuscate the racist narratives of the white racial frame. Another phrase that speaks to the same subterfuge is the subjective, if abstract, concept of the "mutually beneficial relationship." The mutually beneficial relationship functions in this context as a shield to prevent white males in power from having to address the same racial biases and how these biases influence their decision to develop or not develop stronger relationships with associates of color. By elevating the concept of mutuality, which was certainly not a consideration during the more exploitative phases of the evolution of white power in America, the white racial frame is tacitly confessing its inability to grasp the benefit of engaging with people of color in particular context—and perhaps even its failure to grasp the mutual benefits of diversity as a whole. Delia, a fifth-year associate, explained:

> I think opportunities for mentorship are here, but . . . people aren't going to knock you down to mentor you. You kind of have to make it happen yourself. I think really being a mentor is about having a symbiotic relationship, where you bring something to the table, as well, instead of working to bring something to the table while you also try to learn from that particular person.

Like Delia, a number of my respondents reflected the conventional wisdom that a mentor or sponsor relationship has to be "mutually beneficial" in order to work. This phrase casts such a wide, subjective net of interpretation, making it almost indistinguishable from a relationship *perceived to be* mutually beneficial. It is also important to recall that, though it is useful for the firm to encourage black female lawyers to bring something of value to the relationship (apart from, let us assume, their exceptional education and experience), the white racial frame operates to subconsciously perpetuate racialized narratives, stereotypes, and ideologies that posit whites as culturally and intellectually superior to black people. When viewing the world through this distorting lens, it can be difficult to determine what is beneficial about engaging with inferiors in this or any manner that is not paternalistic.[17]

Again, Bonilla-Silva's research illustrates how language is used to code antiblack or color-blind racist views in the post–civil rights era, suggesting the impressive subtlety it cultivates in seeding racial inequality.[18] Unfortunately, these black female lawyers are generally not valued, and white partners are generally not conditioned to view them as bringing something of value to the table. Therefore, the term *mutually beneficial* is used to exclude black female lawyers from the potential pool of mentees and protégés and, deliberately or not, diminish their chances of success in this setting. The inclusion tax directly levied against black women is done so that it appears as though there are active open inclusionary efforts to diversify the firm, yet it still maintains the status quo. The fact that the inclusion tax forces black women to exhaust time, money, and emotional and mental efforts just to be in white spaces while simultaneously excluding them from opportunity is ironic.

RAIN OR SHINE

> "Over time, what I think we all sort of decided on was, at least in the corporate department, you really had to have the support of one or two of the rainmakers.[19] And there's really one guy that, if you get him on your team, if you're his boy, you're going to make it. Well, he might've actually

promoted, gotten one female partner. One woman made partner while I was there, but otherwise it's guys he's tight with. But that seemed to be the way in. No other partner in that department has as much pull as him, and whomever he liked became partner, and it really was never anyone the associates liked working with. And I don't know what the draw was. These weren't associates that had brought in business, at least not to [my knowledge]. They weren't rainmakers at that point, and you don't have to be a rainmaker to make partner. I think it's just being connected to this guy in some fashion. . . . As far as I can tell, I didn't see any other reason that these people made partner except for their relationships."

—Jocaste, fifth-year associate

Although Jocaste and other respondents did not explicitly state that partners only select white male associates to work with, there is still plenty of implication that partners primarily mentor and sponsor white male and white female associates. As Wilkins and Gulati suggest, like many of us, partners and senior associates gravitate toward those they are comfortable and familiar with.[20] The problem in the case of white males, which may or may not distinguish them from you or me in this regard, is that the patriarchal white racial frame (and some hardly negligible characteristics of class stratification in the United States, which could also merit its own study) severely narrows the field of individuals to those whom white males tend to feel comfortable and familiar with.[21]

Although a significant number of my participants did acknowledge that they received some support from senior lawyers and partners, particularly with respect to formal mentors, with the exception of four, the remainder of my interviewees (sixteen) asserted that the support they receive appears to them to be superficial rather than substantive. Specifically, with regard to formal mentoring programs, the perception that they provide such resources as the opportunity to develop legal and networking skills, for instance, was just not confirmed. This reflects the need for program assessment infrastructure, as mentioned previously, and does beg the question, Are these substantive programs and policies to support associates of color in elite corporate law firms part and parcel of the racial structure to maintain white privilege and power? Through the abstract liberalism frame, formal mentoring programs thus create the appearance that whites are concerned about the status of people of color without significantly addressing the roots of racial inequality in these organizations.[22]

The majority of respondents in this study expressed that they have failed to develop organic relationships with partners, relationships in which they have felt comfortable and fully supported in their professional development and advancement prospects. This is an ominous indicator, being that all-important sponsor relationships are generally conceived as unassignable, instead requiring an organic connection between partner and associate stronger than even the mentorship variety. Only three of twenty respondents reported forming mentor relationships that proved to facilitate their advancement within the firm. Several interviewees even highlighted the existence of formal mentoring programs that *guilt* partners into participating, so one can only imagine the efficacy of those programs and the extent to which they manage to alienate all actors. The bottom line: According to my respondents, firm-instituted mentorship programs are generally more useful in theory than in practice.

WE'RE JUST NOT THAT INTO YOU

Fotoula, a fifth-year associate, reflected that she did not have the support of a mentor or sponsor. Noticing that her colleagues were able to develop relationships with partners that supported their training and development, she wondered whether it was because of their performance or because they were better able to fit in to the existing firm culture:

> I didn't feel like there was someone truly in my corner—not really. So, what I realized was that there were certain people that were kind of being taken under other people's wings, and for whatever reason, they were perceived as being better—either better at their work or better because they fit a mold.

Or a *frame.* The real question becomes, How can one fit a frame that is not built to include them? Although law firms suggest that they are engaging in active efforts to diversify their ranks and maintain inclusionary practices, Fotoula clearly is paying an inclusion tax to be in her firm, one that supposedly does not exist. Fotoula further explained that, during the economic downturn of 2007–2008, her firm laid off a great number of associates of color. She believed that most of the associates of color were easily downsized because they did not have sponsors who could advocate on their behalf when firing decisions were under discussion:

> [The firm] laid off a ton of minorities, which is bizarre. And of course, they say it's random. But look, if you think about it, the people who got laid off were the people who had no one to vouch for them, especially if you were very junior. A lot of times, you don't have someone to vouch for you because there

aren't enough people who are in your corner and who care enough to say, "No, he or she hasn't gotten a lot of work, and their hours haven't been great, but they are this, or they're that." And my hours were good, despite that one year. I did all these things, and it still wasn't enough.

In actuality, Fotoula considered, associates of color may have an especially difficult time finding mentors because partners at the firm were simply not interested in them. She referred to one retired black female partner at her firm who became the "beacon" the firm paraded as their diversity representative and who was the only partner who took an active interest in associates of color employed there:

> But then what happens once they [new associates] get there [to the firm] is pretty much nothing. It's just like, "OK, well now we'll just leave it up to [the black female partner]," you know, who's the beacon woman. She is the person that does the minority stuff, so there's no one else that cares that much. After that, they just want you to work your ass off, and that's it. And again, it's harder, I think, as associates of color to find a mentor.

Like many of the other respondents, Fotoula was reluctant to say flat out that associates of color struggle in law firms because some partners have issues with their race. A silence drapes over the racial dynamics of the corporate law firm, in some respects self-preserving in nature but that can nonetheless be described as color-blind racism. Unless enough people perceive a blatantly racist act, the underlying biases and stereotypes that prevent blacks and other associates of color from accessing mentors and sponsors, thereby curtailing their advancement, is not considered. The problem is that what is blatant racism or sexism or both to one individual is not necessarily obvious to another, especially if they possess different relationships to the organization's center of power.[23] Rather than a solution, what these deflections usually create is more distortion that does not, of course, actually address the problem. Like many in her position, Fotoula ultimately decided to look for opportunities elsewhere:

> I think where [the lack of mentorship/sponsorship] really played a role was in not having those people to stand for you, those people to say, . . . "Make sure you're at this event. Make sure you speak up and say this. Make sure that you ask about this," those types of things. Or just those ones to say, "You know what? I heard about a deal that's happening at such and such. I'm going to make sure that this partner knows that you're interested." I'm not saying I was entitled to it, but I didn't have it, and so I know that would've made a difference. I would've maybe made different choices.

Although Fotoula resolved that the only way to advance is to have the backing of a power sponsor, which she suggested is difficult for associates of color to develop, there is a sense of hope that this can change. Again, she acknowledged that, however difficult it would be to shift the ways in which white male partners think about associates of color, it is left to the associates of color to do the work of fixing the perceptions of white male partners, clearly referring to the invisible labor clause[24]:

> But it's got to start somewhere, and I think it's harder to change the mind-set of the white male partner. Not that hard, but I think it's harder. I think that it's really, a lot of times, the onus is on us unfortunately. So that comes to mind.

To further expand on this idea, I return to Nikoleta, a third-year associate who practices law at a so-called white-shoe firm, which she argued has a firmly set culture that defines and shapes its partnership track.[25] The fact that this culture is tailored to suit a white male standpoint is not unsurprising; it is not even necessarily the problem. The problem is the impermeability and fundamental inflexibility of that culture:

> Other associates of color complained a lot at [the firm] about mentorship. [They said that] they don't have those types of connections. They don't feel that people take a genuine interest, and again, I think that that is twofold. I think a part of that is that the culture is kind of set in terms of, "This is what a successful associate/partnership track looks like," and that is very geared toward a white male perspective. That has been set in place. Now what they've tried to do is say, "Oh, we didn't think that female associates might have a different experience in terms of maybe they have to bear children or they have to do these things, so let's set this flextime schedule in there," and they put all these great programs. But still, the criteria for doing well is set on this; the culture's already pretty much set. And then, "Oh, we have diverse candidates. They also need mentors because their situation is special. Let's force a mentorship program." But again, what is the successful associate/partnership track? [It] doesn't look like what that mentorship program looks like.

Reasonably enough, Nikoleta believes that the firm could do better at creating a mentorship program that successfully uses methods already proven successful for lawyers who have become partners, regardless of race or gender. This would result in more people, particularly associates of color, having access to opportunities that lead to advancement, rather than having a program that is manicured toward one particular group and goes nowhere. Forcing mentorship interaction is not going to create meaningful results for black female attorneys or anyone. Rather, it is work on both sides of the color and gender lines to dismantle systemic racism and systemic sexism in these spaces. Nikoleta continued:

> I think they [the firm] have the right idea. It's just that they have an interest in doing some diverse things or accommodating, but it's just that: It's accommodating. It's not necessarily, "Let's look at our whole structure and how we define what successful is here at [the firm] and look at what who was actually successful and how they've done it and how we can kind of make that available to a diverse group of people versus a certain type of person." And so, because of that, I think that a lot of people don't feel like their interactions are genuine and people actually care about what they are doing. And part of that is just the business model of a law firm.

ADDENDUM: WHITE KNIGHTS

The two partners and counsel interviewed in this study, the most professionally advanced respondents, expressed in no uncertain terms that they would not have progressed to the positions they hold had it not been for the distinct white male partners who took a genuine interest in their professional development and eventual career advancement. These partners and sponsors began as mentors, and their relationships with these women developed into a trusting coalition working toward common goals. At the same time, it must be said that the respective partners who took on these mentees and sponsored them already exhibited a history of mentoring diverse associates. According to Iris, Rhebekka, and Xena, there is something intrinsic about each of their respective sponsors' interest in supporting associates of color, which was demonstrated throughout their tenures at their three respective firms. When the will is there, the resources certainly are.

THE HOURS

> "I could start with just the basic in terms of how assignments were distributed. I found that, as a junior, there's really not that many really good assignments that you get. But when there were opportunities to do really interesting work, it essentially would go to the white men over any of the women, regardless of race. And this was something that really consistently happened in terms of cases and assignments, and that was something that all my female colleagues that I talked to would complain about. Also, there was an issue of certain partners only working with

men, and I don't know if this was just a coincidence, but it just seemed very strange that you would see these same partners, and then their whole entire case happens to be staffed with men, each and every time."

—Sophie, third-year associate

In the previous two sections, I discuss the boys' club and how systemic gendered racism in the everyday actions of elite white male actors limit black female lawyers' access to the royal jelly that catalyzes their advancement. This is evidenced largely through the lack of mentor and sponsor relationships and the quality insight, advocacy, and work assignments that derive from those crucial connections.[26] In this section, I discuss the "billable hour model," another structural barrier that plays off the same disadvantages by implementing a putatively "neutral," merit-based system designed to establish advancement qualifications.[27] Firms advertise the model as an objective way of assessing the progress and work of associates, whereby the numerical representation of hours logged, like grades or Law School Admissions Test (LSAT) scores, are used to determine the competence and quality of individual attorneys' work.

What complicates the suggestion of neutrality when it comes to this system is the fact that it ignores gross disparities in the allocation of and access to quality work, as these disparities, many of which I have already discussed, occur along complex racial and gender fault lines. If I am a black attorney who receives a different caliber of guidance, advocacy, and training, any apparent deficits will almost certainly affect whom I bill and how, what assignments fall on my desk (and with what frequency), how I go about executing those assignments, the channels that assist me in my efforts, and how that work is ultimately evaluated within the organization. The fact that any and every stage of this process is susceptible to some degree of the subjectively inspired biases and obstructions erected by patriarchal white racial framing, including what the work is to begin with, effectively nullifies the concept of a neutral evaluation model. This neutral evaluation model, in any context, must be predicated on the assurance of an even playing field among all actors to permit the accurate implementation of objective criteria.

Presentation of the billable hour model as a neutral metric for evaluating associate performance falls into the category of what Bonilla-Silva would describe as color-blind racism manifested through the use of "rhetorical strategy": using language that projects the illusion of equality while maintaining a system that is, in fact, highly contingent and highly subjective.[28] The discursive shift in language frames "neutral" processes determined to be objective by a racist and sexist system designed to reinforce white privilege and power and relieves whites from the responsibility of acknowledging the racialized social structure that facilitates their dominance and taking appropriate steps to change it.[29]

Like the LSAT, the billable hour model places a great deal of stress on lawyers, especially because meeting the requirements (generally between 1,800 to 2,100 hours annually) can be very difficult, depending on the allocation of work assignments. Moreover, the measurement of so-called substantive billable hours, which target the number of quality assignments that provide excellent training and development ("royal jelly") are even less accessible to lawyers without access to the right partners.[30] The difference between substantive work and rote work is equivalent to the difference between visibility and invisibility in this setting—indicating which side, so to speak, of the partnership track one happens to reside on.

All my respondents observed that quality assignments are necessary for on-the-job training and the development of essential skills to practice law efficiently.[31] Theoretical learning is valuable, of course, but nothing compares to the ways in which the application of knowledge in real-world situations cultivates critical thinking skills and judgment on complex transactions, such as drafting deal agreements and negotiating with clients, third parties, and outside counsel. It comes as no surprise, therefore, that pretty much unanimously, our respondents described how the quality of assignments has shaped their learning (or not) and influenced their advancement prospects (for better or worse).

In a field that incurs so much educational debt for its entry-level professionals, as well, it is no small thing that meeting the billable hour requirement is directly linked to performance review and compensation structure, including bonuses. My respondents reported working on average between twelve and sixteen hours per day, sometimes more. This often includes working in the office overnight or from home at odd hours after leaving for the day and on weekends, holidays, and even during vacation, if they are lucky enough to take one. In addition to refining one's critical thinking skills and ability to analyze complex legal matters, substantive work assignments lay the groundwork for cultivating enhanced legal judgment.[32]

Finding themselves locked out of crucial learning opportunities, the majority of my respondents (sixteen) reported that they often receive rote assignments that do not facilitate their training and help develop the necessary skills to become better lawyers and shine within their practice groups. The royal jelly is thus withheld from them, creating a vicious cycle within the billable hour model. Without the insights of adequate mentorship or the advocacy of sponsorship, without substantive hours to become visible and receive the performance reviews that lead to higher- and higher-quality, *visible* work—and thus the royal jelly that engenders invitation to the partnership track—marginalized groups remain outside the door, mere tokens or merely supporting those seated at the table. In other words, by not being assigned to transactions with substantive learning opportunities, the respondents argued that they are not given the same opportunity to develop their craft and access to partners. This also prevents them from developing relationships with higher-ups who have significant influence within the organization and field in general. This added invisible labor that is not valued by the firm, yet the firm benefits from it, does not help black female lawyers obtain the visible work that would eventually lead to better access and opportunity.

Sophie's quote at the beginning of this section describes the prevalence of white male privilege when it comes to allocation and indicates a clear disadvantage for women and associates of color. Chloe, a third-year associate, emphasized that, although she does typically meet her billable hour requirements, the caliber of those assignments is a matter of concern:

> Very frequently I'm working twelve- to thirteen-hour days, sometimes longer. When I'm on deals I can work fourteen, fifteen hours. Yes, I have billable hours. I mean, I do. There's a concern that I'm not getting good work. I think I was a little worried about that. I just kind of felt that I wasn't getting the same attention. And so in the financing group class that I'm in, three of us now, two females and a male, but I feel like this other female, and she's white, is getting more support from this particular female partner who I would love to work with because I know I could learn a lot. But I just have not had the chance to, and it's . . . making me feel that no one cares about me here. I'm not getting the right matters. I'm just kind of being left to the whim of the assigning system, and no one's really looking out for me.

The fact that much of the rote work in elite corporate firms requires an equivalent time commitment and effort for a vastly smaller reward further demoralizes black female associates, who find both their workloads and personal lives dominated by it. Jocaste, who was a fifth-year associate when she left her firm and lateralled into a noncorporate firm, recalled the long and unpredictable work hours that kept her running in place:

> Even though I wasn't doing substantive work, there was a lot of it, and I was always staffed on big deals that were super time sensitive. So everyone had something to do. Everyone was in the office weekends. I definitely had no life. I worked so many Friday nights and Saturdays and Sundays. . . . I absolutely had no life. My social life definitely suffered. And that was when I wasn't gunning for work.

Primarily assigned to due-diligence work, the rote assignments Jocaste found herself inordinately occupied by did not increase her skill level, advancement prospects, or confidence, and she felt that her presence was not in any way valued.

The vicious cycle perpetuated by this model extends to a point that arose in several interviews: Partners typically choose to invest in associates they believe will be at the firm long term. But if attrition rates are highest for lawyers who receive the least opportunities, there is no means in place to achieve the recognition that attracts such investment. Gia, a fifth-year associate, expressed these sentiments and the consequences:

> Why spend the time developing someone who they know is probably not going to be here? Which is, that's the reality. I remember it was last year, and they [partners] had quite a few sessions with us [associates of color], asking us about, "Do we feel that we're not getting quality work?" And, a lot of the people in litigation said they think that the good work is going to nonblack associates. They felt like, if you don't have that social connection with the partners, you're not going to get the good work. And a few of them have left because of that—a number of them actually, not just a few.

Echoed in the literature, Wilkins and Gulati express this very sentiment: "partners have less incentive to invest scarce training resources in associates who they think are unlikely to be at the firm long enough for them to recoup their investment."[33] Partners have misconceptions of black associates not being committed to staying at the firm long-term, which leads them to withhold the royal jelly, which in turn forces black female associates out of the firm, further fueling this vicious cycle of advancement-denying "prophecies" for associates from marginalized groups.[34]

Not being selected to receive the royal jelly creates a revolving door for most associates. Evidence does reveal, however, that associates of color are disproportionately affected by this phenomenon.[35] The dilemma faced by many associates of color is, therefore, whether to stick out the tenure of obstructions in hopes of getting the training necessary to be successful or deciding to lateral elsewhere in hopes of a different reception and proper training in a new environment. Either way, the fact that partners are reluctant to take on associates of color in substantive deals undeniably creates a cyclical effect, whereby they expressly or inadvertently push associates of color out of the firms—inevitably leading to the high attrition rates that causes their reluctance to begin with. Lydia, a third-year associate, recounts a conversation with a black partner at her firm who indicated that the monthly reports partners receive about lawyer utilization, which detail billable hours logged, show that the numbers from associates of color typically reflect the least number of billable hours across all corporate practice groups. This same partner then divulged that the difference in billable hours led other firm partners to believe that associates of color were idler and less interested in working hard:

> Partners in general were just confused about why [associates of color always ranked the lowest]. And so this partner [a black male] was saying that, for many people there, the assumption is just that we're lazier, that we aren't interested in working as hard as the other associates are, without even thinking to dig deeper into possible other explanations for it.

Of course, what this scenario illustrates is a phenomenon common to white institutional spaces (and individuals influenced by the white racial frame within them) when encountering distinctions that do not flatter a stigmatized group. Rather than investigating the difference in billable hours to determine the factors involved, ideally without bias, the firm partners mentioned here instead ascribe to existing cultural deficiency narratives about people of color in general and their work ethic: "They're lazy."[36] Among other disadvantages to this racist reflex, such framing works to automatically immunize the institution from scrutiny and thereby legitimize continued racial inequalities that black associates encounter while never actually addressing the problem, which is more likely a question of access. White racial framing of blacks as lazy allows partners to fall back on historical racial stereotypes that posit people of color as inferior to whites, thereby reinforcing white privilege and legitimizing the dominant position of whites in the firm.[37] Case closed.

Another reality, Lydia suggested, is a difference in billing practices between associates of color and their white male colleagues, for example. She noted that associates of color may not feel comfortable billing a client for certain things, such as thinking about strategies to navigate a deal, whereas white associates are trained to do so through the guidance they receive from partners about proper billing procedure:

> It goes back to staffing. Oftentimes, we [associates of color] aren't the ones who are initially staffed on a lot of things. And then secondly, billing practices tend to differ. There are all kinds of things that other people are talking about that we aren't always aware of, like what people are billing for. And they're legitimately doing things where, if you were just sitting here thinking about, "OK, how am I going to do this? Let me just spend some time planning my mode of attack," where a lot of times minorities, particularly women, wouldn't

bill for that time. Whereas the white guys are billing when they're sitting thinking about how they're going to do something, or they're in the gym and they're thinking about whatever. Since they are actively thinking about whatever their matter [deal] is, then they're going to bill that time. Whereas we aren't doing that, so then we are always going to end up being farther down in the list of hours. It's all kinds of little things like that that we are often missing out on that other associates know because some partner at some point told them informally this is how you should do this, and so we don't get that information.

Again, analogous to Wilkins and Gulati's findings, Lydia noted that associates of color usually do not have access to the same informal mentoring and soft skill development infrastructure that helps white associates confidently traverse the legal landscape of the firm.[38] The white racial frame operates to make whites, and white males in particular, feel at ease in this environment that is catered to their interests, while making it difficult for blacks and other associates of color to maneuver in an environment that mostly tolerates or accommodates their presence rather than embracing it.[39]

Sophie, a third-year associate, mentioned her efforts to proactively go out and ask partners to place her on deals that were substantive in training and offered learning opportunities to build her lawyering skills:

I felt that my substantive assignments were actually pretty rare in terms of being assigned. I felt that I was able to get more substantive work by kind of going out there and requesting it. And I think that if I had, because in our group we actually had an assigning coordinator who would give out assignments based on what assignments were available and how busy people were. And as I stated earlier, because of this kind of bias for assignments that weren't that great to go to someone, I kind of would try to feel out what was going on in certain cases and try and get myself on cases or on assignments where I could get substantive work because it was really important to me to develop a skill set. But even with making those efforts, I still felt that I wasn't getting enough exposure and on-the-job training.

Ultimately, this was one of the primary reasons she ended up leaving her firm. The inadequacies of institutional support and corollary training apparatuses, the vicious cycle perpetuated by the billable hour model, and the narratives of bias and cultural deficiency that dictate access to such indispensable mentor and sponsor relationships all conspired to place that coveted *and necessary* jar of royal jelly on a shelf far higher than most black female lawyers, and associates of color in general, are able to reach due to the structural obstacles that dog, and in many cases doom, their advancement. Until elite corporate firms do more to either help extend their reach or bring that royal jelly closer (ideally, they will do both) with measurable efforts that achieve results and dismantle some of the corrosive framework that inhibits the integration of firm culture with the twenty-first century, such trends are unlikely to shift. Black female lawyers will continue to pay an inclusion tax, "spending" additional resources just to be included in white spaces. They will continue to be required to work harder and be better than their white counterparts through the invisible labor clause just to be recognized or seen. Black women will encounter obstacles without the same guarantee of benefits, only to be excluded from the real opportunity of advancement.

7

CONCLUSION

The Importance of Being Earnest

"Shallow understanding from people of good will is more frustrating than absolute misunderstanding from people of ill will. Lukewarm acceptance is much more bewildering than outright rejection."[1]

"In the everyday lives of black women there are distinctive combinations of racial and gender factors. They face not only the 'double jeopardy' condition of having to deal with both racism and sexism but also the commonplace condition of unique combinations of the two. Because racial and gender characteristics are often blended, they may trigger individual and collective reactions by whites that are also fused. This real-world blending often makes it difficult to know the separate contributions of each element in particular situations that involve both racial and gender barriers to social mobility and personal achievement."[2]

This book began as an exploration of the experiences of black women in elite corporate law firms, raising the question, Why are there so few black female partners in elite corporate law firms? I argue that race and gender affect the advancement prospects of black female lawyers and that systemic gendered racism and white racial framing affect attrition rates. To tease out the ways in which race and gender figure prominently in the experiences of black female lawyers, I draw from critical race theories and scholarship on how systemic gendered racism, white racial framing, patriarchal normativity, color-blind racist ideology, and white institutional spaces operate to maintain white privilege and power, legitimizing the dominant position of whites in racialized social structures.[3] Using these frameworks to methodically analyze the challenges that black female lawyers face in elite law firms provides insight into how gendered racism is so pernicious in its subtle attacks.

Furthermore, centering this research on black women shifts the discourse of diversity in elite corporate law firms toward the realities of race and gender discrimination that permeate black female lawyers' everyday experiences. The twenty black women interviewed provided rich and nuanced descriptions of how they are treated in elite white law firms and why so few of them hold the coveted position of partner.[4] To systematically discuss the penetrating issues that culminate in barriers to becoming partner for black women lawyers, this book targets how race and gender, whether combined, intersecting, or overlapping, affect their experiences, especially (1) their appearance; (2) a continuing tokenistic environment; (3) their differences and similarities based on shared gender or racial identity; (4) the boys' club; and (5) limited access to substantive training, mentors, and (most of all) sponsors.

Throughout this book, what is evidently clear is that racial and gender discrimination has a negative impact on the chances of black female lawyers becoming partners. I argue that systemic gendered racism and the white racial frame operate to entrench patriarchal white normativity supported by color-blind racist ideology, all of which is created, controlled, reproduced, and perpetuated, both consciously and subconsciously, by elite white men through institutional law firm practices.[5] Furthermore, the patriarchal normativity in the firm specifically works to privilege white male lawyers above all other lawyers. The responses of the black women in this book reflect the various ways racism and sexism are both pervasive and subtle in promoting racial inequality and male privilege. They also highlight six obstacles that black female lawyers face.

First, language is a powerful means of control. The ways in which the firm uses language to maintain systems of exclusion are prevalent in the interviews. Describing processes as "objective," such as in recruiting ("fitting in"), mentor and sponsor relationships ("mutually beneficial"), and the billing hour model ("neutral evaluation system"), the firm can exclude black female lawyers from gaining access to opportunities and advancement without appearing racist or sexist. Such terms as *good fit* and *mutually beneficial* are coded to avoid overt racism while still allowing the subtlety of racist practices to persist. Racial codes permit the firm to disguise color-blind racism as objective mechanisms to determine access and opportunity, all the while reinforcing white privilege and upholding racial inequality.[6] Moreover, the neutrality and objectivity discourse perpetuates abstract liberalism because it encourages institutions that historically exclude people of color to reject policies and programs that ameliorate the effects of systemic racism on marginalized groups, such as affirmative action and formal mentoring programs.[7]

Second, silencing racially subordinated groups effectively prevents change. Elite white men have created an extremely successful system for maintaining and reproducing white power and privilege. The white racial frame that benefits white men silences black female lawyers because addressing racial and gender inequality reinforces and adds to their everyday invisible labor to resist the discriminatory actions of elite white men in law firms. Black female lawyers expend emotional, mental, and physical labor that their white counterparts do not have to endure when negotiating white spaces. This burden adds to the everyday pressures of working in elite white law firms and further disadvantages black female lawyers.[8] The function of the invisible labor clause, how black female lawyers are required to perform added invisible labor as described in the book, is key to understanding the seemingly insurmountable obstacles beyond the scope of the universal job description. As discussed in the introduction, the black experience is fettered to the continual invisible labor enshrined within the American social contract and projected onto all professional and personal settings, where interaction within a power dynamic exists. This system was designed by elite white men, is controlled by elite white men, and continues to be run by elite white men in an effort to benefit elite white men.

Third, blaming racially subordinated groups for their own exclusion and lack of advancement perpetuates narratives of cultural deficiency and avoids fundamental discourse about the real implications of tokenism in white spaces. Cultural deficiency and minimization of racism arguments suggest that black female lawyers are not interested in advancing and staying in law firms long term.[9] This rhetorical strategy used by white partners through their white racial framing of blacks as unreliable and incompetent allows them to exclude black female lawyers from training, mentoring, and sponsorship access, which invariably creates a vicious cycle, where black female lawyers end up leaving the firms because of this exclusion that denies them opportunity to advance.[10] This becomes a self-fulfilling prophesy for black female lawyers, exacerbating high attrition rates based on their interactions with partners and the ways in which they are stigmatized.

Fourth, the ubiquitous juxtaposition of black women as both hypervisible and invisible in white spaces is key to understanding their experiences.

Color-blind racist ideology used to promote white narratives of affirmative action causes self-doubt among some black female lawyers and diminishes their accomplishments and achievements by constantly scrutinizing their presence. These narratives aid in making black female lawyers both hyper-visible and invisible in white spaces. By simultaneously scrutinizing and ignoring black women, their intellect and abilities are questioned, deepening an outsider feeling that can lead them to avoid using "official" programs to help them overcome obstacles derived from systemic and institutionalized practices that target their race and gender.[11] The inclusion tax concept introduced in this book speaks directly to the emotional, mental, physical, and monetary cost levied against black women to be in white spaces. This tax is demonstrated in every instance where the participants describe the toll of being both black and female in elite white spaces.

Fifth, the dominant white male culture is prevalent in elite corporate law firms and operates to normalize the white male experience, excluding all other racial groups and creating essentially a baseline of white normativity. Lawyers of color, particularly black women, need to be able to navigate in white spaces—from elite law schools into elite law firms. The lawyers interviewed, along with other racially subordinated individuals in law firms, often are required to put their own experiences aside to fit in to the existing culture. Common in corporate America are social events catered toward a white palate. This is most notably demonstrated in such events as golfing or skiing, which frequently isolate black women. Social and professional interactions that center on white normativity automatically excludes a significant number of people of color, and these "actions reveal the practices that maintain white space and normative assumptions of whiteness within that space."[12] As demonstrated in this book, the boys' club is borne out of this dominate white male culture, and although they may at times offer entrance to nonwhite males, women as a whole are generally not invited.

Last, the notion that intention is important in determining whether actions are racist or sexist is repeatedly mentioned throughout the responses of the lawyers interviewed. "Intention" clouds the discourse on racism and sexism because it is extremely difficult to argue about someone's intentions. Attempting to put an objective framing to something that is subjective is extremely arduous. When dealing with racist encounters, "sometimes these types of incidents are said to be unintentional and therefore not racially significant; sometimes they are dismissed as mere figments of the imagination."[13] The fact remains that discrimination is not always overt and easily identifiable. At the same time, discrimination may not always be maliciously intended, which is irrelevant, as recipients of discrimination face social outcomes based on an act that is detrimental to their life chances. What makes it so pervasive is that discrimination comes in different gradations and is oftentimes hard to untangle. Because of this, racially subordinated groups, particularly women of color, continue to face real, albeit subtle, challenges to their career development.

All of the obstacles described here affect how black women lawyers navigate the firm. However well-intentioned diversity initiatives, affinity groups, formal mentoring programs, and diversity workshops may be in law firms, they remain ineffective when the experiences of black female lawyers clearly indicate that their outcomes are not changing. Good intentions are not leading to the outcome of partnership success and black lawyer retention, and this is what I demonstrate in this book. The discourse is complicated because it is a conversation about objectivity and subjectivity, simply because of how subjective the white racial frame is endemically and the way in which it infiltrates our objectivity.

What I uncover in this book are the ways that black professionals as a whole, and racially subordinated groups overall, may experience similar trajectories in white institutional spaces. This research fits in with the growing body of literature on the effects of race and gender on black professionals in the workplace. Moreover, it engages the discourse of gender and racial disparity as it pertains to recruitment, professional development, training, networking, access to mentorship and sponsorship, and advancement.

This book extends the literature on intersectionality by addressing the varied experiences of black female lawyers in elite corporate law firms, organizations that are overwhelmingly white and male. Through highlighting the lived experiences of women of color, specifically black women, in the workplace, this book adds to dialogues concerning professional women of color and black women, opportunities for blacks within elite companies, and institutional commitments to diversity in the workplace. Moreover, this book adds to the scholarship on diversity and inclusion in the workplace by addressing the extent to which the economic utility of these women to the firm outweigh their racial and gender differences. The book also contributes to the discussion of how systemic gendered racism, white racial framing, and color-blind racism maintained in white spaces continue to benefit whites by reinforcing their privilege and power and thereby safeguarding racial inequality.

Based on the findings of this book, future research should challenge existing notions that numerical representation of diversity is more important than the lived experiences of individuals and suggest that race and gender discrimination are no longer prevalent in American institutions. The theoretical framework laid out can be applied to the study of black women professionals in other fields, such as academia, finance, and the sciences. Additionally, future research can examine the experiences of other marginalized women in elite white spaces through the use of the sociological lens of this study. The fact remains that systemic racism and patriarchal normativity must be challenged and rooted out in order to create spaces where racially subordinated groups are not subjected to the daily racial and gender microaggressions that lead to emotional, physical, mental, economic, social, political, educational, and occupational disadvantages.[14]

My immediate research goal, which is beyond the scope of this book, is to further examine and develop the concept of the invisible labor clause, specifically the added emotional, mental, and physical labor expended by black women lawyers just to be seen or recognized in the firm. I aim to examine the added invisible labor they must engage in while navigating the firm. I also want to counterbalance this narrative by showing what enables black women lawyers to be resilient despite their obstacles. I want to contrast their experiences in elite law firms with the support systems that exist among black professionals via the family and community networks that they may reach out to for help in resisting or healing from the microaggressions sustained while navigating the firm. Additionally, further developing the inclusion tax concept is entwined in understanding the nuanced experiences of black women in law firms and other professional spaces that are predominantly white-male-centric.

In learning about the obstacles black women face in law firms, which point directly to the existence of daily racial and gender microaggressions, I am reminded of how law firms are celebrated today for their diversity. As I show in this book, the celebration is premature and contradictory to the experiences of black women. Law firms distinguished for their diversity, inclusion, and advancement opportunities of all lawyers irrespective of racial and gender identification do not correlate with the low number of racially subordinated lawyers in law firms, particularly black and Latinx lawyers. The problem with diversity ranking systems is that they celebrate racial diversity broadly but do not address the disproportionate progress, or lack thereof, of black lawyers. Returning to the American Lawyer's (AML) *2017 Diversity Scorecard*, if the number 1 ranked law firm can be celebrated for their diversity while having only 20 black associates (out of 448) and 3 black partners (out of 203) across five offices nationwide, then my assessment is correct: Scorecards only provide superficial representations of diversity that give law firms agency to ignore the underlying causes of low numbers of black lawyers, particularly retention and advancement.[15] While the aggregate scores on the diversity scorecard demonstrate progress across racially marginalized groups, black lawyers remain grossly underrepresented in elite law firms. This is a fact.

I suggest we change the diversity discourse by shifting the focus away from quantifying the number of associates of color and partners in firms to actually discussing how racial and gender discrimination plays a significant role. Instead of looking at the symptoms reflected through diversity rankings, we need to start looking at the root causes of high attrition, low recruitment, and challenges to advancement opportunities. This can only happen by making the lived experiences of black female lawyers part of the overall discourse on diversity and by not treating these lawyers as though they are the problem. Inclusion cannot occur by creating artificial categories and initiatives. Rather, the cultural changes can only occur if black women are in a position to assume leadership roles and associated equity stakes to shape the strategic determinants that govern law firms. If this change does not occur, we will continue to have diversity initiatives targeting "them," being the "other," as opposed to initiatives that benefit "us," being a fully inclusive and integrated environment that affords everybody the opportunity to advance.

As I reflect on why so few black female partners exist in elite corporate law firms and I engage in this dialogue, I am reminded that black women lawyers are not alone in this struggle to reach the top echelons of leadership positions in corporate America. Only recently, the departure of two black chief executive officers, Ursula Burns of Xerox and Kenneth Chenault of American Express, significantly lowered the number of black executives in Fortune 500 companies from five to three, with no black female CEO in the Standard & Poor's 500 Index.[16] Also, a recent study reports that, among Harvard Business School's black female graduates in the last forty years, only 13 percent have reached corporate America's top ranks.[17] This recent finding and the departure of Burns and Chenault add to the relevance of what is happening to black women in law firms, and black professionals overall, suggesting that this debate is on the rise. What happens in these law firms is relevant to not just black female lawyers but also black professionals across many fields, from entertainment, as with Lupita Nyong'o's and Solange Knowles's appearance, to the boardroom, with black Harvard Business School graduates. The path to success for black professionals is inhibited by white racial framing and systemic gendered racism, stunting the growth, advancement, and attainment of that promised partnership.

After the interviews took place, several participants indicated that this experience was therapeutic, allowing them to explore deep-seated and

troubling interactions that create and sustain implicit barriers to their success. One interviewee in particular discussed how she often doubted her
ability to succeed as a partner, as well as the difference in treatment and
training she received from the training of white male associates who came
after her yet became partner. Six months after the interview, she contacted
me to acknowledge the impact that this dialogue had on her decision to finally move forward to partner. Almost a year after the interview took place,
she reached out again to notify me that she had been promoted to partner.
Her note read, "Tsedale, . . . I wanted to share some news with you [link
to a notice of her being voted into the partnership]. Thank you so much. I
remember so clearly talking to you in my office and what an impact it had
on my decisions going forward—so thank you!" This is why this book is
important, and as renowned legal scholar David B. Wilkins recently said,
"Integration of elite spaces in society is a civil rights struggle."[18] I echo his
words, acknowledging that the integration of elite spaces is key to addressing the civil rights issues of today that span from the streets to the towers.

As reflected in the epigraph of this chapter by the brilliant revolutionary
civil rights activist Rev. Dr. Martin Luther King Jr., I urge all readers to
go beyond a shallow understanding of the experiences of the black women
highlighted in this book and earnestly consider their obstacles in attempting
to gain equal opportunity and access to the top and how we can clear that
path of obstructions.

APPENDIX

Research Methodology

I conducted anonymous, in-depth, semistructured interviews with twenty black female lawyers in the top twenty-five ranked firms located in a metropolitan city in the northeastern region of the United States. The interviews provided crucial information about how the participants believe their success and failures are affected by race and gender. The questions that led the interviews center on (1) recruitment, including influences on becoming a lawyer, getting into law firms, steps to partnership, similarities and differences with black male and white female associates, and outsider status; (2) professional development and inclusivity, including diversity in firms, exclusion from social and professional networking, discrepancies in feedback and performance reviews, assignment allocation, and work–life balance expectations; and (3) obstacles to advancement, including collegial support, training, and mentorship and sponsorship access, all of which troublingly point to the real effects of systemic gendered racism, white racial framing, and the invisible labor clause.

The top twenty-five firms were determined based on various ranking systems, including *U.S. News and World Report*, *The AM Law 100*, *Vault*, and *The American Lawyer Diversity Scorecard*. The target population of participants was analyzed using data from the National Association of Law Placement (NALP) *Directory of Legal Employers* (*DLE*) website.[1] NALP's *DLE* collects employment data annually from national law firms, including small, midsize, and large private firms, as well as government offices. Of the twenty-five target law firms in this study in this northeastern city in the United States, twenty-two firms provided NALP with data on their lawyer demographics, including the total number of lawyers, broken down into the total number of partners, associates, counsel, staff, and other unidentified titles. These groups were further categorized by gender and race (white, black, Asian, Hispanic, and other). The "other" category includes individuals who identify as American Indian, Alaska Native, Native Hawaiian, other Pacific Islander, and two or more races. Table A.1 outlines the breakdown of the lawyer demographics for the twenty-two targeted firms.

According to the data available at the time of the study, within the twenty-two target law firms, the total number of lawyers was 9,127. Of this total number, there were 2,378 partners (1,928 males and 450 females); 5,634 associates (3,145[2] males and 2,489[3] females); and 718 counsels (487[4] males and 231 females). The target population of potential black female lawyer participants consisted of 17 partners, 169 associates, and 8 counsels. Black male partners across all twenty-two firms accounted for .88 percent of the total male partners; black female partners made up 3.78 percent of the total number of female partners within these firms. Black female associates made up 6.79 percent of all female associates, and black female counsels made up 3.46 percent of all female counsels.

IDENTIFYING POTENTIAL RESPONDENTS

By employing the data available on the NALP's *DLE* website, I was able to gather information on the total number of potential participants (194) for my study. Potential participants were identified by using photos of them available on targeted firm websites and my personal assessment of whether I perceived them as black based on physical appearances. During this process, I came across several firms that did not include profile pictures of the lawyers. I was, therefore, unable to determine the race of the lawyers listed and recruit from these firms. At the time the study was conducted from the twenty-five target firms, nineteen had directories that included the lawyer pictures. I reviewed the profiles of all the lawyers I perceived as being a black female, which amounted to 104 potential participants. I organized each potential participant in an Excel spreadsheet that included firm name, attorney name, practice group, e-mail address, and phone number.

Table A.1. Firm Demographics by Race, Gender, and Position

	Partners		Associates		Counsel		Other		Staff		Total		Total
	Male	Female	Male	Female	Male	Female	Male	Female	Male	Female	Male	Female	(Male and Female)
Black	17	17	108	169	6	8	9	14	0	4	140	212	352
	(0.88)	(3.78)	(3.43)	(6.79)	(1.23)	(3.46)	(7.14)	(10.22)	(0.00)	(6.78)	(2.43)	(6.30)	(3.86)
White	1,811	375	2,489	1,725	447	204	88	85	66	46	4,901	2,435	7,336
	(93.93)	(83.33)	(79.14)	(69.30)	(91.79)	(88.31)	(69.84)	(62.04)	(88.00)	(77.97)	(85.07)	(72.34)	(80.38)
Asian	57	35	351	403	24	12	13	19	6	7	451	476	927
	(2.96)	(7.78)	(11.16)	(16.19)	(4.93)	(5.19)	(10.32)	(13.87)	(8.00)	(11.86)	(7.83)	(14.14)	(10.16)
Hispanic	39	18	125	111	6	6	12	15	3	1	185	151	336
	(2.02)	(4.00)	(3.97)	(4.46)	(1.23)	(2.60)	(9.52)	(10.95)	(4.00)	(1.69)	(3.21)	(4.49)	(3.68)
Other	4	5	72	81	4	1	4	4	0	1	84	92	176
	(0.21)	(1.11)	(2.29)	(3.25)	(0.82)	(0.43)	(3.17)	(2.92)	(0.00)	(1.69)	(1.46)	(2.73)	(1.93)
Total (counted)	1,928	450	3,145	2,489	487	231	126	137	75	59	5,761	3,366	9,127
	(100)	(100)	(100)	(100)	(100)	(100)	(100)	(100)	(100)	(100)	(100)	(100)	(100)
Total (reported)	1,928	450	3,147	2,496	471	231	131	138	91	59	5,768	3,374	9,142

Note: This data was retrieved in February 2014. The numbers may fluctuate based on new hires and attrition. Numbers in parentheses are percentages of lawyers for respective columns.

Source: National Association for Law Placement (NALP), "The Representation of Women and Minorities among Equity Partners Sees Slow Growth, Broad Disparities Remain," press release, April 2014, https://www.nalp.org/0414research.

PHENOMENOLOGICAL APPROACH TO INTERVIEWING

This study examines the career experiences of black female lawyers using a phenomenological approach to interviewing in order to fully capture the experiences of the participants. As described by Irving Seidman in his 2013 book *Interviewing as Qualitative Research: A Guide for Researchers in Education and the Social Sciences*, a "phenomenological approach to interviewing focuses on the experiences of respondents and the meaning they make of that experience."[5] The goal of phenomenological interviewing is for the researcher to come as close as possible to understanding the true essence of a participant's experience based on her subjective point of view, understanding that the experience is both temporal and transitory. The interview is a representation of the participant's lived experience in their own words after it has actually happened, which is then communicated through language, where interviewees reconstruct their experiences.

As such, language is very important to this process and is used to guide both the interviewee and interviewer. Also, the phenomenological approach emphasizes the making of meaning of these experiences, essentially encouraging respondents "to engage in that act of attention" and allowing them to reflect on the meanings of their lived experiences.[6] The four themes within phenomenological interviewing are (1) understanding that the human experience is both temporal and transitory, (2) seeking the interviewee's subjective point of view, (3) engaging the respondents' lived experiences as the foundation of "phenomena," and (4) emphasizing meaning and meaning in context. These themes are essential to the structure and approach to analyzing, interpreting, and sharing data within this study.

A qualitative approach is necessary because available data on women of color tends to be subsumed within research focusing on either women or people of color as a whole, thereby leaving the particular voices of women of color, specifically black women, out. In "Multiple Jeopardy, Multiple Consciousness: The Context of a Black Feminist Ideology," Deborah K. King summarizes that black women tend to be subsumed within narratives of gender or race primarily focused on perspectives of white women or black men:

> The experience of black women is apparently assumed, though never explicitly stated, to be synonymous with that of either black males or white females; and since the experiences of both are equivalent, a discussion of black women in particular is superfluous. It is mistakenly granted that either there is no difference in being black and female from being generically black (i.e., male) or generically male (i.e., white).[7]

Similar to King, bell hooks articulates this very dilemma with respect to black women's experiences in her 1981 book *Ain't I a Women: Black Women and Feminism*. She poignantly states, "No other group in America has so had their identity socialized out of existence as have black women. We are rarely recognized as a group separate and distinct from black men, or a present part of the larger group 'women' in this culture. . . . When black people are talked about the focus tends to be on white women."[8]

My goal was to extract meaning from the interviews and analyze the data in order to hear and learn from the experiences of black women navigating white institutional spaces. This book specifically considers the views and perspectives of black female lawyers and how they perceive their experiences in elite corporate law firms, especially with respect to how race, gender, and other factors affect those experiences.

INTERVIEW RECRUITMENT STRATEGY

The interviewees for the study were recruited using two strategies. First, I sent a letter via e-mail directly to the identified lawyers in the targeted firms based on my online search. In the recruitment letter, I described the broader contours of my research interests and asked the individuals to participate in an interview. I provided my contact information and attached the Institutional Review Board's (IRB) approved consent to participate in the research project. The consent form included the purpose of the research, the procedures, possible discomforts and risks, the benefits, voluntary participation, confidentiality, contact information for questions that included IRB approval, and the statement of consent. The recruitment e-mail was distributed in waves, starting with the number 1 rated firm.

The second strategy in recruitment came directly from participants who were interviewed. These interviewees forwarded my initial recruitment e-mail to their contacts within their firms and others and encouraged others to participate. Additionally, I reached out to my personal contacts and networks, which I have developed over the past ten years as a senior corporate paralegal in New York City law firms. The process of recruitment started in February 2013 and lasted until September 2013. During this time, of a total of 104 potential respondents from nineteen law firms, I was able to recruit 20 black female lawyers and 2 lawyers who identified as Asian. The twenty participants represent 19.23 percent of the total targeted sample. The interviewees came from thirteen different law firms, and each signed the consent form and was provided a copy for their records prior to being interviewed. All of the consents were coded for anonymity and are stored in a lockbox.

CONDUCTING THE INTERVIEWS

At the request of each participant, the interviews were held at locations of their choosing. Sixteen respondents chose to have the interviews conducted at their professional offices during lunch hours (between 12:00 p.m. and 2:00 p.m.) or after business hours (between 5:00 p.m. and 9:00 p.m.). Two interviews were scheduled at their homes, and two were conducted via Skype. The Skype interviews were conducted in the same manner, with consents being obtained before the interviews began. The interview locations were chosen because of convenience and privacy concerns. Generally, the semistructured interviews lasted approximately between 90 and 120 minutes, depending on the respondent, with twenty-nine questions as a guide.

Prior to beginning the interview, I explained the research and the consent to each participant in order to ensure them of the confidentiality and data collection procedures. The interviews were recorded with consent, and I explained with coding the identity of each participant to maintain confidentiality. The tape recording of each interview was crucial to my research methodology, as they allowed for accurate depictions of the respondents' thoughts and consciousness. Tape-recording the interviews also preserved the original data for analysis and accountability, giving respondents confidence that "their words will be treated responsibly."[9] The recording device I used was a Sony ICD PX333 Digital Voice. Only two participants requested that the interviews not be recorded. Of the two, one interview was done in person and took place at her home, while the other interview was done via Skype.

One of the major concerns for most of the participants was being easily identified. Each respondent expressed their interest in being a part of the research, but they were also very clear about their concerns about participating, indicating that their participation may lead to adverse effects on their current employment. This concern stems from the fact that they were one of very few black female lawyers in their firms. As a result, all interview materials were deidentified to ensure the anonymity of each respondent.

TRANSCRIBING THE INTERVIEWS

The interview period lasted from March 20, 2013, to September 21, 2013. A total of twenty-two interviews were conducted. Once the interviews were completed, the recorded audio files were distributed via Dropbox to the transcriber. I provided the transcriber with a nondisclosure statement for execution, outlining the transcription services solicited and the confidentiality measures to strictly adhere to. The audio files were accessed in a centralized location, with login credentials provided by myself. The transcriber was instructed to transcribe the interviews verbatim, carefully outlining the speakers within the recordings and the use of punctuation and interruptions (including nonverbal signals, such as phone calls, coughs, pauses, or outside noises).[10] The transcription service period lasted approximately eight to twelve weeks, with a total of twenty transcripts transcribed verbatim and delivered in the form of Microsoft Word documents.

The transcripts were coded by the date of interview and subsequently labeled as Participant 1 to Participant 20 (P1–P20) for the transcripts used in this study and Participant A and Participant B (PA and PB) for the transcripts not used. All transcripts were printed and inserted into two binders that separated each interview according to participant allocation (P1–P20, PA and PB) based on the date of each interview. The interviews have been transcribed verbatim; however, in the analysis of added quotes, such fillers as *um*, *uh*, *like*, and *you know* and redundancies have been removed for better readability.

RESPONDENT BACKGROUND INFORMATION

The preliminary information on the interview schedule gathered information on the respondent's name, race and ethnicity, age, position at the firm, practice area, law school attended, and family status, which is outlined in table A.2. Nineteen of the twenty respondents self-identified racially as black, and one identified as Middle Eastern. Of the twenty respondents, nine identified ethnically as African American, four as biracial, two as Caribbean American, four as blacks from African countries, and one as black from South America. The age of the respondents ranged from twenty-six to forty years of age. The mean age of the respondents was 32.65 years.

FAMILY BACKGROUND AND SOCIOECONOMIC STATUS

The family background and socioeconomic status (SES) of the respondents varied. In terms of SES, four designations emerged in the study: upper class (four), middle class (six), lower-middle class (one), and lower class (four). Five respondents did not provide information on SES. Family background included such categories as who raised the respondent, siblings, parental occupation and education, location raised, and primary through secondary school education. In terms of who raised the respondents, their family backgrounds varied, with eleven respondents indicating that they were raised in a home with both parents, while seven were raised by single mothers. Two respondents did not provide information about parenting.

Eighteen respondents have one to four siblings, and two indicated that they are an only child. The occupations of the respondents' parents include medical doctors (four), international relations (one), high school guidance counselor (one), school principal (one), assistant at an international corporation (one), corrections officer (one), police officer (one), dentist (one), social worker (one), truck driver (one), working with developmentally disabled adults (two), radio producer (one), pharmacist (one), entrepreneur (two), real estate agent (one), accountant (one), home health aide (one), nurse (one), corporate governance (one), engineer (one), and stay-at-home mothers (two). Four respondents did not provide occupational information for one parent, and seven respondents did not provide this information for both parents.

PRIMARY AND SECONDARY EDUCATION

In terms of primary and secondary school education, ten respondents indicated that they attended public institutions, three attended private institutions, one transitioned from public to private, and six did not provide this information.

UNDERGRADUATE AND LAW SCHOOL EDUCATION

The undergraduate institutions attended by the twenty participants include University of North Carolina (one), Yale University (one), Cornell University (one), Duke University (one), Rutgers University (one), University of Pennsylvania (one), York University (one), Barnard College (one), Smith

Table A.2. Demographic and Personal Information of Participants

Alias*	Age	Race	Marital Status	Kids	Undergraduate School	Law School	Firm Name	Practice Group	Firm Status	Firm Status Notes
Athena	27	Biracial	Single	0	Public	T1	EF1	Banking	3rd year	First firm
Bethania	37	Black	Married	1	Ivy League	T1	EF2	Finance	11th year	Third firm for 5 years
Chloe	27	Black	Single	0	Ivy League	T1	EF2	Finance	3rd year	First firm
Delia	31	Black	Single	0	Private	T1	EF2	Real estate	5th year	First firm
Elissa	33	Black	Single	1	Public	T1	EF2	Finance	5th year	Second firm for 2.5 years
Fotoula	32	Biracial	Married	0	Ivy League	T1	EF3	Finance, banking	5th year (L)	Start-up for 3 years
Gia	35	Black	Married	0	International	T4	EF1	Private funds	5th year	First firm
Hanna	39	Black	Single	0	Ivy League	T1	EF4	Securities, CM	5th year (L)	In-house counsel for 6 years
Iris	40	Black	Single	0	Private	T1	EF2	Investment funds	Counsel	First firm
Jocaste	39	Black	Single	0	Ivy League	T1	EF2	M&A	5th year (L)	Entertainment firm for 5 years
Kallisto	34	Black	Married	2	Private	T1	EF5	Corporate finance	6th year (L)	Professional development manager for 2 years
Lydia	32	Black	Single	0	Private	T1	EF6	M&A	3rd year	First firm
Maria	28	Black	Single	0	International	T1	EF7	CM	3rd year	First firm
Nikoleta	31	Black	Married	Pregnant	Public	T4	EF5	Leveraged finance	3rd year	First firm
Olympia	29	Biracial	Single	0	Ivy League	T1	EF8	Latin American group	3rd year	First firm
Philomena	26	Black	Single	0	Private	T1	EF10	Banking, CM	3rd year	Second firm for 2 years
Rhebekka	35	Black	Single	0	Ivy League	T1	EF11	Corporate restructuring	Partner	First firm
Sophie	29	Black	Single	1	Ivy League	T1	EF5	Corporate litigation	3rd year (L)	SC div. clerk for 3 years
Theodora	30	Black	Single	0	Private	T2	EF9	M&A, securities	4th year	First firm
Xena	37	Black	Married	1, Pregnant	Public	T4	EF12	Corporate restructuring	Partner	First firm

Abbreviations: T = tier; EF = elite firm; M&A = mergers and acquisitions; CM = capital markets; L = left firm; SC div. = Supreme Court division

* Participant aliases were derived from the Female Greek Names website at http://www.20000-names.com/female_greek_names_03.htm.

College (one), Brown University (one), New York University (one), Vanderbilt College (one), University of Utrecht (one), University of Virginia (one), Princeton University (two), Long Island University (one), Harvard Radcliffe College (one), Boston University (one), and University of Houston (one).

The law schools the participants attended include Brooklyn Law School (one), Columbia Law School (four), Fordham Law School (one), Georgetown Law School (two), Harvard Law School (one), Howard Law School (one), Michigan Law School (one), New York University Law School (three), Stanford Law School (two), Toro Law School (two), University of Pennsylvania Law School (one), and University of Virginia Law School (one).

MARITAL STATUS AND CHILDREN

At the time the interviews were conducted, thirteen participants were single, six were married, and one was in the process of getting a divorce. Five participants indicated that they have children. One of these participants has two children, and the other four have one child each. Additionally, two respondents were pregnant at the time of the interviews.

CURRENT POSITIONS AND PRACTICE AREAS

The positions held at the time of the interviews include third-year associates (eight), fourth-year associate (one), fifth-year associates (six), sixth-year associate (one), eleventh-year associate (one), counsel (one), and partners (two). All participants worked in the corporate departments of their law firms. The practice areas within the corporate department varied among the participants: finance, including banking, corporate, and leveraged finance (eight); mergers and acquisitions (three); capital markets (three); corporate restructuring (two); Latin American group (one); corporate litigation (one); real estate (one); investment funds (one); private funds (one); and securities (two).[11] Three respondents worked in at least two practice groups. At the time of the interviews, twelve participants still worked in the first firms that hired them out of law school. The remaining participants either lateralled into other law firms or left for in-house work.

NOTES

FOREWORD

1. Elwood D. Watson, *Outsiders Within: Black Women in the Legal Academy after* Brown v. Board (Lanham, MD: Rowman & Littlefield, 2008).

2. See Joe R. Feagin and Kimberley Ducey, *Racist America: Roots, Current Realities, and Future Reparations*, 4th ed. (New York: Routledge, 2019).

3. For example, Louwanda Evans, *Cabin Pressure: African American Pilots, Flight Attendants, and Emotional Labor* (Lanham, MD: Rowman & Littlefield, 2013).

INTRODUCTION

1. "America's culture wars" refers to the ongoing struggle to define America. This struggle is marked by the fervent separation over distinct ideas of what America was in the past, what America is today, and what America will be in the future. The culture war is fueled by the polarization of ideas among conservatives/traditionalists and liberals/progressives.

2. Associates are lawyers who do not hold an ownership interest in law firms but who have an opportunity to become a partner through the partnership track. Associates range from first-year (straight out of law school) to midlevel (three to five years of practice) and senior level (five-plus years of practice).

3. Minority Corporate Counsel Association and Vault, *2017 Vault/MCCA Law Firm Diversity Survey*, 2017, https://www.mcca.com/wp-content/uploads/2017/12/2017-Vault-MCCA-Law-Firm-Diversity-Survey-Report.pdf.

4. In 2013, Sheryl Sandberg, chief operating officer of Facebook, authored *Lean In: Women, Work and the Will to Lead*, a book that discusses the gender inequality women face and the disproportionate number of women in positions of power. Sandberg attributes the disparity in influence and advancement to the pervasive nature of gender inequality and traditional predispositions that women are faced with in our society; however, she also argues that women can play an integral role in how their successes pan out. Sandberg encourages women to take a seat and lean in at the table where decisions are being made, urging them to let their voices be heard. Sandberg further advises women to choose companions who support their endeavors and not give in to resigning their professional ambitions because of their personal desires to start or maintain their families. It is important to note that, when discussing gender inequality, to a large extent, these dialogues often exclude the experiences of women of color. However, the fact remains that women as a whole experience significant disadvantages compared to men. See Sheryl Sandberg, *Lean In: Women, Work and the Will to Lead* (New York: Alfred A. Knopf, 2013).

5. Alex M. Johnson Jr., "The Underrepresentation of Minorities in the Legal Profession: A Critical Race Theorist's Perspective," *Michigan Law Review* 95, no. 4 (1997): 1005–62, https://doi.org/10.2307/1290052.

6. National Association for Law Placement (NALP), "Representation of Women and African Americans among Law Firm Associates Increases Slightly but Remains below Pre-Recession Levels," press release, December 15, 2017, https://www.nalp.org/uploads/2017NALPReportonDiversityinUSLawFirmsPressRelease.pdf.

7. The American Lawyer (AML), *The 2017 Diversity Scorecard*, May 24, 2017, https://www.wsgr.com/news/PDFs/17diversityscorecard.pdf. Partnership is the highest level a lawyer can attain within a law firm. Once a lawyer demonstrates professional excellence (intellectual ability and judgment, leadership role in client matters, and professional integrity), commitment to the practice and style of the firm, and sustaining legal practice from internal or external sources, he or she can be considered for partnership admission. Partners in a limited liability partnership can either be equity (partners who own a stake in the firm and share in its profits and losses) or nonequity (partners who are paid a fixed salary and granted limited voting rights with firm operations).

8. National Association for Law Placement, Inc. (NALP), *Directory of Legal Employers*, 2017, https://www.nalpdirectory.com.

9. See NALP, *Directory of Legal Employers*. Note that this data was retrieved in July 2017. The numbers may fluctuate based on new hires and attrition. To clarify, AML incorporates statistics of all associates of color and partners in their assessment, including Hispanic American, Asian American, Native American and American Indian, and individuals who identify as multiracial. The inclusion of all

racially subordinated groups increases the potential ranking of law firms that have low numbers of black lawyers, thereby lauding firms for their diversity.

10. Although it appears that expressions of support for diversity in elite law firms and corporations exist through dedicated staff, initiatives, and programs, the numbers are not reflected in these workspaces. The representation of people of color and women is significantly low, and their outcome of success is even smaller, with white upper-class men continuing to dominate in legal and professional careers. See Spencer Headworth, Robert L. Nelson, Ronit Dinovitzer, and David B. Wilkins, *Diversity in Practice: Race, Gender, and Class in Legal and Professional Careers* (Cambridge: Cambridge University Press, 2016).

11. Joe R. Feagin, *Systemic Racism: A Theory of Oppression* (New York: Routledge, 2006), xii, 1–52, 194–95; Joe R. Feagin, *Racist America: Roots, Current Realities, and Future Reparations*, 2nd ed. (New York: Routledge, 2010), 19; Joe R. Feagin, *The White Racial Frame: Centuries of Racial Framing and Counter-Framing*, 2nd ed. (New York: Routledge, 2013), ix–x.

12. Eduardo Bonilla-Silva, *Racism without Racists: Color-Blind Racism and the Persistence of Racial Inequality in America*, 4th ed. (Lanham, MD: Rowman & Littlefield, 2014).

13. Feagin, *Systemic Racism*, 25; Feagin, *Racist America*, 25, 59–96; Feagin, *White Racial Frame*, x–xi, 3, 1–22.

14. Adia Harvey Wingfield, *Doing Business with Beauty: Black Women, Hair Salons, and the Racial Enclave Economy* (Lanham, MD: Rowman & Littlefield, 2008), 6–11.

15. Feagin, *Systemic Racism*, 1–52; Feagin, *Racist America*, 19; Feagin, *White Racial Frame*, ix–x.

CHAPTER 1

1. Joe R. Feagin, *Racist America: Roots, Current Realities, and Future Reparations*, 2nd ed. (New York: Routledge, 2010), 106.

2. James E. Coleman Jr. and Mitu Gulati, "A Response to Professor Sander: Is It Really All about the Grades?" *North Carolina Law Review* 84 (2006): 1823–29, https://scholarship.law.duke.edu/faculty_scholarship/1848; Monique R. Payne-Pikus, John Hagan, and Robert L. Nelson, "Experiencing Discrimination: Race and Retention in America's Largest Law Firms," *Law and Society Review* 44, nos. 3–4, (September 2010): 553–84, https://doi.org/10.1111/j.1540-5893.2010.00416.x; Richard H. Sander, "The Racial Paradox of the Corporate Law Firm," *North Carolina Law Review* 54, (2006): 1755–822, http://scholarship.law.unc.edu/nclr/vol84/iss5/15; David B. Wilkins and Mitu G. Gulati, "Why Are There So Few Black Lawyers in Corporate Law Firms? An Institutional Analysis," *California Law Review* 84 (May 1996): 493–625, http://nrs.harvard.edu/urn-3:HUL.InstRepos:13548823.

3. Sander, "Racial Paradox." The high attrition rate among black lawyers and the paucity of black lawyers in partnership positions is the focus of Sander's article. He argues that, although racially subordinated lawyers make up a significant number of entering lawyers in corporate firms, they continue to lag behind in attaining partnership. This dilemma is what Sander refers to as the racial paradox of corporate law firms. He primarily focuses on black lawyers, arguing that "aggressive racial preferences" in hiring account for the large number of black lawyers working in firms at the onset of their legal careers (1758). Sander defines "aggressive racial preferences" as law firms' preferential hiring of people of color, particularly black law school graduates, to ensure that their firms are diversified. Thus, he contends, it must be that the negative stereotypes and treatment that black lawyers experience lead to a high attrition. For this reason, Sander argues against affirmative action policies, not only in large law firm hiring, but also in law school admissions, because he believes the lower grades that result from aggressive racial preferences pose a substantial handicap for people of color entering large firms.

4. See Wilkins and Gulati, "So Few Black Lawyers," 541. The original analogy of the royal jelly was used by Ian Ayres.

5. See Coleman and Gulati, "Response." Coleman and Gulati argue that Sander's conclusions that grades predict performance and success in firms, which explain high attrition rates among black associates and account for low black partner rates, are too broad and contribute to stereotypes that undermine black associates' potential to succeed in elite law firms (1826). The authors argue that, although Sander does note that some black lawyers succeed within corporate firms, he does not explicitly provide an explanation about why they are successful. Leaving this out gives the impression that most blacks are underqualified as a result of their low grades in law school, resulting in poor law firm performance. Coleman and Gulati maintain that law firms do not recruit white candidates and black candidates in equal measure with respect to law schools. White candidates are recruited from various law schools, whereas black candidates are primarily recruited from elite law schools. The authors also critique Sander's lack of comparative research with respect to similarly situated black and white lawyers in corporate law firms. Furthermore, Coleman and Gulati assert that, in order to examine whether Sander's merit and stereotype discrimination postulations are truly at play, extensive and time-consuming data within a firm would need to be obtained and analyzed. Given the unlikelihood for collecting this evidence, Coleman and Gulati fear that researchers default to the more easily accessible law school GPA data to contend that grades and merit differentials explain why there are not that many black lawyers ascending to partner positions in the firm.

6. See Ronit Dinovitzer, Bryant G. Garth, Robert Nelson, Gabriele Plickert, Rebecca Sandefur, Joyce Sterling, and David Wilkins, *After the JD III: Third Results from a National Study of Legal Careers* (Dallas, TX: American Bar Foundation and the NALP Foundation for Law Career Research and Education, 2014), http://www.americanbarfoundation.org/uploads/cms/documents/ajd3report_final_for_distribu-

tion.pdf; Ronit Dinovitzer, Bryant G. Garth, Richard Sander, Joyce Sterling, and Gita Z. Wilder, *After the JD: First Results of a National Study of Legal Careers* (Overland Park, KS: NALP Foundation for Law Career Research and Education and the American Bar Foundation, 2004), http://www.americanbarfoundation.org/uploads/cms/documents/ajd.pdf; Ronit Dinovitzer, Robert Nelson, Gabriele Plickert, Rebecca Sandefur, and Joyce Sterling, *After the JD II: Second Results from a National Study of Legal Careers* (Chicago: American Bar Foundation and the NALP Foundation for Law Career Research and Education, 2009), http://www.law.du.edu/documents/directory/publications/sterling/AJD2.pdf; US Equal Employment Opportunity Commission (EEOC), *Diversity in Law Firms*, 2003, https://www.eeoc.gov/eeoc/statistics/reports/diversitylaw/lawfirms.pdf; Gita Z. Wilder, *Are Minority Women Lawyers Leaving Their Jobs? Findings from the First Wave of the* After the JD *Study* (Dallas, TX: NALP Foundation for Law Career Research and Education and the National Association for Law Placement, 2008), https://www.nalp.org/assets/1280_ajdminoritywomenmonograph.pdf.; Gita Z. Wilder, *Race and Ethnicity in the Legal Profession: Findings from the First Wave of the* After the JD *Study* (Overland Park, KS: NALP Foundation for Law Career Research and Education and the National Association for Law Placement, 2008), https://www.nalp.org/assets/1064_ajdraceethnicitymonograph.pdf. Several quantitative studies highlight the plight of racially oppressed lawyers and women lawyers in corporate law firms. In 2003, the US Equal Employment Opportunity Commission (EEOC) published *Diversity in Law Firms*. In addition, the National Association of Legal Professionals Foundation for Law Career Research and Education (NALP Foundation; a.k.a., the foundation) in conjunction with the American Bar Foundation (ABF) initiated a national longitudinal quantitative study of the experiences of lawyers within law firms titled *After the JD*.

7. According to US EEOC, *Diversity in Law Firms*, firm characteristics refer to the size, number of offices, locations, prestige, and earnings ranking of a law firm (2).

8. Cynthia Fuchs Epstein, Robert Sauté, Bonnie Oglensky, and Martha Gever, "Glass Ceilings and Open Doors: Women's Advancement in the Legal Profession," *Fordham Law Review* 64 (1995): 291–449.

9. See Dinovitzer et al., *After the JD: First Results*; Dinovitzer et al., *After the JD II*; Dinovitzer et al., *After the JD III*; Wilder, *Are Minority Women Lawyers Leaving*; Wilder, *Race and Ethnicity*. The *After the JD* study was conducted by a highly credentialed group of social scientists and legal scholars. This longitudinal study was initiated in 2000 and followed the careers of law graduates who passed the bar examination through 2012. *After the JD* was intended to empirically examine the career trajectories of almost five thousand new lawyers. It also included a detailed description of how women and racial-ethnic subordinated groups fared in the legal field. The new lawyer sample was pulled from eighteen legal markets, including the four largest (New York City, the District of Columbia, Chicago, and Los Angeles), as well as fourteen other smaller markets. The project was designed to include

three waves of surveyed respondents: the first in 2002–2003 (*After the JD: First Results of a National Study of Legal Careers* [*AJD1*]); the second in 2007–2008 (*After the JD II: Second Results of a National Study of Legal Careers* [*AJD2*]); and the third in 2012 (*After the JD III: Third Results of a National Study of Legal Careers* [*AJD3*]). Essentially, the study captures the first ten years of employment following the graduation of the first wave in 2000.

10. Dinovitzer et al., *After the JD: First Results*, 21, 66, 90. *Minority oversample* is the term used in the *After the JD* study to describe the sample of associates of color.

11. See Deepali Bagati, *Women of Color in U.S. Law Firms: Women of Color in Professional Services Series* (New York: Catalyst, 2009). Deepali Bagati conducted a 2009 study on the retention, development, and advancement of women of color in US law firms. The respondents in the study, 1,242 lawyers across the top twenty-five law firms in the United States according to revenue, responded to a web survey. In addition, interviews were conducted with senior partners and women of color in focus groups. The study combined qualitative and quantitative measures to find out how women of color perceive their experiences at these firms in terms of "workplace culture, the effectiveness of diversity and inclusion efforts, job satisfaction, intent to leave, work-life needs and challenges, and relationships with influential others (supervising attorneys, mentors, and informal networks)" (3). The study found that many firms do not "concentrate on the 'intersectionality' experienced by women of color in the workplace," where *intersectionality* as defined by the study focuses on "how different identities, such as gender, race, ethnicity, immigration status, and class, overlap and combine, creating unique experiences of disadvantage and privilege in the workplace" (2).

12. See American Bar Association (ABA) Commission on Women in the Profession, *Visible Invisibility: Women of Color in Law Firms* (Chicago: American Bar Association, 2006). The American Bar Association (ABA) commissioned a 2006 study on the visibility of women of color in US law firms titled *Visible Invisibility: Women of Color in Law Firms*. The study explored factors that entice women of color to enter the legal profession, whether their practice experiences exceeded expectations or proved to be inadequate, how firms either promoted or hindered job satisfaction, and why there was a high attrition rate of women of color in firms. The study included a quantitative portion comprised of a forty-question anonymous survey distributed to 1,347 lawyers (white women and men and men and women of color) that analyzed the "prevalence of factors that support or undermine the retention and advancement of women of color attorneys." The qualitative section used focus groups to examine the progression and experiences of women of color in firms that have more than twenty-five lawyers. The findings of the study confirm that women of color faced challenges that are particular to them as a result of race and gender. The high attrition rate was caused by perceived feelings of exclusion, lack of mentorship from senior lawyers and partners, lack of access to informal and formal networking, the desire for more challenging work, low billable hours, and few opportunities for growth.

13. See Corporate Counsel of Women of Color (CCWC), *The Perspectives of Women of Color Attorneys in Corporate Legal Departments* (New York: Corporate Counsel Women of Color, 2011). Furthermore, *The Perspectives of Women of Color Attorneys in Corporate Legal Departments*, a 2011 study commissioned by the Corporate Counsel of Women of Color (CCWC), a nonprofit organization created to raise diversity awareness in law firms and corporate environments, discovered an increasing tendency of women of color exiting law firms for in-house practice at corporations as a result of the obstacles they face in law firms. The study cites a 78 percent attrition rate for women of color based on previous research conducted by the CCWC. The study surveyed more than 1,300 female lawyers of diverse backgrounds (African American, Hispanic, Asian American, and Native American) and found the following reasons women of color lawyers leave corporate firms: low visibility of racially subordinated lawyers in prominent positions, the sentiment that their work is devalued, lack of challenging work, and a deficit of advancement opportunities. The study found that these women leave firms for corporations that have a significantly greater percentage of racially subordinated employees, including women of color, resulting from their commitment to diversity in the 1980s. Women of color moved away from firms and toward corporations because, at the time, corporations became increasingly concerned with diversity in anticipation of conducting business with international clients and customers from diverse backgrounds.

14. We cannot talk about race and gender without looking at how other socially constructed identities and categories affect the experiences of black female lawyers. The interconnectedness of these various identities creates oppressive and disadvantageous experiences for black female lawyers. This book uses intersectionality as a tool of inclusion, giving voice to the experiences and perspectives of my research subjects: black female lawyers in elite corporate law firms.

15. National Association for Law Placement (NALP), "Minority Women Still Underrepresented in Law Firm Partnership Ranks: Change in Diversity of Law Firm Leadership Very Slow Overall," press release, November 1, 2007, https://www.nalp.org/minoritywomenstillunderrepresented; NALP, "The Representation of Women and Minorities among Equity Partners Sees Slow Growth, Broad Disparities Remain," press release, April 2014, https://www.nalp.org/0414research; NALP, "Women and Minorities at Law Firms by Race and Ethnicity: An Update," press release, February 2014, https://www.nalp.org/0214research, "Women, Black/African-American Associates Lose Ground at Major U.S. Law Firms," press release, November 9, 2015, https://www.nalp.org/lawfirmdiversity_nov2015.

NALP published statistics on women and racially subordinated lawyers at law firms based on race and ethnicity as an update to their previous bulletin releases. NALP's February 2014 press release lists that, in the United States, there were 1,127 offices and firms employing 110,149 lawyers; 7.10 percent of partners at these firms were people of color, and 2.26 percent were women of color. Black female partners make up only 0.60 percent of all partners, so essentially, of 49,785 partners nationally, there are only 299 black female partners. This number is devastating to black female lawyers aspiring to become partners in law firms, as it does not reflect potential for advancement within law firms. The total number of associates nationally is 45,808, of which 11.29 percent are women of color; black female associates make up 2.43 percent of the total number of associates.

Moreover, in April 2014, NALP released findings that show women and racially subordinated lawyers continue to lag behind in attaining partnership, regardless of equity structure in law firms in the United States. NALP began collecting demographic information of equity and nonequity partners in 2011 and acknowledges that, although many firms with multitiered partnership structures did not provide data, they gathered a substantial amount from 2011 to 2013 to make meaningful assessments of the status of women and people of color. The figures were based on the participation of 262 offices and firms with multitiered partnership structures. Also, racially subordinated lawyers are included in the percentages of both men and women. Overall, the 2013 data provided 63 percent of all partners in the 2013 NALP directory of multitiered partnership firms. The data revealed that men continue to dominate in both equity and nonequity partnership attainment, with 50.3 percent equity and 28.8 percent nonequity. Women comprise 9.9 percent equity and 11.0 percent nonequity. The partners of color, both men and women who are racially subordinated, comprise 3.2 percent equity and 3.6 percent nonequity. Although there was a slight increase in the number of women and people of color attaining equity and nonequity partnership, the numbers do not indicate a growing trend and instead reveal the broad disparities in these institutions between men, women, and people of color.

16. See ABA, *Visible Invisibility*; Lindsay Blohm, Ashley Riveira, and Marcella B. Bary, *Presumed Equal: What America's Top Women Lawyers Really Think about Their Firms* (Bloomington, IN: AuthorHouse, 2006); Coleman and Gulati, "Response"; Deepali, *Women of Color*; Suzanne Nossel and Elizabeth Westfall, *Presumed Equal: What America's Top Women Lawyers Really Think about Their Firms* (Wayne, NJ: Career Press,1998); Payne-Pikus, Hagan, and Nelson, "Experiencing Discrimination"; Sander, "Racial Paradox"; Wilkins and Gulati, "So Few Black Lawyers."

17. Feagin, *Racist America*, 25, 59–96; Joe R. Feagin, *Systemic Racism: A Theory of Oppression* (New York: Routledge, 2006), 25, 272–76; Joe R. Feagin, *The White Racial Frame: Centuries of Racial Framing and Counter-Framing*, 2nd ed. (New York: Routledge, 2013), x–xi, 3, 1–22; Adia Harvey Wingfield, *Doing Business with Beauty: Black Women, Hair Salons, and the Racial Enclave Economy* (Lanham, MD: Rowman & Littlefield, 2008), 6–11.

18. Feagin, *Racist America*, 106; Yanick St. Jean and Joe R. Feagin, *Double Burden: Black Women and Everyday Racism* (Amonk, NY: M. E. Sharpe, 1998).

19. Feagin, *Racist America*, 19; Feagin, *Systemic Racism*, xii, 1–52, 194–95; Feagin, *White Racial Frame*, ix–x.

20. Feagin, *Racist America*, 25, 59–96; Feagin, *Systemic Racism*, 25, 272–76; Feagin, *White Racial Frame*, x–xi, 3, 1–22.

21. Eduardo Bonilla-Silva, *Racism without Racists: Color-Blind Racism and the Persistence of Racial Inequality in America*, 4th ed. (Lanham, MD: Rowman & Littlefield, 2014), 25.

22. Wendy Leo Moore, *Reproducing Racism: White Space, Elite Law Schools and Racial Inequality* (Lanham, MD: Rowman & Littlefield, 2008).

23. Kimberlé Crenshaw, Neil Gotanda, Gary Peller, G., and Kendall Thomas, *Critical Race Theory: The Key Writings That Formed the Movement* (New York: New Press, 1995).

24. Bonilla-Silva, *Racism without Racists*; Feagin, *Systemic Racism*; Bhoomi K. Thakore, "Maintaining the Mechanisms of Colorblind Racism in the Twenty-First Century," *Humanity & Society* 38, no. 1 (February 2014): 3–6, https://doi.org/10.1177/0160597613519229.

25. Bonilla-Silva, *Racism without Racists*, 25–26; Eduardo Bonilla-Silva, *White Supremacy and Racism in the Post-Civil Rights Era* (Boulder, CO: Lynne Rienner, 2001).

26. Bonilla-Silva, *Racism without Racists*, 27.

27. Bonilla-Silva, *Racism without Racists*, 9.

28. Bonilla-Silva, *Racism without Racists*, 9.

29. Bonilla-Silva, *Racism without Racists*, 74–99.

30. Bonilla-Silva, *Racism without Racists*, 76, 78–84.

31. See Eduardo Bonilla-Silva and David Dietrich, "The Sweet Enchantment of Color-Blind Racism in Obamerica," *Annals of the American Academy of Political Science* 634 (2011): 192. Claims that affirmative action disadvantages those who are its intended beneficiaries (e.g., racially oppressed, women) and engages in reverse discrimination allow whites to ignore the historical relevance of these policies.

32. Bonilla-Silva, *Racism without Racists*; Feagin, *Systemic Racism*, 206–8.

33. See Derald Wing Sue, "Microaggressions, Marginality, and Oppression," in *Microaggressions and Marginality: Manifestation, Dynamics, and Impact*, ed. Derald Wing Sue (Hoboken, NJ: Wiley, 2010), 3–22. I acknowledge that there is continuous debate over the use of the term *microaggression*, where some may argue that it does not capture the true reality of the racialized and gendered experiences of both women and men of color. However, in this context, I use Sue's definition of the term:

> [M]icroaggressions are the everyday verbal, nonverbal, and environmental slights, snubs, or insults, whether intentional or unintentional, that communicate hostile, derogatory, or negative messages to target persons based solely upon their marginalized groups membership. In many cases, these hidden messages may invalidate the group identity or experiential reality of target persons, demean them on a personal or group level, communicate they are lesser human beings, suggest they do not belong with the majority group, threaten and intimidate, or relegate them to inferior status and treatment.

The daily racial and gender microaggressions black female lawyers face have a significant impact on their career trajectories, as well as their overall experience as black professionals in corporate America.

34. Bonilla-Silva, *Racism without Racists*, 76, 84–87. Bonilla-Silva presents more on the naturalization frame, particularly as it pertains to neighborhoods, schools, dating, or other forms of socializing.

35. Bonilla-Silva, *Racism without Racists*, 76, 87–90. As Bonilla-Silva describes, cultural racism is found within early research of racially subordinated communities, often described as the "culture of poverty" by scholars looking to diagnose the social and economic status of people of color as deriving from lack of hard work, questionable morals, and familial relations. The "culture of poverty" prognosis is viewed as endemic within communities of color. Oscar Lewis and Oliver La Farge's *Five Families: Mexican Case Studies in the Culture of Poverty* (New York: Basic Books, 1959) formally develops the culture of poverty argument, initially a class-based argument that was later surmised to be an assessment of communities of color because the subjects are of Mexican descent.

36. See Bonilla-Silva and Dietrich, "Sweet Enchantment." Effectively, the cultural racism frame looks at racially subordinated groups and "biologizes their presumed cultural practices and uses that as the rationale for justifying racial inequality . . . 'blaming the victim'—arguing that minorities' standing is the product of their lack of effort, loose family organization, and inappropriate values" (193).

37. See Bonilla-Silva, *Racism without Racists*, 77–78, 91–95; Bonilla-Silva and Dietrich, "Sweet Enchantment." Bonilla-Silva and Dietrich contend that

> whites do not believe that minorities' social standing today is a product of discrimination. Instead, they believe it is due to "their culture," "class," "legacies from slavery," "the culture of segregation," "lack of social capital," "poverty," and so forth. In other words, it is anything but racism. . . . Since most whites . . . believe discrimination has all but disappeared, they regard minorities' claim of discrimination as excuses or as minorities playing the infamous "race card." (193–94)

38. See Bonilla-Silva, *Racism without Racists*. However, Bonilla-Silva acknowledges that "although some whites fight white supremacy and do not endorse white common sense, most subscribe to substantial portions of it, in a casual, uncritical fashion that helps sustain the prevailing racial order" (11). He urges whites to acknowledge white privilege as a facilitator of the continued perpetuation of racial inequality, which is embedded within institutions and their practices. He is keen on moving away from analyzing racialized social systems and systemic inequality as individual practices instead as "collective practices that help reinforce the contemporary racial order" (15). Even the use of particular language (e.g., *prejudice* and *bias*) that implies individual responsibility must shift to address collective institutional practices so as to unpack different levels of the new racism that is pervasive through the color-blind racial ideology. Bonilla-Silva argues that color-blind racism is the dominant racial ideology used today because it "binds whites together and blurs, shapes, and provides many of the terms of the debate for blacks" (219).

39. For a more robust discussion of color-blind racism, see Bonilla-Silva, *Racism without Racists*.

40. Feagin, *Systemic Racism*; Joe R. Feagin and Kimberley Ducey, *Elite White Men Ruling: Who, What, When, Where, and How* (New York: Routledge, 2017), 9–44.

41. Wilkins and Gulati, "So Few Black Lawyers."

42. Feagin, *Systemic Racism*.

43. Sander, "Racial Paradox"; Wilkins and Gulati, "So Few Black Lawyers."

44. Feagin, *White Racial Frame*.

45. Feagin, *Racist America*, 18–20; Feagin, *Systemic Racism*, 1–52; Feagin, *White Racial Frame*, ix–x.

46. Feagin and Ducey, *Elite White Men Ruling*.

47. Feagin and Ducey, *Elite White Men Ruling*.

48. Moore, *Reproducing Racism*, 15.

49. Moore, *Reproducing Racism*.

50. Moore, *Reproducing Racism*, 22.

51. For a thorough discussion on the origins and theoretical frames of intersectionality, see Hae Y. Choo and Myra M. Ferree, "Practicing Intersectionality in Sociological Research: A Critical Analysis of Inclusions, Interactions, and Institutions in the Study of Inequalities," *American Sociological Association, Sociological Theory* 28, no. 2 (2010): 129–49, https://doi.org/10.1111/j.1467-9558.2010.01370.x; Patricia H. Collins, *Black Feminist Thought: Knowledge, Consciousness, and the Politics of Empowerment* (New York: Routledge, 2000); Patricia H. Collins, *Black Sexual Politics: African Americans, Gender, and the New Racism* (New York: Routledge, 2005); Patricia H. Collins, "It's All in the Family: Intersections of Gender, Race and Nation," *Hypatia* 13, no. 3 (1998): 62–82, http://www.jstor.org/stable/3810699; Patricia H. Collins, "Learning from the Outsider Within: The Sociological Significance of Black Feminist Thought," *Social Problems* 33, no. 6 (1986): 14–32, https://doi.org/10.2307/800672; Combahee River Collective Staff, *The Combahee River Collective Statement: Back Feminist Organizing in the Seventies and Eighties* (Brooklyn, NY: Kitchen Table/Women of Color Press, 1986), https://combaheerivercollective.weebly.com/the-combahee-river-collective-statement.html; Kimberlé Crenshaw, "Mapping the Margins: Intersectionality, Identity Politics, and Violence against Women of Color," *Stanford Law Review* 43, no. 6 (1991): 285–320, https://doi.org/10.2307/1229039; Kathy Davis, "Intersectionality as Buzzword: A Sociology of Science Perspective on What Makes a Feminist Theory Successful," *Feminist Theory* 9 (2008): 67–85, https://doi.org/10.1177/1464700108086364; Leslie McCall, "The Complexity of Intersectionality," *Signs* 30, no. 3 (Spring 2005), 1771–1800, http://www.journals.uchicago.edu/doi/pdfplus/10.1086/426800; Jennifer C. Nash, "Re-thinking Intersectionality," *Feminist Review* 89 (2008): 1–15, http://www.jstor.org/stable/40663957; Sylvia Walby, Jo Armstrong, and Sofia Strid, "Intersectionality: Multiple Inequalities in Social Theory," *Sociology* 46, no. 2 (April 2012): 224–40, https://doi.org/10.1177/0038038511416164; Adia Harvey Wingfield, "Comment on Feagin and Elias," *Ethnic and Racial Studies* 36, no. 6 (February 2013): 989–93, https://doi.org/10.1080/01419870.2013.767920; Nira Yuval-Davis, "Intersectionality

and Feminist Politics," *European Journal of Women's Studies* 13, no. 3 (August 2006): 193–209, https://doi.org/10.1177/1350506806065752.

52. Philomena Essed, *Understanding Everyday Racism* (Newbury Park, CA: Sage, 1991). See also St. Jean and Feagin, *Double Burden*, for more discussion on gendered racism.

53. Essed, *Understanding Everyday Racism*.

54. Wingfield, *Doing Business with Beauty*, 6–11.

55. See Judy Trent Ellis, "Sexual Harassment and Race: A Legal Analysis of Discrimination," *Journal of Legislation* 8, no. 1, article 3, http://scholarship.law. nd.edu/jleg/vol8/iss1/3. Judy Trent Ellis endeavors to clarify the nature of sexual harassment by examining it through the lens of race. She argues that black women are in a unique position because of their race and gender classification, where they "may face discrimination based on race, sex, or sex-race" in the workforce (44).

56. Louwanda Evans and Wendy L. Moore, "Impossible Burdens: White Institutions, Emotional Labor, and Micro-Resistance," *Social Problems* 62 (2015): 439–54, https://doi.org/10.1093/socpro/spv009.

CHAPTER 2

1. Adia Harvey Wingfield, *Doing Business with Beauty: Black Women, Hair Salons, and the Racial Enclave Economy* (Lanham, MD: Rowman & Littlefield, 2008), 6–11.

2. Joe R. Feagin, *Racist America: Roots, Current Realities, and Future Reparations*, 2nd ed. (New York: Routledge, 2010), 25, 59–96; Joe R. Feagin, *Systemic Racism: A Theory of Oppression* (New York: Routledge, 2006), 25, 272–76; Joe R. Feagin, *The White Racial Frame: Centuries of Racial Framing and Counter-Framing*, 2nd ed. (New York: Routledge, 2013), x–xi, 3, 1–22.

3. Christine Hauser, "Black Doctor Says Delta Flight Attendant Rejected Her; Sought 'Actual Physician,'" *New York Times*, October 14, 2016, https://www. nytimes.com/2016/10/15/us/black-doctor-says-delta-flight-attendant-brushed-her-aside-in-search-of-an-actual-physician.html.

4. Yanick St. Jean and Joe R. Feagin, *Double Burden: Black Women and Everyday Racism* (Amonk, NY: M. E. Sharpe, 1998), 44–45.

5. Minority Corporate Counsel Association and Vault, *2017 Vault/MCCA Law Firm Diversity Survey*, 2017, https://www.mcca.com/wp-content/uploads/2017/12/2017-Vault-MCCA-Law-Firm-Diversity-Survey-Report.pdf, 3. The findings in this survey reflect information as of December 31, 2016, reported by 229 participating law firms.

6. See Minority Corporate Counsel Association and Vault, *2017 Vault/MCCA*, 6, table 1, "Overall Law Firm Demographics." Black lawyers make up 3.14 percent of the total lawyer population (100,503). The breakdown of black lawyers consists of 2L summer associates (6.57 percent); associates (4.41 percent); equity partners

(1.80 percent); non-equity partners (2.44 percent), and of counsel (2.72 percent). Black women make up an even smaller demographic. Out of the 100,503 attorneys in law firms in 2016 nationwide, there were only 1,648 black female attorneys and 1,508 black male associates. And although black female attorneys outnumber black male associates, black male equity partners (1.17 percent) continue to double black female equity partners (0.63 percent), making this statistic even more startling.

7. See Minority Corporate Counsel Association and Vault, *2017 Vault/MCCA*, 37, table A3, "African-American/Black, Asian American and Hispanic/Latino Lawyers Among Surveyed Firms: 2016 vs 2007." Vault and MCCA compare the number of black female associates, partners, and counsel in 2007 and 2016, noting that, from 2007 to 2016, the percentage of black female lawyers (associates, partners, and counsel) has decreased from 1.98 percent in 2007 to 1.64 percent in 2016.

8. See Minority Corporate Counsel Association and Vault, *2017 Vault/MCCA*, 12, table 2, "Attorney Departures among Largest Racial/Ethnic Groups in 2016 as Percentage of Their Overall Law Firm Population." Attrition is highest among all black lawyers (16.5 percent); black female lawyers, though, have a higher attrition rate (18.4 percent) than black male lawyers (14.3 percent), Hispanic and Latino male lawyers (13.1 percent), Hispanic and Latina female lawyers (12.4 percent), Asian male lawyers (14.9 percent), Asian female lawyers (14.4 percent), white female lawyers (11.6 percent), and white male lawyers (9.1 percent).

9. David B. Wilkins and Mitu G. Gulati, "Why Are There So Few Black Lawyers in Corporate Law Firms? An Institutional Analysis," *California Law Review* 84 (May 1996): 493–625, http://nrs.harvard.edu/urn-3:HUL.InstRepos:13548823.

10. See Cynthia Fuchs Epstein, "Reaching for the Top: 'The Glass Ceiling' and Women in Law," in *Women in Law*, ed. Shimon Shetreet (London: Kluwer Law International, 1998), 105–30; Cynthia Fuchs Epstein, "Women in the Legal Profession at the Turn of the Twenty-First Century: Assessing Glass Ceilings and Open Doors," *Kansas Law Review* 49 (2001): 733–60; Cynthia Fuchs Epstein, *Women in Law* (Urbana, IL: University of Chicago, 1981); Cynthia Fuchs Epstein, Robert Sauté, Bonnie Oglensky, and Martha Gever, "Glass Ceilings and Open Doors: Women's Advancement in the Legal Profession," *Fordham Law Review* 64 (1995): 291–449; Suzanne Nossel and Elizabeth Westfall, *Presumed Equal: What America's Top Women Lawyers Really Think about Their Firms* (Wayne, NJ: Career Press, 1998).

11. American Bar Association (ABA) Commission on Women in the Profession, *Visible Invisibility: Women of Color in Law Firms* (Chicago: American Bar Association, 2006); Deepali Bagati, *Women of Color in U.S. Law Firms: Women of Color in Professional Services Series* (New York: Catalyst, 2009); Lindsay Blohm, Ashley Riveira, and Marcella B. Bary, *Presumed Equal: What America's Top Women Lawyers Really Think about Their Firms* (Bloomington, IN: AuthorHouse, 2006); Corporate Counsel of Women of Color (CCWC), *The Perspectives of Women of Color Attorneys in Corporate Legal Departments* (New York: Corporate Counsel Women of Color, 2011; Nossel and Westfall, *Presumed Equal.*

12. Minority Corporate Counsel Association and Vault, *2017 Vault/MCCA*, 12.

13. Susan L. Bryant, "The Beauty Ideal: The Effects of European Standards of Beauty on Black Women," *Columbia Social Work Review* 6 (2013): 80–81; St. Jean and Feagin, *Double Burden*, 45–46; 73–98, 204–7.

14. Bryant, "Beauty Ideal"; Cheryl Thompson, "Black Women, Beauty, and Hair as a Matter of Being," *Women's Studies: An Interdisciplinary Journal* 38, no. 8 (2009): 831–56, https://doi.org/10.1080/00497870903238463.

15. Wingfield, *Doing Business with Beauty*, 37.

16. Wingfield, *Doing Business with Beauty*, 6–11.

17. Joe R. Feagin and Kimberley Ducey, *Elite White Men Ruling: Who, What, When, Where, and How* (New York: Routledge, 2017), 9–44.

18. Feagin, *White Racial Frame*; Feagin, *Racist America*; Feagin, *Systemic Racism*.

19. See Eduardo Bonilla-Silva, *Racism without Racists: Color-Blind Racism and the Persistence of Racial Inequality in America*, 4th ed. (Lanham, MD: Rowman & Littlefield, 2014); St. Jean and Feagin, *Double Burden*, 45–46; 73–98, 204–7. As Bonilla-Silva argues, racialized social systems are in place to confer systemic benefits to whites over nonwhites; therefore, "society's racial structure [is] the totality of the social relations and practices that reinforce white privilege" (9).

20. See Graham Ruddick, "Lupita Nyong'o Accuses Grazia of Editing Her Hair to Fit 'Eurocentric' Ideals," *Guardian*, November 10, 2017, https://www.theguardian.com/film/2017/nov/10/lupita-nyongo-grazia-editing-hair-eurocentric; Graham Ruddick, "Solange Knowles Tells Evening Standard: 'Don't Touch My Hair,'" *Guardian*, October 20, 2017, https://www.theguardian.com/music/2017/oct/20/solange-knowles-tells-evening-standard-dont-touch-my-hair; St. Jean and Feagin, *Double Burden*, 45–46, 73–98, 204–7. Recently, both Lupita Nyong'o and Solange Knowles accused magazines of editing out their hair to fit a white aesthetic of beauty.

21. Paulette M. Caldwell, "A Hair Piece: Perspectives on the Intersection of Race and Gender," *Duke Law Journal* (1991): 383, https://scholarship.law.duke.edu/dlj/vol40/iss2/5.

22. Caldwell, "Hair Piece"; D. Wendy Greene, "Black Women Can't Have Blonde Hair . . . in the Workplace," *Journal of Gender, Race and Justice* 14, no. 2 (June 2011): 405–30; Tina R. Opie and Katherine W. Phillips, "Hair Penalties: The Negative Influence of Afrocentric Hair on Ratings of Black Women's Dominance and Professionalism," *Frontiers in Psychology* 6 (2015): 1311, https://doi.org/10.3389/fpsyg.2015.01311; Tracey O. Patton, "Hey Girl, Am I More than My Hair? African American Women and Their Struggles with Beauty, Body Image, and Hair," *National Women's Studies Associate* 18, no.2 (Summer 2006): 24–51, https://doi.org/10.1353/nwsa.2006.0037; Carla D. Pratt, "Sisters in Law: Black Women Lawyers' Struggle for Advancement," *Michigan State Law Review* (2012): 1777–95, http://dx.doi.org/10.2139/ssrn.2131492; Ashleigh Shelby Rosette

and Tracy L. Dumas; "The Hair Dilemma: Conform to Mainstream Expectations or Emphasize Racial Identity," *Duke Journal of Gender, Law, & Policy*
(2007): 14407–22, https://scholarship.law.duke.edu/djglp/vol14/iss1/13; St. Jean
and Feagin, *Double Burden*; Rose Weitz, "Women and Their Hair: Seeking Power
through Resistance," *Gender & Society* 15, no. 5 (Fall 2001): 667–86, https://doi.
org/10.1177/089124301015005003.

23. Caldwell, "Hair Piece," 384; Opie and Phillips, "Hair Penalties."

24. Opie and Phillips, "Hair Penalties."

25. Opie and Phillips, "Hair Penalties." According to Opie and Phillips, blacks
who "believe that dominance is a negative trait and that Whites consider blacks to
be dominant . . . may have heightened negativity toward Black women's dominance
because they think White people negatively stereotype such behavior. Blacks may
have concerns that Black women's dominance displays will reinforce negative stereotypes about Blacks" (2).

26. Wendy Leo Moore, *Reproducing Racism: White Spaces, Elite Law Schools,
and Racial Inequality* (Lanham, MD: Rowman & Littlefield, 2008).

27. See Erving Goffman, *Stigma: Notes on the Management of Spoiled Identity*
(Englewood Cliffs, NJ: Prentice-Hall, 1963) for a comprehensive exploration on
interaction and how impression management is most visible among marginalized
individuals and groups, such as mental patients, people who are disfigured, individuals labeled as criminals, and others. According to Goffman, stigma is defined
as an "attribute that is deeply discrediting," and the individual who is stigmatized is
lessened "from a whole and usual person to a tainted, discounted one" (3).

28. Hauser, "Black Doctor."

29. Bonilla-Silva, *Racism without Racists*; Feagin, *Systemic Racism*; Moore,
Reproducing Racism.

30. Bonilla-Silva, *Racism without Racists*; Moore, *Reproducing Racism*.

31. Wilkins and Gulati, "So Few Black Lawyers." See also Spencer Headworth,
Robert L. Nelson, Ronit Dinovitzer, and David B. Wilkins, *Diversity in Practice:
Race, Gender, and Class in Legal and Professional Careers* (Cambridge: Cambridge
University Press, 2016), 12, for hiring practices at large law firms that

> perpetuate patterns of demographic inequality. This in part reflects the continuing
> importance of credentialing as a *de facto* requirement for gaining entry to the profes-
> sional elite. . . . Elite firms continue to concentrate their recruitment and interviewing
> efforts at the most prestigious, expensive, and exclusive universities, thus functionally
> eliminating from consideration those who do not meet this fundamental eligibility
> threshold. (12)

32. Erving Goffman, *The Presentation of Self in Everyday Life* (New York:
Doubleday, 1959), 225.

33. Bonilla-Silva, *Racism without Racists*.

34. Bonilla-Silva, *Racism without Racists*.

35. See Bonilla-Silva, *Racism without Racists*. Bonilla-Silva acknowledges, "language of color blindness is slippery, apparently contradictory, and often subtle" (101).

36. See Derald Wing Sue, "Microaggressions, Marginality, and Oppression," in *Microaggressions and Marginality: Manifestation, Dynamics, and Impact*, ed. Derald Wing Sue (Hoboken, NJ: Wiley, 2010), 3–22.

37. See Peter Geraghty, "Of Counsel, Special Counsel, Senior Counsel: What Does It All Mean?" *American Bar Association—Eye on Ethics*, October 2015, https://www.americanbar.org/publications/youraba/2015/october-2015/of-counsel—special-counsel—senior-counsel—what-does-it-all-me.html. Counsel is a lawyer who maintains a "close, personal, continuous, and regular relationship" with the firm. A lawyer with the position of counsel does not have the same business development responsibilities or workload as a partner but is still more senior and specialized than an associate. Counsel positions are offered to associates whom the firm would like to maintain a relationship with, if the partner track is not offered or desired.

38. Feagin, *Racist America*; Feagin, *Systemic Racism*; Feagin, *White Racial Frame*.

39. See Devon W. Carbado and Mitu Gulati, "Working Identity," *Cornell Law Review* 85, no. 5 (July 2000): 1267–70, http://scholarship.law.cornell.edu/clr/vol85/iss5/4 (discusses how developing and managing workplace identity is important for all individuals but that members of "minority" groups, including women, subordinated racial groups, and LGBTQ, face institutionalized and structural barriers that make this process burdensome because of the cultural stereotypes they must counter in their working identities) and Goffman, *Presentation of Self* (emphasizes impression management as a tool to shape how others perceive an individual).

40. Louwanda Evans and Wendy L. Moore, "Impossible Burdens: White Institutions, Emotional Labor, and Micro-Resistance," *Social Problems* 62 (2015): 439–54; Feagin, *Racist America*; Feagin, *Systemic Racism*; Feagin, *White Racial Frame*; Moore *Reproducing Racism*.

41. Carbado and Gulati, "Working Identity."

CHAPTER 3

1. Joe R. Feagin, *Racist America: Roots, Current Realities, and Future Reparations*, 2nd ed. (New York: Routledge, 2010), 19; Joe R. Feagin, *Systemic Racism: A Theory of Oppression* (New York: Routledge, 2006), xii, 1–52, 194–95; Joe R. Feagin, *The White Racial Frame: Centuries of Racial Framing and Counter-Framing*, 2nd ed. (New York: Routledge, 2013), ix–xi.

2. Feagin, *Racist America*, 18–20; Feagin, *Systemic Racism*, 1–52; Feagin, *White Racial Frame*, ix–x.

3. Devon W. Carbado and Mitu Gulati, "Working Identity," *Cornell Law Review* 85, no. 5 (July 2000): 1267–70, http://scholarship.law.cornell.edu/clr/vol85/iss5/4.

4. Feagin, *Systemic Racism*, 35–52.

5. Feagin, *Systemic Racism*, 25; Feagin, *White Racial Frame*, xi, 3.

6. Wendy Leo Moore, *Reproducing Racism: White Spaces, Elite Law Schools, and Racial Inequality* (Lanham, MD: Rowman & Littlefield, 2008), 48.

7. Joe R. Feagin and Kimberley Ducey, *Elite White Men Ruling: Who, What, When, Where, and How* (New York: Routledge, 2017), 9–44.

8. Eduardo Bonilla-Silva, *Racism without Racists: Color-Blind Racism and the Persistence of Racial Inequality in America*, 4th ed. (Lanham, MD: Rowman & Littlefield, 2014); Feagin, *Racist America*; Feagin, *White Racial Frame*; Moore, *Reproducing Racism*.

9. Moore, *Reproducing Racism*, 162–63.

10. Moore, *Reproducing Racism*.

11. Moore, *Reproducing Racism*, 54.

12. Moore, *Reproducing Racism*.

13. Feagin, *Racist America*, 84–86; Feagin, *Systemic Racism*, 178–81, 231–32; Feagin, *White Racial Frame*, 51. See also Angela Davis, *Women, Race and Class* (New York: Vintage Books, 1983), which discusses black women's perspective in relation to education and liberation. Davis notes that, according to the prevailing racist ideology,

> Black people were allegedly incapable of intellectual advancement. After all, they had been chattel, naturally inferior as compared to white epitomes of humankind. But if they really were biologically inferior, they would have manifested neither the desire nor the capability to acquire knowledge. Ergo, no prohibition of learning would be necessary. In reality, of course, Black people had always exhibited a furious impatience as regards the acquisition of educations. (101)

14. See Bonilla-Silva, *Racism without Racists*, for a discussion of the abstract liberalism frame.

15. Moore, *Reproducing Racism*, 149.

16. See Moore, *Reproducing Racism*, for a discussion of how white narratives of affirmative action negatively affect perceptions of law students of color and their abilities while simultaneously minimizing their accomplishments, both academic and professional.

17. Feagin, *Racist America*, 25, 59–96; Feagin, *Systemic Racism*, 25, 272–76; Feagin, *White Racial Frame*, x–xi, 3, 1–22; Moore, *Reproducing Racism*, 149.

18. Franz Kafka, "A Little Fable," in *The Complete Stories*, ed. Nahum N. Glatzer (New York: Schocken Books, 1971). Again, we see the impact of the invisible labor clause on black female lawyers. The invisible labor clause is enacted in various ways, forcing added invisible labor on the women's already-strenuous path.

19. David B. Wilkins and Mitu G. Gulati, "Why Are There So Few Black Lawyers in Corporate Law Firms? An Institutional Analysis," *California Law Review* 84 (May 1996): 493–625, http://nrs.harvard.edu/urn-3:HUL.InstRepos:13548823.

CHAPTER 4

1. Adia Harvey Wingfield, *Doing Business with Beauty: Black Women, Hair Salons, and the Racial Enclave Economy* (Lanham, MD: Rowman & Littlefield, 2008), 6–11.

2. See Minority Corporate Counsel Association and Vault, *2017 Vault/MCCA Law Firm Diversity Survey*, https://www.mcca.com/wp-content/uploads/2017/12/2017-Vault-MCCA-Law-Firm-Diversity-Survey-Report.pdf, 12, table 2, "Attorney Departures among Largest Racial/Ethnic Groups in 2016 as Percentage of Their Overall Law Firm Population." See also Gita Z. Wilder, "Are Minority Women Lawyers Leaving Their Jobs? Findings from the First Wave of the *After the JD* Study," Dallas, TX: NALP Foundation for Law Career Research and Education and the National Association for Law Placement, 2008), https://www.nalp.org/assets/1280_ajdminoritywomenmonograph.pdf. As demonstrated in chapter 2, attrition is highest among black lawyers (16.5 percent); however, black female lawyers have the highest attrition rate, at 18.4 percent, compared to black men (14.3 percent); Hispanic and Latino men (13.1 percent), Hispanic and Latina women (12.4 percent), Asian men (14.9 percent), Asian women (14.4 percent), white women (11.6 percent), and white men (9.1 percent).

3. See Minority Corporate Counsel Association and Vault, *2017 Vault/MCCA*, 24.

4. Joe R. Feagin, *Racist America: Roots, Current Realities, and Future Reparations*, 2nd ed. (New York: Routledge, 2010), 25, 59–96; Joe R. Feagin, *Systemic Racism: A Theory of Oppression* (New York: Routledge, 2006), 25, 272–76; Joe R. Feagin, *The White Racial Frame: Centuries of Racial Framing and Counter-Framing*, 2nd ed. (New York: Routledge, 2013), x–xi, 1–22.

5. See Arlie Hochschild and Anne Machung, *The Second Shift* (New York: Avon Books, 1990). The double shift refers to the unpaid labor performed by women at home in addition to the paid labor in the public sector. Their "second shift" begins when they arrive home from work.

6. See Minority Corporate Counsel Association and Vault, *2017 Vault/MCCA*, 24.

7. Minority Corporate Counsel Association and Vault, *2017 Vault/MCCA*, 11, 37. According to the *2017 Vault/MCCA Law Firm Diversity Survey*, black men outnumber black women by nearly double among equity partners.

8. See Gloria T. Hull and Barbara Smith, *All the Women Are White, All the Blacks Are Men, but Some of Us Are Brave: Black Women's Studies* (Westbury, NY: Feminist Press, 1982). The phrase originates in this book, which is a comprehensive

collection of black feminist scholarship addressing the politics of black women's studies and engaging race and gender discourse of black women in American society.

9. Joe R. Feagin and Kimberley Ducey, *Elite White Men Ruling: Who, What, When, Where, and How* (New York: Routledge, 2017), 9–44.

10. Katty Kay, "100 Women: Katty Kay on How the 'Confidence Gap' Holds Women Back," *BBC News*, October 2, 2017, http://www.bbc.com/news/world-41444682; Katty Kay and Claire Shipman, *The Confidence Code* (New York: HarperCollins, 2014); Katty Kay and Claire Shipman, "The Confidence Gap," *Atlantic*, May 2014, https://www.theatlantic.com/magazine/archive/2014/05/the-confidence-gap/359815/.

11. Kay, "100 Women"; Kay and Shipman, *Confidence Code*; Kay and Shipman, "Confidence Gap."

12. See Ronit Dinovitzer, Robert Nelson, Gabriele Plickert, Rebecca Sandefur, and Joyce Sterling, *After the JD II: Second Results from a National Study of Legal Careers* (Chicago: American Bar Foundation and the NALP Foundation for Law Career Research and Education, 2009), http://www.law.du.edu/documents/directory/publications/sterling/AJD2.pdf. This study (*AJD2*) discusses how respondents measured their prospects of becoming partners. The results revealed that women consistently appraised their chances of becoming partners as being less than men. *AJD2* discovered that, in large firms (101–250 lawyers), women believed that they had significantly less chances of becoming partners (46 percent), in comparison to the beliefs of their male peers (70 percent). Additionally, women in large firms were more likely to indicate the unlikelihood of their chances of attaining partnership, in comparison to women's advancement prospect estimations in other legal practice settings (64). *AJD2* postulates that women's low self-estimation of their chances to become partner are due to the fact that (1) some women do not aspire to become partners and so do not invest in this career path and (2) some women who remained at the firm in order to assess their chances of attaining partnership will usually know by the seventh year if that is a possibility. Both men and women who have remained at the firm up to the point of assessing their chances for partnership find that their chances of making partner are low. Regardless of the reasons, women's lower estimation of their potential for success compared to men, in terms of partnership attainment, would alert us to significant divergences in women's career paths (64).

13. Kay and Shipman, "Confidence Gap."

14. See David B. Wilkins and Mitu G. Gulati, "Why Are There So Few Black Lawyers in Corporate Law Firms? An Institutional Analysis," *California Law Review* 84 (May 1996): 493–625, http://nrs.harvard.edu/urn-3:HUL.InstRepos:13548823.

15. I acknowledge that these statements are heterosexist assumptions about men having women at home. The participants were speaking primarily within a heterosexist context, not including the possibility of men with male partners and women with female partners.

16. Hochschild and Machung, *Second Shift*.

17. See Wilder, *Are Minority Women Lawyers Leaving*, 9, where she cites National Association for Law Placement (NALP), *Keeping the Keepers II: Mobility and Management of Associates* (Dallas, TX: NALP Foundation for Law Career Research and Education, 2003), 32–35. Given the number of female associates of color entering the legal profession, the staggeringly low numbers of racially subordinated female partners is often attributed to the high attrition rate that firms suffer. Further data indicate that 64 percent of racially subordinated women who enter law firms as entry-level associates tend to leave the firm within fifty-five months of their start (Wilder, *Are Minority Women Lawyers Leaving*, 9). Comparable figures for the attrition rates of all entry-level hires and all entry-level female hires are 53 percent and 55 percent, respectively. Because the number of female associates of color in law firms tends to be smaller than white males, white females, and minority men, the attrition rate of racially subordinated women is dramatic and quite visible.

18. See Anne-Marie Slaughter, "Why Women Still Can't Have It All," *Atlantic*, July/August 2012, https://www.theatlantic.com/magazine/archive/2012/07/why-women-still-cant-have-it-all/309020/, for a discussion on the obstacles women face in trying to "have it all," managing a professional and personal life. .

19. See Bruce G. Link and Jo C. Phelan, "Conceptualizing Stigma," *Annual Review of Sociology* 27 (2001): 363–85, http://dx.doi.org/10.1146/annurev.soc.27.1.363, for a robust discussion on how categorization of stereotypes linked to individuals based on particular markers (stigmatization) lead to negative effects on the *stigmatized* individual.

20. Philomena is citing Debora L. Spar, *Wonder Women: Sex, Power, and the Quest for Perfection* (New York: Sarah Crichton Books, 2013), and the associated Debora L. Spar, "Why the Woman Who "Has It All" Doesn't' Really Exist," *Glamour*, August 14, 2013, https://www.glamour.com/story/why-women-cant-have-it-all-according-to-barnard-college-president-debora-l-spar, discussing precisely the subject of work–life balance for females and the need to be "perfect" in all aspects of their lives.

21. See Irene Padavic and Barbara Reskin, *Women and Men at Work*, 2nd ed. (Thousand Oaks, CA: Pine Forge Press, 2005), for a discussion on the role that gender plays in the workplace.

22. Padavic and Reskin, *Women and Men at Work*, 100–101, 153.

23. Philomena Essed, *Understanding Everyday Racism* (Newbury Park, CA: Sage, 1991); Yanick St. Jean and Joe R. Feagin, *Double Burden: Black Women and Everyday Racism* (Amonk, NY: M. E. Sharpe, 1998). See also Hae Y. Choo and Myra M. Ferree, "Practicing Intersectionality in Sociological Research: A Critical Analysis of Inclusions, Interactions, and Institutions in the Study of Inequalities," *American Sociological Association, Sociological Theory* 28, no. 2 (2010): 129–49, https://doi.org/10.1111/j.1467-9558.2010.01370.x; Patricia H. Collins, *Black Feminist Thought: Knowledge, Consciousness, and the Politics of Empowerment*

(New York: Routledge, 2000); Patricia H. Collins, *Black Sexual Politics: African Americans, Gender, and the New Racism* (New York: Routledge, 2005); Patricia H. Collins, "It's All in the Family: Intersections of Gender, Race and Nation," *Hypatia* 13, no. 3 (1998): 62–82, http://www.jstor.org/stable/3810699; Patricia H. Collins, "Learning from the Outsider Within: The Sociological Significance of Black Feminist Thought," *Social Problems* 33, no. 6 (1986): 14–32, https://doi.org/10.2307/800672; Combahee River Collective Staff, *The Combahee River Collective Statement: Back Feminist Organizing in the Seventies and Eighties* (Brooklyn, NY: Kitchen Table/Women of Color Press, 1986), https://combaheerivercollective.weebly.com/the-combahee-river-collective-statement.html; Kimberlé Crenshaw, "Mapping the Margins: Intersectionality, Identity Politics, and Violence against Women of Color," *Stanford Law Review* 43, no. 6 (1991): 285–320, https://doi.org/10.2307/1229039; Kathy Davis, "Intersectionality as Buzzword: A Sociology of Science Perspective on What Makes a Feminist Theory Successful," *Feminist Theory* 9 (2008): 67–85, https://doi.org/10.1177/1464700108086364; Leslie McCall, "The Complexity of Intersectionality," *Signs* 30, no. 3 (Spring 2005): 1771–1800, http://www.journals.uchicago.edu/doi/pdfplus/10.1086/426800; Jennifer C. Nash, "Re-thinking Intersectionality," *Feminist Review* 89 (2008): 1–15, http://www.jstor.org/stable/40663957; Sylvia Walby, Jo Armstrong, and Sofia Strid, "Intersectionality: Multiple Inequalities in Social Theory," *Sociology* 46, no. 2 (April 2012): 224–40, https://doi.org/10.1177/0038038511416164; Adia Harvey Wingfield, "Comment on Feagin and Elias," *Ethnic and Racial Studies* 36, no. 6 (February 2013): 989–93, https://doi.org/10.1080/01419870.2013.767920; Nira Yuval-Davis, "Intersectionality and Feminist Politics," *European Journal of Women's Studies* 13, no. 3 (August 2006): 193–209, https://doi.org/10.1177/1350506806065752.

24. See Feagin, *Racist America*, 189–219. See also Donna Bobbitt-Zeher, "Gender Discrimination at Work," *Gender and Society* 25, no. 6 (December 2011): 764–86; https://doi.org/10.1177/0891243211424741, for a discussion on gender inequality and gender discrimination in the workplace. See Walter T. Martin and Dudley L. Poston Jr., "The Occupational Composition of White Females: Sexism, Racism and Occupational Differentiation," *Social Forces* 50, no. 3 (March 1972): 349–55, https://doi.org/10.1093/sf/50.3.349, for a discussion on the degree of occupational differentiation between white women and men and white women and nonwhite women. See Peggy McIntosh, "White Privilege and Male Privilege: A Personal Account of Coming to See Correspondences through Work in Women's Studies," in *The Teacher in American Society: A Critical Anthology*, ed. Eugene F. Provenzo Jr. (Los Angeles: Sage, 2011), 121–34, for a discussion on white privilege and male privilege and the unwillingness to acknowledge and fully recognize its benefits on those who occupy these identity traits. See Padavic and Reskin, *Women and Men*, for a discussion on women and men's experiences in the workplace and how they may differ from or reflect each other. St. Jean and Feagin, *Double Burden*, on the racial oppression and stigmatization of black women, notes that

racial oppression is multifaceted, with a number of important dimensions. These include the weighing down of a target group with "heavy burdens," the literal meaning of "oppression." These burdens include harshly applied white-power plays that take the form of racial domination, discrimination, exploitation, and cultural devaluation. In addition to the burdens and barriers of racial oppression, there are also the privileges and power that come to whites from this system of oppression. (11)

25. Dorothy E. Roberts, "Racism and Patriarchy in the Meaning of Motherhood," *Journal of Gender and the Law* 1, no. 1 (1993): 2, http://scholarship.law.upenn.edu/faculty_scholarship/595.

26. Roberts, "Racism and Patriarchy," 2.

27. See Roberts, "Racism and Patriarchy, for a discussion of how racism and patriarchy interact to create unique experiences for black women. Roberts notes,

Racism and patriarchy are not two separate institutions that intersect only in the lives of Black women. They are two interrelated, mutually supporting systems of domination and their relationship is essential to understanding the subordination of all women. Racism makes the experience of sexism different for Black women and white women. But it is not enough to note that Black women suffer from both racism and sexism, although this is true. Racism is patriarchal. Patriarchy is racist. We will not destroy one institution without destroying the other. I believe it is the recognition of that connection—along with the recognition of difference among women—that is truly revolutionary. (3)

28. See Minority Corporate Counsel Association and Vault, *2017 Vault/MCCA*, 12, table 2, "Attorney Departures among Largest Racial/Ethnic Groups in 2016 as Percentage of Their Overall Law Firm Population."

29. Enobong Hannah Branch, *Opportunity Denied: Limiting Black Women to Devalued Work* (New Brunswick, NJ: Rutgers University Press, 2011), 98. Branch continues, noting that "in all areas where there is a competition for desirable resources, the systematic exclusion or limitation of the racialized and/or gendered Other' permits the advantaged group to preserve those resources for itself" (98).

30. Branch, *Opportunity Denied*, 98; Feagin, *Racist America*, 189–219; McIntosh, "White Privilege"; St. Jean and Feagin, *Double Burden*, 11.

31. See National Association for Law Placement, *2017 Report on Diversity in U.S. Law Firms* (Washington, DC: National Association of Law Placement, 2017), https://www.nalp.org/uploads/2017NALPReportonDiversityinUSLawFirms.pdf, 9, table 1, "Women and Minorities at Law Firms—2009–2017"; Minority Corporate Counsel Association and Vault, *2017 Vault/MCCA*, 46–47, table A6, "Women among Surveyed Firms: 2016 vs. 2007."

32. Branch, *Opportunity Denied*, 98; Feagin, *Racist America*, 189–219; McIntosh, "White Privilege"; St. Jean and Feagin, *Double Burden*, 11, 123–50.

33. See Wilkins and Gulati, "So Few Black Lawyers," 568–72.

34. Eduardo Bonilla-Silva, *Racism without Racists: Color-Blind Racism and the Persistence of Racial Inequality in America*, 4th ed. (Lanham, MD: Rowman & Lit-

tlefield, 2014); Branch, *Opportunity Denied*, 98; Feagin, *Racist America*, 189–219; McIntosh, "White Privilege"; St. Jean and Feagin, *Double Burden*, 11.

35. Bonilla-Silva, *Racism without Racists*, 76, 84–87.

36. See Wilkins and Gulati, "So Few Black Lawyers."

37. The explanatory power of intersectionality as a theoretical and political tool is crucial in this analysis because it aids in the conceptualization of a viable theory that empowers marginalized identities and elaborates on complexities of oppression.

38. The invisible labor clause diminishes black female lawyers' chances of becoming a partner.

39. *Scandal*, season 3, episode 1, "It's Handled," directed by Tom Verica, written by Shonda Rhimes, featuring Kerry Washington, Columbus Short, and Scott Foley, aired October 3, 2013, on ABC.

40. Feagin, *Racist America*, 19; Feagin, *Systemic Racism*, xii, 1–52, 194–95; Feagin, *White Racial Frame*, ix–x; Wendy Leo Moore, *Reproducing Racism: White Space, Elite Law Schools and Racial Inequality* (Lanham, MD: Rowman & Littlefield, 2008).

41. Louwanda Evans and Wendy L. Moore, "Impossible Burdens: White Institutions, Emotional Labor, and Micro-Resistance," *Social Problems* 62 (2015): 439, https://doi.org/10.1093/socpro/spv009.

42. Black professionals and people of color overall experience the dynamics of the invisible labor clause.

43. See Minority Corporate Counsel Association and Vault, *2017 Vault/MCCA*, 6, table 1, "Overall Law Firm Demographics."

44. See Elijah Anderson, *Code of the Street* (New York: Norton, 1999), 36.

45. See Hanifa Barnes, "Talking White and Living Black: The Art of Code Switching," *For Harriet* (blog), April 11, 2014, http://www.forharriet.com/2014/04/talking-white-and-living-black-art-of.html#ixzz3tfc5Rnxh; Mary B. Zeigler and Viktor Osinubi, "Theorizing the Postcoloniality of African American English," *Journal of Black Studies* 32, no. 5 (2002): 588–609, http://journals.sagepub.com/doi/pdf/10.1177/002193470203200506.

46. Anderson, *Code of the Street*, 36.

47. Link and Phelan, "Conceptualizing Stigma."

48. See Ronit Dinovitzer, Bryant G. Garth, Robert Nelson, Gabriele Plickert, Rebecca Sandefur, Joyce Sterling, and David Wilkins, *After the JD III: Third Results from a National Study of Legal Careers* (Dallas, TX: American Bar Foundation and the NALP Foundation for Law Career Research and Education, 2014), http://www.americanbarfoundation.org/uploads/cms/documents/ajd3report_final_for_distribution.pdf, 80. This observation falls directly in line with findings of the third *After the JD* study, which reports that black and Latinx associates are disproportionately burdened by educational debt.

49. Feagin, *Racist America*, 18–20; Feagin, *Systemic Racism*, 1–52; Feagin, *White Racial Frame*, ix–x.

50. See Minority Corporate Counsel Association and Vault, *2017 Vault/MCCA*, 6, table 1, "Overall Law Firm Demographics."

51. St. Jean and Feagin, *Double Burden*, 3–15, 26–29, 99–113.

52. Feagin, *Racist America*, 112.

53. Feagin, *Racist America*. Moreover, as Feagin demonstrates in reference to the sports world, "black male athletes are seen by whites as less intelligent and more animal-like than white male athletes" (112).

54. See Feagin, *Racist America*, for a discussion on the limited interaction that whites have with blacks. Feagin points out how, due to the

> racial demography and spatial ecology of everyday life, the majority of blacks spend much more time interacting with whites than the majority of whites spend interacting with blacks. Most black Americans work or shop with large numbers of whites, whereas relatively few whites do the same with large numbers of blacks. The racial views of most white Americans are not likely to be shaped by numerous equal status contacts with black Americans. The sense of white superiority is reinforced by the continuing process in which most whites live separated from black Americans or other Americans of color. (130)

55. See Erica Chito Childs, "Looking behind the Stereotypes of the 'Angry Black Woman': An Exploration of Black Women's Responses to Interracial Relationship," *Gender and Society* 19, no. 4 (2005): 544–61. In her article, sociologist Chito Childs describes how "there is little acknowledgement or concern for the larger issues that may be the root of Black women's perceived anger and hostility" (546).

While the "angry black man" trope is also ubiquitous, the more successful stereotype—and fear—that black males are fundamentally animalistic anyway may tend to trump (no pun intended) the influence of this depiction. The matter is certainly open to debate.

56. Moore, *Reproducing Racism*, 153–54.

57. Moore, *Reproducing Racism*, 149.

58. Feagin, *Systemic Racism*; Moore, *Reproducing Racism*.

59. See Deborah K. King, "Multiple Jeopardy, Multiple Consciousness: The Context of a Black Feminist Ideology," *Signs* 14, no. 1 (1988): 42–72, http://www.jstor.org/stable/3174661, for a discussion on the distinct nature in which black women tend to be subsumed within narratives of gender or race primarily focused on perspectives of white women or black men.

60. Choo and Ferree, "Practicing Intersectionality."

61. Collins, *Black Feminist Thought*.

CHAPTER 5

1. Joe R. Feagin, *Racist America: Roots, Current Realities, and Future Reparations*, 2nd ed. (New York: Routledge, 2010), 25, 59–96; Joe R. Feagin, *Systemic*

Racism: A Theory of Oppression (New York: Routledge, 2006), 25, 272–76; Joe R. Feagin, *The White Racial Frame: Centuries of Racial Framing and Counter-Framing*, 2nd ed. (New York: Routledge, 2013), x–xi, 3, 1–22.

2. Joe R. Feagin and Kimberley Ducey, *Elite White Men Ruling: Who, What, When, Where, and How* (New York: Routledge, 2017), 9–44.

3. See David B. Wilkins and Mitu G. Gulati, "Why Are There So Few Black Lawyers in Corporate Law Firms? An Institutional Analysis," *California Law Review* 84 (May 1996): 493–625, especially 534–42, http://nrs.harvard.edu/urn-3:HUL.InstRepos:13548823. There is a tournament-like structure of competition for promotion within elite law firms, which is essentially a competition for partnership.

4. Adia Harvey Wingfield, *Doing Business with Beauty: Black Women, Hair Salons, and the Racial Enclave Economy* (Lanham, MD: Rowman & Littlefield, 2008), 6–11.

5. See Feagin, *Systemic Racism*. Feagin discusses the boys' club phenomenon noting,

> Given the continuing racial hierarchy of the U.S. workplace, with whites in most positions of power to hire and promote . . . much racial favoritism for whites seems to involve a social cloning whereby whites prefer and choose yet other whites to fill positions traditionally held by whites. Favoritism proceeds along critical white "old boy" (less often, "old girl") networks. (203)

6. Jonathan A. Segal, "Boys' Club: The Invisible Affinity Groups," *Bloomberg Business*, January 10, 2012, 1, http://www.bloomberg.com/bw/management/boys-clubs-the-invisible-affinity-groups-01102012.html#p2.

7. Feagin and Ducey, *Elite White Men*; Wendy Leo Moore, *Reproducing Racism: White Space, Elite Law Schools and Racial Inequality* (Lanham, MD: Rowman & Littlefield, 2008).

8. See Feagin, *Racist America*, 74–75. Feagin discusses how social Darwinism claims that "certain 'racially inferior' races were less evolved, less human and more ape-like than the 'superior races,'" thereby arguing that black Americans belonged to a "degenerate race" whose alleged "immorality was a natural trait" used to propagate "racists doctrines with defenses of other societal oppression, particularly sexism and class oppression" (74).

9. Moore, *Reproducing Racism*, 98–99.

10. Eduardo Bonilla-Silva, *Racism without Racists: Color-Blind Racism and the Persistence of Racial Inequality in America*, 4th ed. (Lanham, MD: Rowman & Littlefield, 2014), 102; Moore, *Reproducing Racism*, 137.

11. Of course, this statement assumes that underdeveloping the skills (and contacts) of associates from marginalized groups is not a deliberate strategy to maintain white patriarchal control over these institutions. But in that case, the only way to convince elite corporate firms to enhance their diversity efforts or make them more effective is to somehow convince the boys' club that greater inclusivity might

actually lead to greater white male privilege and power, a somewhat circular argument. In any case, the argument for widening access must be directed to good-faith institutions, perhaps deeply infiltrated by the white racial frame but seeking to lift the proverbial veil of systemic racist, gendered ignorance from those institutions.

12. See Erica Chito Childs, "Looking behind the Stereotypes of the 'Angry Black Woman': An Exploration of Black Women's Responses to Interracial Relationship," *Gender and Society* 19, no. 4 (2005): 544–61. Given how much discomfort with people of color the white racial frame invokes in various sectors of US culture, it is a testament to the normalization, invisibility, and level of ignorance of the other that, in 2018, so many whites still allow such a "suffocating emotional straitjacket to be clasped around their worldview," as a colleague so vividly described it.

13. Bonilla-Silva, *Racism without Racists*; Feagin, *Racist America*; Feagin, *Systemic Racism*; Moore, *Reproducing Racism*.

14. See Bruce G. Link and Jo C. Phelan, "Conceptualizing Stigma," *Annual Review of Sociology* 27 (2001): 363–85, http://dx.doi.org/10.1146/annurev. soc.27.1.363, for a discussion on how negative labeling has real consequences to those stigmatized. According to Link and Phelan, status loss as a result of labeling and stereotyping leads to both individual and structural discrimination. Individual discrimination, which may be subtle or overt, resulting from negative labels can cause stigmatized persons to experience inequality in many facets, such as job rejection, housing, or educational opportunities. Structural discrimination in the form of institutional racism, for example, does not necessarily require an actual interaction leading to behavior that disadvantages one group over another, but rather the ingrained attitudes or beliefs about particular groups can lead to institutions operating in a manner that disadvantages certain groups (372).

15. See Wilkins and Gulati, "So Few Black Lawyers," 541. The "royal jelly," as described by Wilkins and Gulati, is the training that allows lawyers to shine and develop into potential stars for partnership track. Receiving the royal jelly is confirmation from the firm the associate has the potential to become a partner. The original analogy of the royal jelly was used by Ian Ayres.

16. Ida O. Abbot, *Sponsoring Women: What Men Need to Know* (Golden, CO: Attorney at Work, 2014).

17. See Cynthia Fuchs Epstein, "Reaching for the Top: 'The Glass Ceiling' and Women in Law," in *Women in Law*, ed. Shimon Shetreet, 105–30 (London: Kluwer Law International, 1998); Cynthia Fuchs Epstein, *Women in Law* (Urbana, IL: University of Chicago, 1981); Cynthia Fuchs Epstein, "Women in the Legal Profession at the Turn of the Twenty-First Century: Assessing Glass Ceilings and Open Doors," *Kansas Law Review* 49 (2001): 733–60; Cynthia Fuchs Epstein, Robert Sauté, Bonnie Oglensky, and Martha Gever, "Glass Ceilings and Open Doors: Women's Advancement in the Legal Profession," *Fordham Law Review* 64 (1995): 291–449.

18. See Feagin, *Racist America*, 74–75.

19. Yanick St. Jean and Joe R. Feagin, *Double Burden: Black Women and Everyday Racism* (Amonk, NY: M. E. Sharpe, 1998), 123–50.

20. National Association for Law Placement (NALP), "Women and Minorities at Law Firms—What Has Changed and What Has Not in the Past 25 Years," press release, February 2018, https://www.nalp.org/0218research.

21. Moore, *Reproducing Racism*, 149.

CHAPTER 6

1. See David B. Wilkins and Mitu G. Gulati, "Why Are There So Few Black Lawyers in Corporate Law Firms? An Institutional Analysis," *California Law Review* 84 (May 1996): 493–625, especially 534–42. http://nrs.harvard.edu/urn-3:HUL.InstRepos:13548823. Wilkins and Gulati describe a pyramid and tournament structure that law firms use to weed out associates from the pool of potential partners. Firms are not invested in spending resources to develop every associate they hire because it would take away from the pyramid and tournament structure they have developed.

2. See Wilkins and Gulati, "So Few Black Lawyers," 541. Ian Ayres is credited for the original analogy of the royal jelly. Wilkins and Gulati provide us with a grounded understanding of what the missing piece to advancement often times entails, namely, the royal jelly. The royal jelly is the quality training that partners bestow on associates they believe are worthy. If an associate does not receive the royal jelly, which exposes her to worthwhile assignments, partners, and clients, she will not have an opportunity to develop her brand within the firm and become a viable candidate for advancement. Therefore, the royal jelly is essential for any lawyer's success in the firm.

3. Joe R. Feagin, *Racist America: Roots, Current Realities, and Future Reparations*, 2nd ed. (New York: Routledge, 2010), 19, 25, 59–96; Joe R. Feagin, *Systemic Racism: A Theory of Oppression* (New York: Routledge, 2006), xii, 1–52, 194–95, 272–76; Joe R. Feagin, *The White Racial Frame: Centuries of Racial Framing and Counter-Framing*, 2nd ed. (New York: Routledge, 2013), ix–xi, 1–22.

4. Feagin, *Racist America*, 60; Feagin, *Systemic Racism*.

5. Ida O. Abbott, *Sponsoring Women: What Men Need to Know* (Golden, CO: Attorney at Work, 2014).

6. Sylvia Anne Hewlett, "Mentors Are Good. Sponsors Are Better," *New York Times*, April 13, 2013, http://www.nytimes.com/2013/04/14/jobs/sponsors-seen-as-crucial-for-womens-career-advancement.html.

7. Abbott, *Sponsoring Women*.

8. Abbott, *Sponsoring Women*, 15.

9. Abbott, *Sponsoring Women*.

10. Hewlett, "Mentors Are Good," 2.

11. See Abbott, *Sponsoring Women*, and Sylvia Ann Hewlett, *(Forget a Mentor) Find a Sponsor: The New Way to Fast-Track Your Career* (Boston: Harvard Business School, 2013), for an in-depth discussion on the importance of a sponsor in advancing the career of individuals, particularly women.

12. Abbott, *Sponsoring Women*. See also Ida O. Abbott, "How Does a Lawyer Find a Sponsor?" *Attorney at Work* (blog), September 2015, https://www.attorney-atwork.com/how-does-a-lawyer-find-sponsor/; and Cynthia Fuchs Epstein, Robert Sauté, Bonnie Oglensky, and Martha Gever, "Glass Ceilings and Open Doors: Women's Advancement in the Legal Profession," *Fordham Law Review* 64 (1995): 291–449, for a discussion on the difficulties women face developing meaningful mentorship relationships.

13. Abbott, *Sponsoring Women*, 15.

14. Abbott, "How Does a Lawyer," 1.

15. Minority Corporate Counsel Association and Vault, *2017 Vault/MCCA Law Firm Diversity Survey*, 2017, https://www.mcca.com/wp-content/uploads/2017/12/2017-Vault-MCCA-Law-Firm-Diversity-Survey-Report.pdf.

16. Eduardo Bonilla-Silva, *Racism without Racists: Color-Blind Racism and the Persistence of Racial Inequality in America*, 4th ed. (Lanham, MD: Rowman & Littlefield, 2014), 76, 78–84.

17. As a colleague brought to my attention, this logic fuels much of the debate over so-called entitlements, as well, the sense that any potential sharing of power, resources, or privilege that occurs between the races is inevitably some form of charity from whites given (sometimes forced out of them) for the exclusive benefit of the other.

18. Bonilla-Silva, *Racism without Racists*.

19. Patricia K. Gillette, "Rainmakers: Born or Bred?" *Law Practice Today*, 2014, http://www.lawpracticetoday.org/article/rainmakers-born-bred/. *Rainmaker* is an informal term to describe an employee who is able to bring to the firm a substantial amount of business through client relationships and negotiating deals. According to Gillette, a partner at Orrick, Herrington, and Sutcliff, a rainmaker is a partner who has at least four million dollars in business annually.

20. See Wilkins and Gulati, "So Few Black Lawyers," 569n273. As suggested by Wilkins and Gulati, potential mentors and sponsors look for protégés who remind them of themselves.

21. It is a lamentable state of affairs for everyone, as this phenomenon also severely locks white males into a stiflingly limited frame of reference. (Pun intended.)

22. Bonilla-Silva, *Racism without Racists*, 76, 78–84.

23. See Eduardo Bonilla-Silva, *White Supremacy and Racism in the Post–Civil Rights Era*, (Boulder, CO: Lynne Rienner, 2001). Bonilla-Silva suggests that the color-blind racism that exists within the structural framework of white spaces, such as elite law firms, creates a subtlety in the ways in which racism becomes pervasive but eerily dismissed, thereby perpetuating white privilege and power.

24. The exhaustive emotional and mental work lawyers of color are forced to exert in order to navigate the firm was prevalent throughout the interviews, demonstrating the effectiveness of the invisible labor clause.

25. Peter Lattman, "What's a 'White-Shoe' Firm Anyway," *Law Blog: On Cases, Trends and Personalities in Business*, March 10, 2006, http://blogs.wsj.com/ law/2006/03/10/whats-a-white-shoe-firm-anyway/. *White-shoe firm* is a term to describe an institution, generally in legal or finance, that has been in existence for more than a century and retains high-end clients. Also, the leadership of the institution tends to be white Anglo-Saxon Protestant (WASP) men who typically hail from Ivy League institutions, where these men used to wear white-laced buckskin shoes. Today the term still refers to the same, including "large law and financial firms and their employees, conservative, staid, well-established, financially powerful; formerly and less frequently today, elitist, WASPy; the opposite of blue-collar."

26. As discussed previously, these formal mentoring programs often have insignificant positive effects on the advancement prospects of racially subordinated associates because these programs are often forced.

27. See Epstein et al., "Glass Ceilings." Epstein and colleagues describe the billable hour model:

> Everyone points to the increasing expectations regarding billable hours as one of the greatest impediments to women's movement up the career ladder at large law firms. The "greedy" nature of such a law practice necessitates not only putting in considerable hours that are billable but also expending time to develop business and participate in the organizational activity that enhances a career. Billable hours not only reflect actual time spent on a case; they have also become a benchmark for ascertaining commitment to the firm. As one of the few measurable elements in a system of evaluation marked by subjective criteria, billable hours are also symbolic in expressing dedication and willingness to sacrifice for the good of the firm. (378–79)

28. Bonilla-Silva, *Racism without Racists*, 101–21, 212–17.

29. Bonilla-Silva, *Racism without Racists*; Feagin, *Systemic Racism*; Wendy Leo Moore, *Reproducing Racism: White Space, Elite Law Schools and Racial Inequality* (Lanham, MD: Rowman & Littlefield, 2008).

30. Wilkins and Gulati, "So Few Black Lawyers."

31. David B. Wilkins, "Why Are There *Still* So Few Black Lawyers in Corporate Law Firms: An Institutional Analysis in the New Global Age of More For Less," Fordham Law School Diversity and Inclusion Speaker Series, inaugural event, February 21, 2018; Wilkins and Gulati, "So Few Black Lawyers.".

32. Richard H. Sander, "The Racial Paradox of the Corporate Law Firm," *North Carolina Law Review* 54, (2006): 1755–822, http://scholarship.law.unc.edu/nclr/ vol84/iss5/15; Wilkins and Gulati, "So Few Black Lawyers."

33. Wilkins and Gulati, "So Few Black Lawyers," 570.

34. Monique R. Payne-Pikus, John Hagan, and Robert L. Nelson, "Experiencing Discrimination: Race and Retention in America's Largest Law Firms," *Law and*

Society Review 44, nos. 3–4, (September 2010): 553–84, https://doi.org/10.1111/j.1540-5893.2010.00416.x.

35. Ronit Dinovitzer, Bryant G. Garth, Richard Sander, Joyce Sterling, and Gita Z. Wilder, *After the JD: First Results of a National Study of Legal Careers* (Overland Park, KS: NALP Foundation for Law Career Research and Education and the American Bar Foundation, 2004), http://www.americanbarfoundation.org/uploads/cms/documents/ajd.pdf; Ronit Dinovitzer, Robert Nelson, Gabriele Plickert, Rebecca Sandefur, and Joyce Sterling, *After the JD II: Second Results from a National Study of Legal Careers* (Chicago: American Bar Foundation and the NALP Foundation for Law Career Research and Education, 2009), http://www.law.du.edu/documents/directory/publications/sterling/AJD2.pdf; Ronit Dinovitzer, Bryant G. Garth, Robert Nelson, Gabriele Plickert, Rebecca Sandefur, Joyce Sterling, and David Wilkins, *After the JD III: Third Results from a National Study of Legal Careers* (Dallas, TX: American Bar Foundation and the NALP Foundation for Law Career Research and Education, 2014), http://www.americanbarfoundation.org/uploads/cms/documents/ajd3report_final_for_distribution.pdf; Gita Z. Wilder, *Are Minority Women Lawyers Leaving Their Jobs? Findings from the First Wave of the* After the JD *Study* (Dallas, TX: NALP Foundation for Law Career Research and Education and the National Association for Law Placement, 2008), https://www.nalp.org/assets/1280_ajdminoritywomenmonograph.pdf.; Gita Z. Wilder, *Race and Ethnicity in the Legal Profession: Findings from the First Wave of the* After the JD *Study* (Overland Park, KS: NALP Foundation for Law Career Research and Education and the National Association for Law Placement, 2008), https://www.nalp.org/assets/1064_ajdraceethnicitymonograph.pdf; Wilkins and Gulati, "So Few Black Lawyers."

36. Bonilla-Silva, *Racism without Racists*, 76–77, 87–90.

37. Bonilla-Silva, *Racism without Racists*; Feagin, *Racist America*; Feagin, *Systemic Racism*; Feagin, *White Racial Frame*.

38. Wilkins and Gulati, "So Few Black Lawyers."

39. Feagin, *Racist America*; Feagin, *Systemic Racism*; Feagin, *White Racial Frame;* Wendy L. Moore, "Maneuvers of Whiteness: 'Diversity' as a Mechanism of Retrenchment in the Affirmative Action Discourse," Critical Sociology 37, no. 5 (2011): 597–613.

CHAPTER 7

1. Rev. Dr. Martin Luther King Jr., "Letter from a Birmingham Jail," April 16, 1963, retrieved from the Africana Studies Center, University of Pennsylvania, https://www.africa.upenn.edu/Articles_Gen/Letter_Birmingham.html.

2. Yanick St. Jean and Joe R. Feagin, *Double Burden: Black Women and Everyday Racism* (Amonk, NY: M. E. Sharpe, 1998), 16.

3. Eduardo Bonilla-Silva, *Racism without Racists: Color-Blind Racism and the Persistence of Racial Inequality in America*, 4th ed. (Lanham, MD: Rowman & Littlefield, 2014); Joe R. Feagin, *Racist America: Roots, Current Realities, and Future Reparations*, 2nd ed. (New York: Routledge, 2010), 25, 59–96; Joe R. Feagin, *Systemic Racism: A Theory of Oppression* (New York: Routledge, 2006), 25, 272–76; Joe R. Feagin, *The White Racial Frame: Centuries of Racial Framing and Counter-Framing*, 2nd ed. (New York: Routledge, 2013), x–xi, 3, 1–22; Wendy Leo Moore, *Reproducing Racism: White Space, Elite Law Schools and Racial Inequality* (Lanham, MD: Rowman & Littlefield, 2008); Adia Harvey Wingfield, *Doing Business with Beauty: Black Women, Hair Salons, and the Racial Enclave Economy* (Lanham, MD: Rowman & Littlefield, 2008), 6–11.

4. See Irving Seidman, *Interviewing as Qualitative Research: A Guide for Researchers in Education and The Social Sciences* (New York: Teachers College Press, 2013), and the appendix to this book, "Research Methodology," for a discussion on phenomenological approach to interviewing.

Phenomenological interviewing was used to fully capture the experiences of twenty black female lawyers. These interviews provided crucial information about how they believe their success and failures are affected by race and gender. The questions that led the interviews center on (1) recruitment, including influences on becoming a lawyer, getting into law firms, steps to partnership, similarities and differences with black male and white female associates, and outsider status; (2) professional development and inclusivity, including diversity in firms, exclusion from social and professional networking, discrepancies in feedback and performance reviews, assignment allocation, and work–life balance expectations; and (3) obstacles to advancement, including collegial support, training, and mentorship and sponsorship access, all of which illicit troubling encounters that point to the real effects of systemic gendered racism and white racial framing.

5. Bonilla-Silva, *Racism without Racists*; Feagin, *Systemic Racism*; Joe R. Feagin and Kimberley Ducey, *Elite White Men Ruling: Who, What, When, Where, and How* (New York: Routledge, 2017).

6. Bonilla-Silva, *Racism without Racists*; Feagin, *Racist America*; Feagin, *Systemic Racism*; Feagin, *White Racial*; Moore, *Reproducing Racism*.

7. Bonilla-Silva, *Racism without Racists*, 76, 78–84.

8. Moore, *Reproducing Racism*.

9. Bonilla-Silva, *Racism without Racists*, 76–78, 87–90, 91–95.

10. Bonilla-Silva, *Racism without Racists*, 101–21, 212–17; Monique R. Payne-Pikus, John Hagan, and Robert L. Nelson, "Experiencing Discrimination: Race and Retention in America's Largest Law Firms," *Law and Society Review* 44, nos. 3–4 (September 2010): 553–84, https://doi.org/10.1111/j.1540-5893.2010.00416.x.

11. See Moore, *Reproducing Racism*. This is similar to Moore's findings, where she suggests that white narratives of affirmative action affect law students of color by "question(ing) their own abilities, to downplay their educational and professional achievements, and sometimes even to avoid the programs and institutional supports

designed to assist students of color in overcoming systemic racism so that they can be successful law students and lawyers" (149).

12. Moore, *Reproducing Racism*, 101.

13. Moore, *Reproducing Racism*, 101–2.

14. See Derald Wing Sue, "Microaggressions, Marginality, and Oppression," in *Microaggressions and Marginality: Manifestation, Dynamics, and Impact*, ed. Derald Wing Sue (Hoboken, NJ: Wiley, 2010), 3–22.

15. The American Lawyer (AML), *The 2017 Diversity Scorecard*, May 24, 2017, https://www.wsgr.com/news/PDFs/17diversityscorecard.pdf. See also National Association for Law Placement (NALP), *Directory of Legal Employers* (DLE), accessed February 1, 2013, http://www.nalpdirectory.com. Note that this data was retrieved from the NALP *DLE* in July 2017. The numbers may fluctuate based on new hires and attrition.

16. The Standard & Poor's 500 Index is an American stock market index based on the market capitalizations of five hundred large companies having common stock listed on the New York Stock Exchange (NYSE) or National Association of Securities Dealers Automated Quotations (NASDAQ).

17. Laura Morgan Roberts, Anthony J. Mayo, Robin J. Ely, and David A. Thomas, "Beating the Odds," *Harvard Business Review* (March–April 2018), https://hbr.org/2018/03/beating-the-odds. Roberts and colleagues conducted a study that examined the careers of black alumni from Harvard Business School since 1908, specifically those who have gained entry into elite corporate positions, such as chief executive officer, chair, other C-level executive title, or senior managing partner or director in a professional service firm. Of 2,300 alumni, there were 67 women in these positions. Roberts and colleagues interviewed 30 of these women and found that resilience played a key role in their successes, particularly emotional intelligence, authenticity, and agility.

18. David B. Wilkins, "Why Are There *Still* So Few Black Lawyers in Corporate Law Firms: An Institutional Analysis in the New Global Age of More for Less," Fordham Law School Diversity and Inclusion Speaker Series, inaugural event, February 21, 2018.

APPENDIX

1. See National Association for Law Placement (NALP), *Directory of Legal Employers* (DLE), accessed February 1, 2013, http://www.nalpdirectory.com.

2. It is important to note that the actual numbers reported and the numbers I calculated produced a discrepancy of two associates, which can be explained away by looking at other categories where attorneys may have identified themselves.

3. It is important to note that the actual numbers reported and the numbers I calculated produced a discrepancy of seven associates, which can be explained away by looking at other categories where attorneys may have identified themselves.

4. It is important to note that the actual numbers reported and the numbers I calculated produced a discrepancy of sixteen associates, which can be explained away by looking at other categories where attorneys may have identified themselves.

5. See Irving Seidman, *Interviewing as Qualitative Research: A Guide for Researchers in Education and the Social Sciences* (New York: Teachers College Press, 2013), 16

6. Seidman, *Interviewing as Qualitative Research*, 19.

7. Deborah K. King, "Multiple Jeopardy, Multiple Consciousness: The Context of a Black Feminist Ideology," *Signs* 14, no. 1 (1988): 45, http://www.jstor.org/stable/3174661.

8. bell hooks, *Ain't I a Woman: Black Women and Feminism* (Boston: South End Press, 1981), 7.

9. Seidman, *Interviewing as Qualitative Research*, 117.

10. Seidman, *Interviewing as Qualitative Research*, 118–19.

11. In this study, I do not attempt to compare areas within the corporate department with advancement. What is significant is that these participants all worked within a corporate firm, within corporate practice groups. This information simply shows the range of different corporate practice groups that the participants work in.

BIBLIOGRAPHY

Abbott, Ida O. "How Does a Lawyer Find a Sponsor?" *Attorney at Work* (blog). September 2015. https://www.attorneyatwork.com/how-does-a-lawyer-find-sponsor/.

———. *Sponsoring Women: What Men Need to Know*. Golden, CO: Attorney at Work, 2014.

American Bar Association (ABA) Commission on Women in the Profession. *Visible Invisibility: Women of Color in Law Firms*. Chicago: American Bar Association, 2006.

The American Lawyer (AML). *The 2017 Diversity Scorecard*. May 24, 2017. https://www.wsgr.com/news/PDFs/17diversityscorecard.pdf.

Anderson, Elijah. *Code of the Street*. New York: Norton, 1999.

Bagati, Deepali. *Women of Color in U.S. Law Firms: Women of Color in Professional Services Series*. New York: Catalyst, 2009.

Barnes, Hanifa. "Talking White and Living Black: The Art of Code Switching." *For Harriet* (blog). April 11, 2014. http://www.forharriet.com/2014/04/talking-white-and-living-black-art-of.html#ixzz3tfc5Rnxh.

Blohm, Lindsay, Ashley Riviera, and Marcella B. Bary. *Presumed Equal: What America's Top Women Lawyers Really Think about Their Firms*. Bloomington, IN: AuthorHouse, 2006.

Bobbitt-Zeher, Donna. "Gender Discrimination at Work." *Gender and Society* 25, no. 6 (December 2011): 764–86. https://doi.org/10.1177/0891243211424741.

Bonilla-Silva, Eduardo. *Racism without Racists: Color-Blind Racism and the Persistence of Racial Inequality in America*. 4th edition. Lanham, MD: Rowman & Littlefield, 2014.

————. *White Supremacy and Racism in the Post-Civil Rights Era*. Boulder, CO: Lynne Rienner, 2001.

Bonilla-Silva, Eduardo, and David Dietrich. "The Sweet Enchantment of Color-Blind Racism in Obamerica." *Annals of the American Academy of Political Science* 634 (2011): 190–205.

Branch, Enobong Hannah. *Opportunity Denied: Limiting Black Women to Devalued Work*. New Brunswick, NJ: Rutgers University Press, 2011.

Bryant, Susan L. "The Beauty Ideal: The Effects of European Standards of Beauty on Black Women." *Columbia Social Work Review* 6 (2013): 80–81.

Caldwell, Paulette M. "A Hair Piece: Perspectives on the Intersection of Race and Gender." *Duke Law Journal* (1991): 365–96. https://scholarship.law.duke.edu/dlj/vol40/iss2/5.

Carbado, Devon W., and Mitu Gulati. "Working Identity." *Cornell Law Review* 85, no. 5 (July 2000): 1259–308. http://scholarship.law.cornell.edu/clr/vol85/iss5/4.

Childs, Erica Chito. "Looking behind the Stereotypes of the 'Angry Black Woman': An Exploration of Black Women's Responses to Interracial Relationships." *Gender and Society* 19, no. 4 (2005): 544–61.

Choo, Hae Y., and Myra M. Ferree. "Practicing Intersectionality in Sociological Research: A Critical Analysis of Inclusions, Interactions, and Institutions in the Study of Inequalities." *American Sociological Association, Sociological Theory* 28, no. 2 (2010): 129–49. https://doi.org/10.1111/j.1467-9558.2010.01370.x.

Coleman, James E., Jr., and Mitu Gulati. "A Response to Professor Sander: Is It Really All about the Grades?" *North Carolina Law Review* 84 (2006): 1823–29.

Collins, Patricia H. *Black Feminist Thought: Knowledge, Consciousness, and the Politics of Empowerment*. New York: Routledge, 2000.

————. *Black Sexual Politics: African Americans, Gender, and the New Racism*. New York: Routledge, 2005.

————. "It's All in the Family: Intersections of Gender, Race and Nation." *Hypatia* 13, no. 3 (1998): 62–82. http://www.jstor.org/stable/3810699.

————. "Learning from the Outsider Within: The Sociological Significance of Black Feminist Thought." *Social Problems* 33, no. 6 (1986): 14–32. https://doi.org/10.2307/800672.

Combahee River Collective Staff. *The Combahee River Collective Statement: Back Feminist Organizing in the Seventies and Eighties*. Brooklyn: Kitchen Table, Women of Color Press, 1986. https://combaheerivercollective.weebly.com/the-combahee-river-collective-statement.html.

Corporate Counsel of Women of Color (CCWC). *The Perspectives of Women of Color Attorneys in Corporate Legal Departments*. New York: Corporate Counsel Women of Color, 2011.

Crenshaw, Kimberlé. "Mapping the Margins: Intersectionality, Identity Politics, and Violence against Women of Color." *Stanford Law Review* 43, no. 6 (1991): 285–320. https://doi.org/10.2307/1229039.

Crenshaw, Kimberlé, Neil Gotanda, Gary Peller, G., and Kendall Thomas. *Critical Race Theory: The Key Writings that Formed the Movement*. New York: New Press, 1995.

Davis, Angela. *Women, Race and Class*. New York: Vintage Books, 1983.

Davis, Kathy. "Intersectionality as Buzzword: A Sociology of Science Perspective on What Makes a Feminist Theory Successful." *Feminist Theory* 9 (2008): 67–85. https://doi.org/10.1177/1464700108086364.

Dinovitzer, Ronit, Bryant G. Garth, Robert Nelson, Gabriele Plickert, Rebecca Sandefur, Joyce Sterling, and David Wilkins. *After the JD III: Third Results from a National Study of Legal Careers*. Dallas, TX: American Bar Foundation and the NALP Foundation for Law Career Research and Education, 2014. http://www. americanbarfoundation.org/uploads/cms/documents/ajd3report_final_for_distribution.pdf.

Dinovitzer, Ronit, Bryant G. Garth, Richard Sander, Joyce Sterling, and Gita Z. Wilder. *After the JD: First Results of a National Study of Legal Careers*. Overland Park, KS: NALP Foundation for Law Career Research and Education and the American Bar Foundation, 2004. http://www.americanbarfoundation.org/uploads/cms/documents/ajd.pdf.

Dinovitzer, Ronit, Robert Nelson, Gabriele Plickert, Rebecca Sandefur, and Joyce Sterling. *After the JD II: Second Results from a National Study of Legal Careers*. Chicago: American Bar Foundation and the NALP Foundation for Law Career Research and Education, 2009. http://www.law.du.edu/documents/directory/publications/sterling/AJD2.pdf.

Ellis, Judy Trent. "Sexual Harassment and Race: A Legal Analysis of Discrimination." *Journal of Legislation* 8, no. 1, article 3 (1981): 30–45. http://scholarship. law.nd.edu/jleg/vol8/iss1/3.

Epstein, Cynthia Fuchs. "Reaching for the Top: 'The Glass Ceiling' and Women in Law." In *Women in Law*, edited by Shimon Shetreet, 105–30. London: Kluwer Law International, 1998.

———. *Women in Law*. Urbana, IL: University of Chicago, 1981.

———. "Women in the Legal Profession at the Turn of the Twenty-First Century: Assessing Glass Ceilings and Open Doors." *Kansas Law Review* 49 (2001): 733–60.

Epstein, Cynthia Fuchs, Robert Sauté, Bonnie Oglensky, and Martha Gever. "Glass Ceilings and Open Doors: Women's Advancement in the Legal Profession." *Fordham Law Review* 64 (1995): 291–449.

Essed, Philomena. *Understanding Everyday Racism*. Newbury Park, CA: Sage, 1991.

Evans, Louwanda, and Wendy L. Moore. "Impossible Burdens: White Institutions, Emotional Labor, and Micro-Resistance." *Social Problems* 62 (2015): 439–54. https://doi.org/10.1093/socpro/spv009.

Feagin, Joe R. *Racist America: Roots, Current Realities, and Future Reparations*. 2nd ed. New York: Routledge, 2010.

———. *Systemic Racism: A Theory of Oppression*. New York: Routledge, 2006.

———. *The White Racial Frame: Centuries of Racial Framing and Counter-Framing*. 2nd ed. New York: Routledge, 2013.

Feagin, Joe R., and Kimberley Ducey. *Elite White Men Ruling: Who, What, When, Where, and How*. New York: Routledge, 2017.

———. *Racist America: Roots, Current Realities, and Future Reparations*. 4th ed. New York: Routledge, 2019.

Geraghty, Peter. "Of Counsel, Special Counsel, Senior Counsel: What Does It All Mean?" *American Bar Association—Eye on Ethics*. October 2015. https://www.americanbar.org/publications/youraba/2015/october-2015/of-counsel—special-counsel—senior-counsel—what-does-it-all-me.html.

Gillette, Patricia K. "Rainmakers: Born or Bred?" *Law Practice Today*. August 15, 2014. http://www.lawpracticetoday.org/article/rainmakers-born-bred/.

Goffman, Erving. *The Presentation of Self in Everyday Life*. New York: Doubleday, 1959.

———. *Stigma: Notes on the Management of Spoiled Identity*. Englewood Cliffs, NJ: Prentice-Hall, 1963.

Greene, D. Wendy. "Black Women Can't Have Blonde Hair . . . in the Workplace." *Journal of Gender, Race and Justice* 14, no. 2 (June 2011): 405–30.

Hauser, Christine. "Black Doctor Says Delta Flight Attendant Rejected Her; Sought 'Actual Physician.'" *New York Times*, October 14, 2016. https://www.nytimes.com/2016/10/15/us/black-doctor-says-delta-flight-attendant-brushed-her-aside-in-search-of-an-actual-physician.html.

Headworth, Spencer, Robert L. Nelson, Ronit Dinovitzer, and David B. Wilkins. *Diversity in Practice: Race, Gender, and Class in Legal and Professional Careers*. Cambridge: Cambridge University Press, 2016.

Hewlett, Sylvia Ann. *(Forget a Mentor) Find a Sponsor: The New Way to Fast-Track Your Career*. Boston: Harvard Business School, 2013.

———. "Mentors Are Good. Sponsors Are Better." *New York Times*, April 14, 2013. http://www.nytimes.com/2013/04/14/jobs/sponsors-seen-as-crucial-for-womens-career-advancement.html.

Hochschild, Arlie, and Anne Machung. *The Second Shift*. New York: Avon Books, 1990.

hooks, bell. *Ain't I a Woman: Black Women and Feminism*. Boston: South End Press, 1981.

Hull, Gloria T., and Barbara Smith. *All the Women Are White, All the Blacks Are Men, but Some of Us Are Brave: Black Women's Studies*. Westbury, NY: Feminist Press, 1982.

Johnson, Alex M., Jr. "The Underrepresentation of Minorities in the Legal Profession: A Critical Race Theorist's Perspective." *Michigan Law Review* 95, no. 4 (1997): 1005–62. https://doi.org/10.2307/1290052.

Kafka, Franz. "A Little Fable." In *The Complete Stories*, ed. Nahum N. Glatzer (New York: Schocken Books, 1971).

Kay, Katty. "100 Women: Katty Kay on How the 'Confidence Gap' Holds Women Back." *BBC News*, October 2, 2017. http://www.bbc.com/news/world-41444682.

Kay, Katty, and Claire Shipman. *The Confidence Code*. New York: HarperCollins, 2014.

———. "The Confidence Gap." *Atlantic*, May 2014. https://www.theatlantic.com/magazine/archive/2014/05/the-confidence-gap/359815/.

King, Deborah K. "Multiple Jeopardy, Multiple Consciousness: The Context of a Black Feminist Ideology." *Signs* 14, no. 1 (1988): 42–72. http://www.jstor.org/stable/3174661.

King, Rev. Dr. Martin Luther, Jr. "Letter from a Birmingham Jail." Africana Studies Center, University of Pennsylvania. April 16, 1963. https://www.africa.upenn.edu/Articles_Gen/Letter_Birmingham.html.

Lattman, Peter. "What's a 'White-Shoe' Firm Anyway." *Law Blog: On Cases, Trends and Personalities in Business* (blog). March 10, 2006. http://blogs.wsj.com/law/2006/03/10/whats-a-white-shoe-firm-anyway/.

Lewis, Oscar, and Oliver La Farge. *Five Families: Mexican Case Studies in the Culture of Poverty*. New York: Basic Books: 1959.

Link, Bruce G., and Jo C. Phelan. "Conceptualizing Stigma." *Annual Review of Sociology* 27 (2001): 363–85. https://doi.org/10.1146/annurev.soc.27.1.363.

Martin, Walter T., and Dudley L. Poston Jr. "The Occupational Composition of White Females: Sexism, Racism and Occupational Differentiation." *Social Forces* 50, no. 3 (March 1972): 349–55. https://doi.org/10.1093/sf/50.3.349.

McCall, Leslie. "The Complexity of Intersectionality." *Signs* 30, no. 3 (Spring 2005): 1771–800. http://www.journals.uchicago.edu/doi/pdfplus/10.1086/426800.

McIntosh, Peggy. "White Privilege and Male Privilege: A Personal Account of Coming to See Correspondences through Work in Women's Studies." In *The Teacher in American Society: A Critical Anthology*, edited by Eugene F. Provenzo Jr., 121–34 (Los Angeles: Sage, 2011).

Minority Corporate Counsel Association and Vault. *2017 Vault/MCCA Law Firm Diversity Survey*. 2017. https://www.mcca.com/wp-content/uploads/2017/12/2017-Vault-MCCA-Law-Firm-Diversity-Survey-Report.pdf.

Moore, Wendy L. "Maneuvers of Whiteness: 'Diversity' as a Mechanism of Retrenchment in the Affirmative Action Discourse." *Critical Sociology* 37, no. 5 (2011): 597–613.

———. *Reproducing Racism: White Spaces, Elite Law Schools, and Racial Inequality*. Lanham, MD: Rowman & Littlefield, 2008.

Nash, Jennifer C. "Re-thinking Intersectionality." *Feminist Review* 89 (2008): 1–15. http://www.jstor.org/stable/40663957.

National Association for Law Placement (NALP). *2017 Report on Diversity in U.S. Law Firms*. Washington, DC: National Association of Law Placement. https://www.nalp.org/uploads/2017NALPReportonDiversityinUSLawFirms.pdf.

———. *Directory of Legal Employers (DLE)*. Accessed February 1, 2013. http://www.nalpdirectory.com.

———. *Keeping the Keepers II: Mobility and Management of Associates*. Dallas, TX: NALP Foundation for Law Career Research and Education, 2003.

———. "Minority Women Still Underrepresented in Law Firm Partnership Ranks—Change in Diversity of Law Firm Leadership Very Slow Overall." Press release. November 1, 2007. https://www.nalp.org/minoritywomenstillunderrepresented.

———. "Representation of Women and African Americans among Law Firm Associates Increases Slightly but Remains Below Pre-Recession Levels." Press release. December 15, 2017. https://www.nalp.org/uploads/2017NALPReporton DiversityinUSLawFirmsPressRelease.pdf.

———. "The Representation of Women and Minorities among Equity Partners Sees Slow Growth, Broad Disparities Remain." Press release. April 2014. https: www. nalp.org/0414research.

———. "Women and Minorities at Law Firms—What Has Changed and What Has Not in the Past 25 Years." Press release. February 2018. https://www.nalp. org/0218research.

———. "Women and Minorities at Law Firms by Race and Ethnicity—An Update." Press release. February 2014. https://www.nalp.org/0214research.

———. "Women, Black/African-American Associates Lose Ground at Major U.S. Law Firms." Press release. November 9, 2015. https://www.nalp.org/lawfirmdiversity_nov2015.

Nossel, Suzanne, and Elizabeth Westfall. *Presumed Equal: What America's Top Women Lawyers Really Think about Their Firms*. Wayne, NJ: Career Press, 1998.

Opie, Tina R., and Katherine W. Phillips. "Hair Penalties: The Negative Influence of Afrocentric Hair on Ratings of Black Women's Dominance and Professionalism." *Frontiers in Psychology* 6 (2015): 1311. https://doi.org/10.3389/fpsyg.2015.01311.

Padavic, Irene, and Barbara Reskin. *Women and Men at Work*. 2nd ed. Thousand Oaks, CA: Pine Forge Press, 2005.

Patton, Tracey O. "Hey Girl, Am I More than My Hair? African American Women and Their Struggles with Beauty, Body Image, and Hair." *National Women's Studies Associate* 18 no. 2 (Summer 2006): 24–51. https://doi.org/10.1353/nwsa.2006.0037

Payne-Pikus, Monique R., John Hagan, and Robert L. Nelson. "Experiencing Discrimination: Race and Retention in America's Largest Law Firms." *Law and Society Review* 44, nos. 3–4 (September 2010): 553–84. https://doi.org/10.1111/j.1540-5893.2010.00416.x.

Pratt, Carla D. "Sisters in Law: Black Women Lawyers' Struggle for Advancement." *Michigan State Law Review* (2012): 1777. https://doi.org/10.2139/ssrn.2131492.

Roberts, Dorothy E. "Racism and Patriarchy in the Meaning of Motherhood." *Journal of Gender and the Law* 1, no. 1 (1993): 1–38. http://scholarship.law.upenn.edu/faculty_scholarship/595.

Roberts, Laura Morgan, Anthony J. Mayo, Robin J. Ely, and David A. Thomas. "Beating the Odds." *Harvard Business Review* (March–April 2018). https://hbr.org/2018/03/beating-the-odds.

Rosette, Ashleigh Shelby, and Tracy L. Dumas. "The Hair Dilemma: Conform to Mainstream Expectations or Emphasize Racial Identity." *Duke Journal of Gender, Law, and Policy* (2007): 14407–22. https://scholarship.law.duke.edu/djglp/vol14/iss1/13.

Ruddick, Graham. "Lupita Nyong'o Accuses *Grazia* of Editing Her Hair to Fit 'Eurocentric' Ideals." *Guardian*, November 10, 2017. https://www.theguardian.com/film/2017/nov/10/lupita-nyongo-grazia-editing-hair-eurocentric.

———. "Solange Knowles Tells *Evening Standard*: 'Don't Touch My Hair.'" *Guardian*, October 20, 2017. https://www.theguardian.com/music/2017/oct/20/solange-knowles-tells-evening-standard-dont-touch-my-hair.

Sandberg, Sheryl. *Lean In: Women, Work and the Will to Lead*. New York: Alfred A. Knopf, 2013.

Sander, Richard H. "The Racial Paradox of the Corporate Law Firm." *North Carolina Law Review* 54 (2006): 1755–822. http://scholarship.law.unc.edu/nclr/vol84/iss5/15.

Segal, Jonathan A. "Boys' Club: The Invisible Affinity Groups." Bloomberg Business. January 10, 2012. http://www.bloomberg.com/bw/management/boys-clubs-the-invisible-affinity-groups-01102012.html#p2.

Seidman, Irving. *Interviewing as Qualitative Research: A Guide for Researchers in Education and the Social Sciences*. New York: Teachers College Press, 2013.

Slaughter, Anne-Marie. "Why Women Still Can't Have It All." *Atlantic* (July/August 2012). https://www.theatlantic.com/magazine/archive/2012/07/why-women-still-cant-have-it-all/309020/.

Spar, Debora L. "Why the Woman Who "Has It All" Doesn't Really Exist." *Glamour*, August 14, 2013. https://www.glamour.com/story/why-women-cant-have-it-all-according-to-barnard-college-president-debora-l-spar.

———. *Wonder Women: Sex, Power, and the Quest for Perfection*. New York: Sarah Crichton Books, 2013.

St. Jean, Yanick, and Joe R. Feagin. *Double Burden: Black Women and Everyday Racism*. Amonk, NY: M. E. Sharpe, 1998.

Sue, Derald Wing. "Microaggressions, Marginality, and Oppression." In *Microaggressions and Marginality: Manifestation, Dynamics, and Impact*, edited by Derald Wing Sue, 3–22. Hoboken, NJ: Wiley, 2010.

Thakore, Bhoomi K. "Maintaining the Mechanisms of Colorblind Racism in the Twenty-First Century." *Humanity and Society* 38, no. 1 (February 2014): 3–6. https://doi.org/10.1177/0160597613519229.

Thompson, Cheryl. "Black Women, Beauty, and Hair as a Matter of Being." *Women's Studies: An Interdisciplinary Journal* 38, no. 8 (2009): 831–56. https://doi.org/10.1080/00497870903238463.

US Equal Employment Opportunity Commission (EEOC). *Diversity in Law Firms*. Washington, DC: US Equal Employment Opportunity Commission, 2003. https://www.eeoc.gov/eeoc/statistics/reports/diversitylaw/lawfirms.pdf.

Verica, Tom, dir. *Scandal*. Season 3, episode 1, "It's Handled." Aired October 3, 2013, on ABC.

Walby Sylvia, Jo Armstrong, and Sofia Strid. "Intersectionality: Multiple Inequalities in Social Theory." *Sociology* 46, no. 2 (2012): 224–40. https://doi.org/10.1093/socpro/spv009.

Weitz, Rose. "Women and Their Hair: Seeking Power through Resistance." *Gender and Society* 15, no. 5 (Fall 2001): 667–86. https://doi.org/10.1177/089124301015005003.

Wilder, Gita Z. *Are Minority Women Lawyers Leaving Their Jobs? Findings from the First Wave of the After the JD Study*. Dallas, TX: NALP Foundation for Law Career Research and Education and the National Association for Law Placement, 2008. https://www.nalp.org/assets/1280_ajdminoritywomenmonograph.pdf.

———. *Race and Ethnicity in the Legal Profession: Findings from the First Wave of the After the JD Study*. Overland Park, KS: NALP Foundation for Law Career Research and Education and the National Association for Law Placement, 2008. https://www.nalp.org/assets/1064_ajdraceethnicitymonograph.pdf.

Wilkins, David B. "Why Are There *Still* So Few Black Lawyers in Corporate Law Firms: An Institutional Analysis in the New Global Age of More for Less." *Fordham Law School Diversity and Inclusion Speaker Series*, inaugural event, February 21, 2018.

Wilkins, David B., and Mitu G. Gulati. "Why Are There So Few Black Lawyers in Corporate Law Firms? An Institutional Analysis." *California Law Review* 84 (May 1996): 493–625. http://nrs.harvard.edu/urn-3:HUL.InstRepos:13548823.

Wingfield, Adia Harvey. "Comment on Feagin and Elias." *Ethnic and Racial Studies* 36, no. 6 (February 2013): 989–93. https://doi.org/10.1080/01419870.2013.767920.

———. *Doing Business with Beauty: Black Women, Hair Salons, and the Racial Enclave Economy*. Lanham, MD: Rowman & Littlefield, 2008.

Yuval-Davis, Nira. "Intersectionality and Feminist Politics." *European Journal of Women's Studies* 13, no. 3 (August 2006): 193–209. https://doi.org/10.1177/1350506806065752.

Zeigler, Mary B., and Viktor Osinubi. 2002. "Theorizing the Postcoloniality of African American English." *Journal of Black Studies* 32, no. 5 (2002): 588–609. http://journals.sagepub.com/doi/pdf/10.1177/002193470203200506.

INDEX

AAVE. *See* African American Vernacular English

ABA. *See* American Bar Association

Abbott, Ida O., 96–97, 158nn11–12

advancement: of black male lawyers, 68; boys' club and, 81; comfort and, 28, 30–31; at corporate law firms, 8; professional networks for, 36–38; self-doubt and, 44–47; of white women, 92; of women attorneys, 61–62

advancement, of black women lawyers, 7, 50–56, 63–64, 74, 76; dynamics of gender and race impacting, 9–11; hurdles of, 22; as most marginalized group, 1–4; perceptions influence on, 21; prospects for, 25–26; tangible barriers to, 15–18

affirmative action: as aggressive racial preference, 134n3; associates of color and, 13, 28; attrition rate and, 36; for black women lawyers, 44–45; boys' club and, 79; as disparaging designation, 53; diversity outreach

and, 45; good old days and, 77–78; liberalism and, 12, 139n31; mentoring programs and, 115; necessity of, xvi; negative label of, 3; as reverse racist entitlement program, 44–45, 139n31; subordinated groups and, 44–45; tokenism and, 46; white women and, 78

African American professionals, xii, xvi

African American Vernacular English (AAVE), 69–70

After the JD, 8–9, 53, 134n6, 135n9, 136n10, 149n12

aggressive racial preferences, 134n3

Ain't I a Women (hooks), 125

American Bar Association (ABA), 9, 136n12

American beauty, 23–26

American Lawyer (AML), 2–3, 118–19, 121, 132n7, 161n15, 162n15

AM Law 100, 121

Anderson, Elijah, 69–70

ABOUT THE AUTHOR

Tsedale M. Melaku is a sociologist and postdoctoral research fellow with the Institute for Research on the African Diaspora in the Americas and the Caribbean (IRADAC) at The Graduate Center, City University of New York. Her research focuses on how race and gender affect advancement in traditionally white institutional spaces and how white racial framing and systemic gendered racism play a crucial role in the experiences of women of color within predominantly white spaces. She is particularly interested in how the intersection of race, gender, and class operates on the experiences of black women in the workplace. She is developing her theories on invisible labor and its impact on marginalized individuals in the workplace. Dr. Melaku received her PhD and MPhil in sociology from the Graduate Center, City University of New York, and her BA in sociology and Africana studies from New York University. To learn more about her research and interests follow her on Twitter, @TsedaleMelaku or visit her website, www.tsedalemelaku.com.